The EVERYTHING
Father's First Year Book

Dear Reader:

I practically had to write this book in my sleep; after all, I had just gotten through my first year of being a dad to twin boys, and I'm a pediatrician. Although I think I have grown and become a better doctor and a better father, this past year has helped me realize one thing: Being a dad can be hard work! This is especially true during the first year, when kids only seem to sleep, eat, and cry, and not do much else that a dad can easily relate to.

New dads are also usually at a disadvantage compared to new moms. We often don't have a big support network that would allow us to talk about parenting concerns. Dads might gripe to each other about how their kid isn't sleeping all night or cries too much, but they probably aren't offering tips to each other the way a group of moms might. And our first baby is often our first experience with caring for or even touching a baby.

I hope that my book will help dads develop the parenting skills they need to nurture a healthy and loving relationship with their child—one that will last a lifetime.

Vincent Iannelli MD

The EVERYTHING® Series

Editorial

Publishing Director	Gary M. Krebs
Managing Editor	Kate McBride
Copy Chief	Laura M. Daly
Acquisitions Editor	Gina Chaimanis
Development Editor	Christina MacDonald
Production Editors	Jamie Wielgus

Production

Production Director	Susan Beale
Production Manager	Michelle Roy Kelly
Series Designers	Daria Perreault
	Colleen Cunningham
	John Paulhus
Cover Design	Paul Beatrice
	Matt LeBlanc
Layout and Graphics	Colleen Cunningham
	Rachael Eiben
	John Paulhus
	Daria Perreault
	Monica Rhines
	Erin Ring
Series Cover Artist	Barry Littmann

Visit the entire Everything® Series at *www.everything.com*

THE
EVERYTHING®
FATHER'S FIRST YEAR BOOK

A survival guide for the first
12 months of being Dad

Vincent Iannelli, M.D.

Adams Media
Avon, Massachusetts

For my father. I'm proud to say that in all of the
most important ways, I am just like you.

An Everything® Series Book.
Everything® and everything.com® are registered trademarks of F+W Publications, Inc.

Published by Adams Media, an F+W Publications Company
57 Littlefield Street, Avon, MA 02322 U.S.A.
www.adamsmedia.com

ISBN: 1-59337-310-4
Printed in the United States of America.

J I H G F E D C B A

Library of Congress Cataloging-in-Publication Data
Iannelli, Vincent.
The everything father's first year book / Vincent Iannelli.
     p.   cm. — (An everything series book)
ISBN 1-59337-310-4
1. Fatherhood. 2. Fathers. I. Title. II. Series: Everything series.

HQ756.I266 2005
649'.122—dc22
                                        2004026400

This publication is designed to provide accurate and authoritative information with regard to the subject matter covered. It is sold with the understanding that the publisher is not engaged in rendering legal, accounting, or other professional advice. If legal advice or other expert assistance is required, the services of a competent professional person should be sought.

—From a *Declaration of Principles* jointly adopted by a Committee of the American Bar Association and a Committee of Publishers and Associations

Many of the designations used by manufacturers and sellers to distinguish their products are claimed as trademarks. Where those designations appear in this book and Adams Media was aware of a trademark claim, the designations have been printed with initial capital letters.

This book is available at quantity discounts for bulk purchases.
For information, call 1-800-872-5627.

Contents

11 Infant Nutrition / 135

12 Sleep Schedules / 151

13 Infant Safety / 163

14 Choosing Your Pediatrician / 177

15 Going to the Pediatrician / 187

16 Common Medical Problems / 201

Acknowledgments

For helping me to get to a point at which I could write a book like this, I would like to thank:

Everyone involved in my education in medical school and at Children's Hospital in Dallas. I would especially like to thank Dr. Tom Abramo, for helping me gain experience; Dr. Brett Giroir, for building my confidence in my abilities; and Dr. Patty Hicks, for being a great role model of a caring and thoughtful pediatrician. And Dr. Charles Ginsburg, for helping influence the decisions that brought me where I am right now.

The moderators in the Parents' Talk forums at *www.keepkids healthy.com* for their suggestions of things to include in this book and helping watch things while I was busy writing.

My family, especially my mother and father, for all of their love and support over the years. My boys, Collin, Jordan, and Braden, who have helped me see that being a father is one of the most rewarding and important things that I will ever do. And especially my wife, Priscilla. None of what I do would be possible without you. I love you and am very proud of all of the things you do for our family.

Top Ten Things
Every New Father Should Do

1. Be supportive. Be kind. Be available.

2. Don't deliberately try to screw up all of the jobs you are given to do, just so you won't be asked again. It might get you out of doing more work, but it might also get you out of a relationship with your family.

3. Don't take it personally if you don't get as much attention as you are used to, including sex.

4. Instead of just helping take care of the baby, offer to help out with household chores and cooking meals.

5. If your baby is breastfeeding, getting up for some of the feedings at night and bringing the baby to the breast is a big help.

6. Be supportive as long as both the baby and mother would like to continue breastfeeding.

7. Take over some of the daily chores, such as changing diapers, giving the baby a bath, and changing the baby's clothes.

8. Learn to recognize signs of postpartum depression.

9. Learn from your mistakes, instead of using them as an excuse for not helping with the baby's care.

10. Ask for help if you don't know what you're doing.

Introduction

▶ A lot has changed for fathers in recent years. Long gone are the days when a father got the first glimpse of his new baby when she was brought to the waiting room of the hospital. Now a new father is expected to be in the delivery room and is able to play an integral role as his baby comes into the world.

Though most things have changed for the better, it's unfortunate that many other things haven't changed at all. Dads are expected to be full and equal partners when it comes to taking care of their kids, but they aren't always given the resources to be able to do it. They may have difficulty getting time off from work to care for their sick child or go to well-baby visits with their pediatrician, and may not even get any paternity leave. And many people still promote the stereotype of the bumbling, clueless father.

One thing that hasn't changed—and hopefully it never will—is how important it is for children to have an active father figure in their lives. Children who grow up in a household without a father are more likely to drop out of school, abuse drugs, run away from home, and end up in prison. A father who understands his responsibility and takes an active role in raising his sons and daughters is important for his family and for society in general.

If being a good father is so important, then why aren't new fathers given more resources to help them? You won't find as many support groups and clubs for dads as there are for moms, and there are far fewer parenting classes just for new fathers. Other simple things, like diaper-changing tables in the restroom, are often not as widespread for men as they are for women. Why do new fathers still often have a hard time understanding what their role is supposed to be?

Part of the reason is that although the role of fathers is changing, it sometimes still isn't seen as being very "manly" to take on many parenting tasks. Sure, you're a real man if you take your son to a ball game, but what if you help feed your baby or regularly change his diapers? Is that still a "manly" thing to do?

Of course it is. Real men are good fathers and are equal partners when it comes to all aspects of raising a baby. You take care of your baby when she is sick, wake up at night for feedings, and are familiar with how your baby is growing and developing. Understanding this more active parenting role can help you realize what it means to be a good father.

One of the most important aspects of learning to be a good father is understanding all of the general parenting tasks that you are expected to do. This includes changing diapers, feeding your baby, and giving him a bath. Fathers who know how to do these things will be eager to do them, and won't be uncomfortable or afraid of doing something wrong. In *The Everything® Father's First Year Book*, you will learn everything you need to know in order to care for your baby until his first birthday. You will also learn how to support and help your partner through this very enjoyable, but often challenging, first year of your baby's life.

Chapter 1

What Kind of Dad Will You Be?

That probably seems like a silly question. After all, how can you know ahead of time what kind of dad you are going to be? Bad fathers most likely don't start off with the goal of being a poor parent, but then again, not all good dads are just naturally good at fatherhood, either. It takes some work to be a good father, and the first step is to be prepared. It can all start with knowing what it takes to be a good dad, and then deciding what kind of dad you will be.

Your Expectations

Do you know what to expect from fatherhood? Are you planning to go about your regular routines and maybe just change a few diapers now and then? If you don't expect or plan to make more time to be with your family and your new baby, then you aren't going to be a very helpful father. Of course, if you already are a very devoted family man, then spending a lot of time helping around the house and taking care of a child may not be a very big change for you—it may just be that the specific tasks you help with will change.

Changes Dads Should Expect

First-time dads who think that their lives won't change much are in for a very big surprise. Having kids may not change everything, but it will change a big part of your life. You won't be able to go out each night, watch every sporting event on TV, or spend all of your free time playing golf. You will need to use a lot more of what used to be free time taking care of your baby.

ALERT!

Not being able to do things spontaneously is one of the hardest changes for many new fathers to get used to. No longer can you simply go to a movie or dinner on a moment's notice. You now need to plan things in advance, either around your baby's schedule or based on the availability of a baby sitter. Having to do a little planning is a small price to pay for being a dad, though.

Other things that you can expect to change during this first year can include:

- Needing to be more flexible with your time
- Being less spontaneous
- Getting by with less sleep
- Having less time alone with your partner

Of course there are plenty of positives, too. Chief among them is having the unconditional love of your baby. Remember that having a baby is not all about the things that you are going to give up or have less time doing. It just makes things easier in the long run if you go into this new time of your life with a good idea of what to expect.

Prioritizing Your Time

Just because you should be more available to help at home and with your baby doesn't mean that you can't still make time for other things that are important to you. As with other busy times in your life, you just have to set your priorities and give up some of the less important things you used to spend time doing. Take a good look at your usual schedule, and see which things show up more often than they should. Do you really need to go for a drink after work with the guys, spend several hours on the Internet, or watch whatever is on TV at night?

Not everything you do is going to be equally important, so learn to set priorities to better manage your time. Your priorities still can (and should) include some time for yourself. This means that in addition to your new role as the helpful father, you can probably still play your usual rounds of golf if, for example, you give up watching sports on TV in the evening. Or if you like working out at a health club regularly, switch your workouts to the early morning so that you can head home right after work to take over caring for your baby. As long as your top priority is your family, you should be able to balance the rest of your time to fit in the other activities that are important to you.

What Is Expected of You?

In addition to thinking about and understanding what you expect to happen when you become a father, you should know what your partner expects of you. A lot of the conflicts and problems that arise between parents during their baby's first year result from very different expectations about each parent's role. To avoid this, it's a good idea to talk about these roles before the baby comes along.

Unfortunately, many people don't think about this in advance. Too often, each parent has his or her own expectation of what the other is going to do, and these expectations don't match. So a new father might be thinking that as long as he helps around the house a little more, he won't have to bother with diapers or feedings, when the mother is expecting help in both areas.

Sometimes, even when parents-to-be agree on the roles they each will take, their expectations and needs change once the baby comes home. When this happens, parents often can just re-evaluate their roles and try to change the way that they are doing things. Sometimes, though, the situation is more serious and the parents may require counseling. This can happen if either or both parents realize that this isn't what they want to be doing, that they need more help, or that they simply can't handle caring for a baby. If you reach this point, it's likely that you will need some professional help if your family is going to stay together.

Learning to Be a Good Dad

So, what kind of dad are you going to be? It's easy to say that you are going to be the best dad ever, but it is harder to actually earn that honor. Your past experiences with your own father and other role models as well as your personal feelings about fatherhood will all affect the way you act as a father.

Qualities of a Good Father

Do you even know what being a good father means? It's going to mean different things for different families, but it usually isn't about how much money you make, all of the things you can buy your family, or how successful you are at work. It's more about being available and supporting your family with your love and attention.

FACT

Being a good father can be harder if you didn't have a strong role model to lead the way for you. But unless you want your kids to have the same problem once they begin to have kids, learn to be a good role model of fatherhood for them.

Being an equal partner when it comes to taking care of your baby is one of the most important qualities of a good father. Others include:

- Understanding your family's needs
- Offering unconditional love
- Having patience
- Being generous with your time
- Setting a good example
- Staying calm and learning to teach when you discipline (instead of simply relying on physical punishment to stop bad behaviors)
- Being responsible with your family's money

How do you acquire these qualities of a good father? The average dad isn't going to be able to simply choose what type of father he will be. His own experiences, expectations, and overall personality will shape his actions and have a big influence on what type of father he will be.

Like Father, Like Son?

How you were raised is going to be one of the big influences on the type of father that you will be. What role did your own father have when you were growing up? Was he simply a strict disciplinarian, or did he take a more active role in your care? Was your father even around very much?

For good or bad, the type of father you had is likely to influence what kind of father you will become. Because that influence isn't always obvious, understanding the relationship between your father's parenting style and your own is important.

When considering your own father's parenting style, you do have to keep in mind that the role of a father was different when you were growing up. Just because he wasn't in the delivery room and didn't change diapers doesn't mean that he was a bad father. Those things weren't widely expected of fathers back then.

If you do think that your father did a poor job, it doesn't mean that he has to have a negative influence on you. Even having a bad father can help you to be a better dad, because you will have firsthand experience in all of the things that a dad shouldn't do. Do you wish that your father had been more available? Do you think he used physical punishment too much? Then be sure that you don't make those same mistakes.

Other than your own father, other role models may have influenced what kind of father you will be. These might include other family members, friends, and coworkers. Your role models should not be limited to the fathers you see on TV. Unlike the Ward Cleavers and other fathers of the sitcoms of the 1950s and '60s, who often portrayed the qualities of a good father, today's TV dads are more often incompetent and just offer comic relief.

Even though your personal experiences and role models will have a big effect on the type of father you become, you can make a conscious decision to be the best father you can be. Learning about the different types of fathers will help you to learn what to strive for, as well as what *not* to do.

The "Hands-Off" Dad

This is perhaps the worst kind of father to be. In addition to not helping to raise his baby, this type of dad doesn't want anything to do with him. Whether or not he is married to his baby's mother, she is likely to have sole responsibility for raising their child. If they don't all live together, then he may never see his baby at all.

For the hands-off dad, there will be no diaper changes, no sleepless nights, and he will likely never get spit up on. He won't ever take care of his baby when he's sick, won't go to doctor's visits, and won't know whether or not his baby is sleeping through the night. He also most likely won't have a family for very long.

Some men become hands-off dads by simply trying to delay fatherhood for a while—even after the baby is born. The man who does this is the dad who wants to be a big part of his child's life, but not until she is more grown up. He figures there will be plenty of time to bond later, when his kids can play a game of catch, compete in sports, or need help with their homework. This dad doesn't want anything to do with any of the baby stuff. Then he is surprised when the baby grows up and doesn't want to have much to do with him, either.

The worst kind of hands-off dad is the selfish one. In addition to not helping at home or taking care of the baby, he still will want all of his own needs met. He may expect his partner to take care of their baby and their home, cook his dinner, clean his clothes, and do all of the shopping, even if she works outside the home too. Luckily, if you are taking the time and effort to read this book, chances are very good that you won't become such a selfish parent. Making the effort to learn what it takes to be a father is a good sign that you want to be involved in your child's life. Be sure you continue to do whatever it takes to avoid being a dad like this.

The "Clueless" Dad

Unlike fathers who don't want to help at all, the clueless dad may want to help, but he is just lousy at it. He doesn't know how to do anything. Although his intentions may be good, the clueless dad doesn't quickly learn from his mistakes. However, he doesn't go out of his way to do a poor job to ensure that he isn't asked again.

Some signs of a clueless dad include that he:

- Puts diapers on too loose, so that they leak
- Doesn't change his baby's clothes when they are soiled
- Feeds his baby inappropriate foods
- Doesn't know how to put his baby in a car seat correctly
- Forgets to connect the harness in the high chair
- Doesn't know how to mix formula
- Gives the wrong dosage of vitamins or medicines
- Doesn't know when his partner needs his help or support
- Figures each cry means that the baby wants to breastfeed, so he hands her off to mom
- Freaks out every time the baby cries, jerks, or passes gas

As you can see, it can be downright dangerous to leave a baby with a clueless dad. Fortunately, unless he is being clueless on purpose, this type of dad can be helped, and can evolve into a father who is more supportive and helpful. The keys to becoming a better dad include recognizing when you need help and then asking for it, and learning from your mistakes. Obviously, if you're a first-time father there are going to be things that are new to you, and things you don't know how to do. The important thing is that you realize this and get the help you need in order to learn the basics.

ALERT!

Don't try to trick your partner by being clueless on purpose. Leaving your baby in a dirty diaper so that he gets a rash, not responding to his cries, or not feeding him on time is going to hurt your baby (and your relationship with your partner).

The clueless dad who doesn't want to learn to do a better job is really just a hands-off dad in disguise. Instead of being honest about not wanting to be a good father, this type of dad is trying to fool his partner or himself about how helpful (or unhelpful) he is, in order to avoid helping.

The "Somewhat Supportive" Dad

The dad who is somewhat supportive wants to help, tries to help, and does a pretty good job at it, but only some of the time. He may change a few diapers, but he can probably count on two hands all of the diapers he had to change during his baby's whole first year. And if he does tackle a more difficult task, like giving his baby a bath or waking up at night with her, he is likely to give up quickly if it doesn't go well.

This type of dad will just want to help when it is convenient for him. Maybe he will watch his baby while she is sleeping, or after a meal when she is alert and happy. But at other times, especially if a lot of work or crying is involved, he will probably be less likely to help.

Not only does the somewhat supportive dad not help very often, but when he does do something that is helpful, he may make his partner feel guilty about it. Instead of being eager to help, this type of dad will probably complain about the work he does and make it seem like it's a hassle. That does make it less likely that he will be asked to help again, but it will also hurt his relationship with his partner.

Don't let yourself become this type of dad, either. Such a halfhearted approach won't get you anywhere in terms of bonding with your child. Also, be sure you realize from the outset that parenting is a full-time job. Your baby will need constant love and attention, and not just from his mother.

The "Mostly Helpful" Dad

The father who is mostly helpful is a very good father, at least most of the time. It's likely that he helps around the house, changes a lot of diapers, and understands how his baby is growing and developing. He probably even goes to most of his baby's visits to his pediatrician and is involved in most aspects of his care.

If you are a mostly helpful father, go the extra step to be Father of the Year. With a few small changes, you can develop a much better relationship with both your baby and your partner. If you aren't sure what it is that you aren't doing, just ask your partner.

The reason that he is just mostly helpful is that there is *something* he is leaving out. He may have most of the qualities of a good father, but there is still that one thing that keeps him from getting Father of the Year honors. The one thing that he leaves out may be that he:

- Doesn't change dirty diapers
- Won't wake up to share nighttime duties
- Doesn't clean up after himself when he is caring for his baby
- Helps a lot with the baby, but doesn't help around the house
- Is very helpful, but still spends a little too much time away doing stuff like playing golf
- Is very helpful when he has time, but works very long hours and so isn't home as much as he should be

- Does great with the baby and helping around the house, but could pay a little more attention to his partner
- Is eager to help, but has to be told what to do each time

If there are more than one or two things on this list that a dad isn't doing, then he probably doesn't qualify for being mostly helpful and is more like a somewhat supportive dad. If the thing he doesn't do is very important to his partner, then he may lose a few more points and be knocked down even further.

How can he leave out some of these very important tasks and still be considered a good father? Basically, he is so good at the other things he does that he makes up for it. If he doesn't help at night, maybe he lets his partner sleep in each morning, or at least on weekends, so that she can catch up on her rest. Or, he completely takes over once he gets home from work until his baby's bedtime. And he probably spends so much time with his baby that he has bonded well and they have a good relationship together.

Father of the Year

This is the dad that every mother wants for her baby and every father should strive to be. This type of father is truly an equal with his partner in all aspects of his family's care. He is a good father, but also a good husband or boy-friend to his baby's mother. Even if the parents are no longer a couple, he is still supportive and takes his parenting duties seriously.

If there is something he doesn't do, it is because both caregivers have compromised on the matter and he makes up for it somewhere else. If both parents work, then he shares in parenting duties when they both get home. If his partner is a stay-at-home mom, he gives her a break in the evening, either by helping care for the baby or doing some of the chores around the house when he gets home from work.

The Father of the Year dad isn't afraid to change a dirty diaper, give his baby a bath, or stay up with her when she is sick. He knows his baby's routine and doesn't need a detailed list of things to do every time he cares for the baby. He knows what his baby is eating and drinking, how much, and when to feed it to her. And he knows and has met his baby's pediatrician on many occasions.

QUESTION?

How can I become a "Father of the Year"?
A good start is learning more about your baby, about being a father, and also about parenthood in general. Next, be more observant about the needs of your family and take the initiative to eagerly do what needs to be done, instead of always waiting to be asked. Last, learn to be loving, kind, and supportive of your family.

By definition, a stay-at-home dad usually qualifies for Father of the Year honors, as long as he isn't simply acting as a baby sitter. If he just watches the baby all day when his partner is at work, but neglects all of the other daily chores, including housework, shopping, and nighttime duties, he will fall to being just somewhat supportive, mostly helpful, or even clueless. A dad who stays home still needs to be equal partners with the baby's mother and share household and parenting duties.

Chapter 2

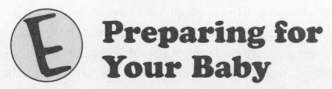

Preparing for Your Baby

Expecting dads have a lot of work to do to prepare for the baby, such as helping stock up on supplies, choosing a crib and bedding, and designing the nursery. This is also a good time to think about important medical topics, like cord blood banking, newborn screening, and whether or not to circumcise your baby boy. It is also important to get your home babyproofed before your baby is born.

Your Baby's First Car Seat

Although parents often take their kids out of a car seat and start using regular seat belts well before the recommended age of eight years or weight of 80 pounds, putting a baby in a car seat is a no-brainer, even for first-time fathers.

Shopping for a car seat, with so many different brands and types available, can be overwhelming. There are different basic guidelines to follow depending on the car you drive and the type of seat you're looking for. Remember, as the American Academy of Pediatrics states, there is no "safest" or "best" car seat. You will find many brands and styles of seats that fit the guidelines, so in the end your choice will come down to personal preference. Just be sure to read the manufacturer's instructions so that you install and use the seat correctly.

FACT

Car seats have always been hard to use, and most experts estimate that 85 percent of parents use them incorrectly. LATCH (Lower Anchors and Tethers for Children) is a new system that is installed in newer cars and car seats to make them much easier to install and use.

Infant-Only Carriers

Your first car seat will probably be an infant-only seat. This seat is designed for young infants and the rear-facing position that is safest for them. One of the best features of an infant-only seat is that after installing a detachable base into the back seat of your car, you can just snap the seat into the base when you are ready to go. When you reach your destination, detach the seat and use it as a carrier to transport your baby. Without this type of seat, you will have to buy a separate carrier, use a sling, or simply carry your baby around in your arms.

Most infant seats can only be used for babies that weigh less than 20 pounds. If you use an infant seat and your baby reaches 20 pounds before his first birthday, then you will have to get a convertible seat and use it in the rear-facing position for a while.

Convertible Car Seats

This type of seat is "convertible" because it can be used in both the rear-facing and forward-facing positions, accommodating newborns, infants, and most toddlers. These seats can be used until a child weighs about 40 pounds. There are even some with higher weight limits that can be used as a belt-positioning booster seat for children up to 65–80 pounds. While this means that you might be able to use just one car seat until your child is three years old (and therefore buy only one), a convertible seat might not fit your newborn well and it can't be used as a carrier.

Car Seat Positioning

Where exactly to put the car seat is another common source of confusion. Most dads know that the back seat is safest, but where in the back seat? Should you put your baby behind the driver or passenger, or in the middle?

Although it sometimes depends on how many other kids you have seated in the car and where the seat fits best, in almost all cases your baby will be safest in the middle of the back seat. In addition to keeping him away from side-impact collisions, it protects him from any danger from side air bags. Whichever seat you choose, remember to place your baby in the rear-facing position until he weighs 20 pounds and is twelve months old.

ALERT!

Although you can apply to get permission to turn your air bag off or install an air bag on-off switch, your baby would still be safer in the back seat of a car. Try to make other arrangements (such as using another vehicle to travel in with your baby), and consider turning off your air bag only as a last resort.

Alternative Arrangements

Rear-facing car seats cannot be used in a seat with an air bag. Since your younger child must be seated rear-facing in the car, you will have to make other arrangements if your car or truck doesn't have a back seat.

One alternative is to turn off your passenger-side air bag when you have your baby in the car. The National Highway Traffic Safety Administration (NHTSA) has a form that you can use to request an air bag on-off switch if you have an infant who must ride in the front seat. You can learn more about air bag on-off switches and download a copy of the request form at the air bag section of the NHTSA's Web site (*www.nhtsa.gov*).

Get Your Home Ready

Many of the things you will do to childproof your house (found in Chapter 13) can wait until your baby is getting around on his own, but there are a few things you should take care of immediately to keep your baby safe. These include checking the temperature on your hot water heater and eliminating secondhand smoke.

Hot Water Heater Temperature

Younger children, especially newborns, are very sensitive and their skin can burn easily. They also usually are not able to quickly pull away from burning water or let you know if the water is too hot, so it is important to protect your child from hot water to prevent scalding burns.

Simply testing the water is not enough, because your infant may turn the water faucet on herself and quickly get burned if the water temperature is too hot. The best precaution to take is to turn down the temperature of your hot water heater now, before you even bring the baby home.

How quickly can a child get a third-degree burn?

- In only 2 seconds if the water temperature is 150° Fahrenheit
- In only 5 seconds if the water temperature is 140° Fahrenheit
- In 30 seconds if the water temperature is 130° Fahrenheit
- In about 5 minutes if the water temperature is 120° Fahrenheit

Could you get your baby away from the water in two or even five seconds if she is playing with the hot water tap and manages to turn it on? Probably not, and that's all the reason you need to lower your hot water heater temperature to no hotter than 120° Fahrenheit. It's not always easy to see exactly what temperature a water heater is set at, so even after lowering your heater's temperature, it is a good idea to test the water with a cooking thermometer.

Also be sure to test the water before you use it near your baby each time, especially if you are lowering her into a bath, and never leave your kids unsupervised in the bathroom or kitchen.

Setting your hot water heater temperature is not always easy, especially because many thermostats don't actually include a temperature gauge on them. If you need help, call your electric company, gas company, or the water heater manufacturer for detailed instructions.

Eliminate Secondhand Smoke

One of the healthiest things that you can do, for your baby and yourself, is to make your home smoke-free. If you smoke, the best time to quit is now, before your baby is born and you bring him home.

If you had been planning to just smoke outside, understand that really isn't enough to keep your baby healthy. Many studies have shown that babies whose parents smoke are more likely to have ear infections, allergies, and asthma, and are at greater risk of Sudden Infant Death Syndrome (SIDS). This is true even if the smoking isn't done directly around the babies. Your doctor or a good Web site, like *quitsmoking.about.com*, can help you stop smoking before it's time to bring your baby home.

Fire Safety

It's obvious that infants depend completely on you or another older family member to get them out of the house if there is a fire. Having working smoke alarms installed properly throughout the house can help you create an early warning system in case of such an emergency. A fire escape plan will help you handle an emergency situation as calmly and efficiently as possible, to allow everyone in your family make it to safety. As you install smoke detectors in your house, consider going the extra step and installing carbon monoxide detectors as well. Otherwise you may not know this harmful gas is in your house until it's too late.

Installing Smoke Alarms

Every floor or level of your house should have a working smoke alarm. They are especially important inside or just outside each and every bedroom. To prevent false or nuisance alarms, don't install a smoke alarm inside the kitchen or bathrooms. The manufacturer's instructions and your local building and safety codes can also help you find the best places in your home for a smoke alarm.

QUESTION?

What's the best way to position a smoke alarm?
Smoke alarms should be installed on the ceiling or high up on a wall, about 6 to 12 inches from the ceiling. Don't install them near outside windows or doors or near an air duct.

To make sure that your smoke alarm is in good working condition, change the batteries at least once a year and test the alarm each month.

Fire Escape Plan

No matter how safe your home is and how many smoke alarms you have, if you don't have a plan for everyone to get out of the house, your family may still not be safe in case of a fire. A well-planned and regularly practiced fire escape plan can help to make sure that everyone gets out safely. As part of your fire escape plan, you should decide who will get each of your children out of the house, how they will get out, a backup route in case the first is blocked or unusable, and where you will meet outside. This way you won't have to worry about anyone rushing back into the house trying to reach a child who is already out safely.

Installing Carbon Monoxide Detectors

Carbon monoxide is a colorless and odorless gas that can quickly be poisonous. It is produced by cars and appliances that burn fuel such as charcoal, natural gas, coal, wood, oil, kerosene, and liquefied petroleum.

Most people understand the need for having smoke alarms in their home, but carbon monoxide detectors are often overlooked, even though the Consumer Product Safety Commission recommends that every home have one. Carbon monoxide detectors are especially important if you have a garage attached to your home or if you have any fuel burning, nonelectric appliances in your home. These can include:

- furnaces
- fireplaces
- stoves
- water heaters
- space heaters

In addition to having these types of appliances professionally inspected each year and providing them with adequate ventilation, you should have carbon monoxide alarms to help alert you to any leaks before they can poison your family. Like smoke alarms, they should be installed near your bedrooms and on every floor of your house.

FACT

Because both are important and they are installed in the same areas, it makes sense to install a combination smoke and carbon monoxide detector instead of having to install two separate alarms. You should be able to find a combination detector at your local hardware store.

Get the Lead Out

Lead, which is especially toxic for children, was banned from household paint in the 1970s and as an additive to gasoline in the 1980s. Since these laws went into effect, lead poisoning is not as big of a problem as it used to be. However, now that it has gone out of the spotlight, many people have forgotten about lead poisoning, even though about 2 percent of children still have high lead levels, putting them at risk of behavior problems, learning disabilities, and more serious neurological problems. Lead poisoning may not be as common as it once was, but children can still suffer from it if the proper precautions are not taken.

The biggest exposures to lead these days is from lead paint in older homes, especially those built before 1950 and homes built before 1978 that are being remodeled, and soil that is contaminated with lead. If your house was built during the time when lead-based paint was still used, keep a close eye out for peeling, chipping paint that your baby might try to eat. Also watch for lead dust that can be created when a door or window is repeatedly opened and closed.

Drinking Water and Lead

Lead may also be used in pipes, which means that drinking water is likely to be the biggest source of exposure to lead for your baby. Although only homes built before 1930 are likely to have lead pipes, the pipes in newer homes may have been connected with lead solder. And keep in mind that even "lead-free" pipes can be made with up to 8 percent lead.

If your plumbing might have lead in it, be sure to only use cold water from the tap to make formula or for cooking and drinking, because hot water can have higher lead levels than cold water. You should also let the water run for fifteen to thirty seconds before using it, to help flush your pipes so that the water has less lead in it. A water filter might also help to reduce the amount of lead in your drinking water.

Other Sources of Lead

Lead is still used today in many products, including batteries and solder, which means that if you work in certain industries you may present a potential risk to your children because lead dust can get on your clothes. Among the jobs and hobbies that can be a risk to your family are:

- Auto repair
- Welding

- Construction
- Radiator repair
- Battery repair
- Making pottery
- Making stained glass

If you spend time doing any of these activities you should wash and change your clothes and shoes before leaving your place of work or entering your home. Washing your work clothes separately from the rest of the family's clothes is also a good idea to keep them from getting contaminated.

Certain home remedies and medicines, such as pay-loo-ah, azarcon, and ghasard, can also be sources of lead to children and should be avoided.

ALERT!

A recent report has shown that many people do not know how old their home is and so may underestimate their children's risk of lead poisoning. If you live in an older home or apartment, but aren't sure how old it really is, ask your pediatrician to test your infant for lead poisoning.

Cord Blood Banking

There are few things that you can invest your money in that have the potential to save your child's life. Sure, buying a car seat, getting your child vaccinated, and having working smoke and carbon monoxide alarms in your home can save your child, but none of these will cure her if she gets sick.

Unlike these preventive strategies, storing your baby's umbilical cord stem cells in a cord blood bank does have the potential to save her if she someday gets seriously sick. Once collected, stored, and saved, umbilical cord stem cells can later be used for a stem cell transplant if your child develops a genetic disease or a type of blood disorder or cancer that can be treated with a bone marrow transplant.

In recent years, many for-profit programs that collect and store umbilical cord stem cells have been developed. You probably have seen advertising in parenting magazines and may even have received brochures in the mail describing these services. Because your baby's cord blood must be collected at the time she is born, you will have to think about and be prepared to have her cord blood collected while you are still expecting. It is not a decision you can make later.

FACT

If you have a child with sickle cell disease, thalassemia, leukemia, lymphoma, or another cancer, you may be eligible for free collection and storage of the umbilical cord stem cells of your future children through the Children's Hospital Oakland Research Institute Sibling Donor Cord Blood Program (☞*www.chori.org*).

The marketing of the cord blood banks that describe a "once-in-a-lifetime opportunity" can be persuasive, but the procedure is expensive. After a one-time "banking fee" of about $1,500 to $1,700, you will have to pay about $95 a year to store the stem cells. Even with payment plans, that is a lot of money for most new parents.

It doesn't hurt your baby to take the blood from the cut umbilical cord, and this blood would just be thrown out if you decided not to save it. That seems to leave money as the main deciding factor. So should you pay to bank your baby's umbilical cord stem cells? If it is something that you can afford and you feel better knowing that you are storing your baby's stem cells in case you ever need them, then signing up with a cord blood bank might be for you.

When making your decision, keep in mind the clinical report on cord blood banking by the American Academy of Pediatrics (AAP), which concluded that "private storage of cord blood as 'biological insurance' is unwise." In other words, the AAP doesn't think that it is necessary for the average parent to store their child's cord blood. However, it may be a good idea if you already have a family member who needs or may need a stem cell transplant because they have leukemia, a severe hemoglobinopathy, or other disorder, both because they may be able to use your baby's cord blood for a transplant and because your child may be at increased risk of developing these conditions too. The AAP does recommend that parents donate their babies' stem cells to nonprofit centers, like the National Marrow Donor Program cord blood banks, so that they can be used for stem cell transplants in unrelated recipients.

Newborn Screening Tests

Not all birth defects can be easily recognized at birth, because many don't cause symptoms until weeks or even years later. However, some birth defects can be found through newborn screening tests. Many of the illnesses that are screened for can cause severe mental retardation or even death.

Among the disorders that can be easily screened for are the following:

- Phenylketonuria (PKU)
- Galactosemia
- Congenital Hypothyroidism
- Sickle Cell Disease
- Congenital Adrenal Hyperplasia (CAH)
- Homocystinuria
- Maple Syrup Urine Disease (MSUD)
- Cystic Fibrosis
- Medium Chain ACYL-CoA Dehydrogenase (MCAD) Deficiency
- Glucose-6-Phosphate Dehydrogenase Deficiency (G6PD)

Most of these are disorders that cannot be totally cured, but can be easily treated. There are medications for congenital hypothyroidism and CAH, and special diets for PKU, galactosemia, and MSUD. Depending on where you live, your baby may only be screened for PKU and congenital hypothyroidism, or he may be screened for all of them and more. Your pediatrician or state health department can let you know what your baby will be automatically screened for.

For those parents who want more extensive screening, expanded or supplemental screening tests are also available. The blood specimen for these tests can be taken at the same time that the state screen is done. It's possible to test for an additional thirty to fifty diseases from a single specimen of blood. Although each disease that is screened for is rare, the tests are relatively inexpensive, at about $25 to $60 for all of them, and so can be a good idea for those parents that want some additional reassurance. Start thinking now about whether you want to pay for extra tests or check with your insurance company to see if this is a covered benefit.

You can find out how to order a supplemental screening test kit at ✍*www.savebabies.org*. Have the kit ready when your baby is born so that they can send it off at the same time your baby's state screen is sent.

Circumcision

Even though getting a baby boy circumcised can be a controversial topic, parents usually have a strong opinion one way or the other about whether or not a circumcision is a necessary procedure. Circumcision is another thing you and your partner need to think about and discuss before your baby is born, so that you don't feel rushed into making a decision.

If you are considering circumcising your baby boy, keep in mind the new American Academy of Pediatrics Circumcision Policy Statement, which states that "data are not sufficient to recommend routine neonatal circumcision."

So why would anyone circumcise their baby if the AAP doesn't recommend it? One big reason is that although the AAP doesn't formally recommend that babies be circumcised, they don't actually recommend against it, either. Instead they conclude that "parents should determine what is in the best interest of the child," which leaves open many reasons for why a baby might be circumcised, including religious or cultural reasons, or just because dad or an older sibling is already circumcised.

Still, there are many reasons why you may not want to circumcise your baby. One of the biggest is that although it is a minor procedure, it is still a surgical procedure. And like most medical or surgical procedures, there can be risks, including excessive bleeding and infections. Other risks or complications can include your doctor taking off too much skin or too little skin, so that the circumcision has to be repeated at some later time. Even though these side effects are uncommon, if you add in the fact that the benefits are also small, such as the small decrease in the rate of urinary tract infections, choosing to not have your baby circumcised is a valid decision.

ALERT!

If your child is going to be circumcised, you should insist that the doctor use some type of analgesia to try to decrease the pain your baby may feel. This might include a topical anesthetic, like EMLA cream, or an injection of lidocaine in a penile nerve block. The days of believing that babies don't feel pain are long over.

Don't let anyone try to tell you that all boys are circumcised. In some parts of the world outside the United States, circumcision is quite rare. Even in this country, the rates of circumcision vary widely. While on average 65 percent of male newborns are circumcised, the rates range from a low of 37 percent in the West to 64 percent in the South, 65 percent in the Northeast, and 81 percent in the Midwest. Whether or not to have your son circumcised is a personal decision that each family should make individually.

Baby Names

Choosing a name for your new baby can be one of the most fun things you can do before your baby is born—but it can also be one of the most difficult. How on earth do you even begin to decide on the name your baby will live with for the rest of his life? Do you choose a family name, a popular name, a unique name?

It can be hard for both parents to agree on the same name for their baby, but you should be prepared to offer your own favorites and suggestions and try to compromise if you can't decide on a name that both of you like.

Popular Baby Names

Choosing a popular name doesn't usually mean naming your baby after your favorite movie star, singer, or character on TV or in the movies. It means choosing a name that many other people are also going to choose, leading to classrooms with two or three Matthews and several Emilys. Here's a list of the most popular names from a few years ago that you can review if you are looking for (or trying to avoid) a name for your baby that a lot of other babies will have too.

Top 10 Baby Names of 2003		
	Boy Names	**Girl Names**
1.	Jacob	Emily
2.	Michael	Emma
3.	Joshua	Madison
4.	Matthew	Hannah
5.	Andrew	Olivia
6.	Joseph	Abigail
7.	Ethan	Alexis
8.	Daniel	Ashley
9.	Christopher	Elizabeth
10.	Anthony	Samantha

from the U.S. Social Security Administration

Middle Names

The baby's middle name might simply include a name that you like, or the name of a friend or family member whom you want to honor. Be sure to check for words that the initials spell out so that your child doesn't end up with initials like FAT or PIG. If your partner had to make a compromise on the choice of the baby's first name, it might be nice to let her choose the middle name she wants.

Starting Your Own Traditions

Sticking to a family tradition for naming your baby can be a good way to honor or remember your ancestors, but whose tradition do you follow?

What if both mom's and dad's families have a tradition of naming the first-born child after their own grandparents?

In this kind of situation, if you can't reach a compromise, you might come up with your own "tradition." Maybe name all of your children with names that start with a certain letter: Charlie, Chace, and Chad. Or name your first girl after the mom's mother and your first boy after the dad's father.

Making a Will

Younger couples often overlook the need to have a will. After all, they don't expect anything to happen to them anytime soon and they probably haven't built up many assets yet. Once a baby is born, the need for a will becomes essential.

FACT

You should hire a lawyer if you need more than just a basic will. In complicated situations—for example, if you are not married to your baby's mother, have children from a previous marriage, or already have a lot of financial assets—then a lawyer should help you prepare your will.

Without a will, if both you and your baby's mother die, you will have no control over who becomes your baby's guardian. Do you want family members to fight over your baby, have a court pick someone, or have your baby go to a foster home? Or would you rather put some thought into who would best raise your baby, and make sure that they have the legal right to do so?

For most new parents, unless they already have a lot of money or financial assets, the cost of preparing a will shouldn't be a big issue. A basic will that is easy to prepare is likely to be all you need, and you may not even need a lawyer to do it. There is a wide choice of software and self-help books to help you prepare a simple will on your own, inexpensively.

Special Situations

In addition to all of the regular things that parents have to do as they prepare for a new baby, there are some extra things to think about in certain situations. For example, there are a lot of extra baby products to get if you are having twins, triplets, or even more babies. You will also have different things to do if you are adopting a baby or if you will be a single parent caring for the baby on your own.

Expecting Multiples

In general, parents have about a 3 percent chance of having twins or other multiples, like triplets or quadruplets. For older couples or those who used fertility treatments, the chances are even higher. Although each bundle of joy is definitely a blessing, if you are going to have more than one at once, there is a lot more preparation to do.

QUESTION?

Does having twins run in the family?
Not always. While your chance of having twins is increased if there are fraternal twins in your family, there is no increased chance if other family members only have identical twins. Identical twins are thought to occur randomly and are not tied to genetics.

Having multiples means buying more of everything as you prepare for your babies. You will need more clothing, more diapers, and more of just about everything else. You will need more than one car seat and eventually, more than one crib. Of course that means having to spend more money than you would if you only had one baby at a time, and it also means that you are likely to need more help caring for them. This is a situation in which a father might try to take more paternity leave or ask another family member to come help with the babies. Fathers of multiples should also expect to help out a lot more than what they might have expected for only one baby.

Adopting a Child

A lot of preparation goes into the whole adoption process, starting with signing up with an adoption agency and going all the way to the day that you actually get to take home your child. There is the paperwork, waiting, and all of the regular preparations to get your home ready for a baby.

If you are adopting a child from another country, there may also be medical issues to prepare for. Does the child have any special health-care needs? Does he need immunizations or screening tests to detect common infectious diseases, like HIV, tuberculosis, and hepatitis? Your pediatrician can help you review your adopted child's health once you adopt your baby.

Single Parenting

Although there are many single parents raising children on their own, it is much more common for this primary caretaker to be the child's mother. Still, fathers sometimes have the sole responsibility of caring for the baby. A single father will have a lot of financial pressures and will need some help and support to care for his baby, much like a single mother would.

Maybe you don't live with and aren't married to the baby's mother. Depending on your situation, you may need to consult a lawyer to help you understand your rights and responsibilities. Will you have partial custody, visitation rights, or any contact at all with your baby? Do everything you can to offer support and be a big part of your baby's life.

Special-Needs Kids

Infants with special needs can be much harder to understand than the average baby. They may need to feed more frequently or more slowly, require special medical attention, or have other things you need to do to help them feed and grow. Of course, these babies really are special, and you will love and care for yours just as you would any other baby.

Whether you have a premature baby who is a little behind in everything, or a child with Down syndrome or a cleft lip and palate, you will have to learn to understand your baby's own special needs. Your pediatrician, a specialist or other health professional, or a support group can help you learn to best take care of your baby with special needs.

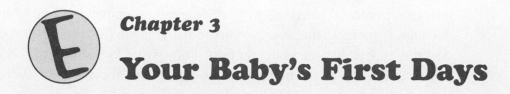

Chapter 3

Your Baby's First Days

If having a baby really changes every-thing, then get ready, because here is where it all starts. Once your baby arrives, it will soon hit you that you're a new dad. Although the first few days can be over-whelming, they are also fun and exciting. This is a time that you will always remem-ber. Knowing what to expect and what is going on with your baby can help make these days even more enjoyable.

At the Hospital

Once your baby is born, a lot of different things can happen in the delivery room. Although it is now routine for fathers to be in the labor and delivery room with the mother when their baby is being born, it can sometimes be hard for an expecting dad to know his place. You probably will be feeling anxious, confused, nervous, excited, or some combination of all of these feelings. Remember that your primary role is going to be to coach and comfort the expecting mother. If you don't know what to do beyond this, just ask someone. No matter how many books you read or classes you take, this experience is not something that you can easily prepare for.

Usually the first thing that will happen once the baby is born is that the cord will be cut. Then, if it was an uncomplicated vaginal delivery, the mother might be given a few moments with the baby. If it was a caesarean section or if the baby is limp or blue, he might immediately be taken away to be resuscitated.

Resuscitation

The term "resuscitation" means to revive someone. This procedure is best suited for a newborn that comes out and is not breathing or doesn't have a heartbeat; however, even crying, healthy newborns often undergo the same basic initial resuscitation procedure. After delivery, a baby who needs resuscitation is handed off to someone from the resuscitation team—a nurse, pediatrician, or some other health professional—who takes him over to an infant warmer. There the baby will be dried off, positioned on the warmer, and have his nose and mouth suctioned. The baby will then have his breathing or heart rate stimulated if necessary, although a crying newborn who is breathing well will likely not need this additional stimulation.

Once on the warmer, the baby will be quickly dried off to prevent heat loss, especially if he seems sick. Next, the baby is positioned so that his airway can be seen, and then his mouth is suctioned to get any leftover fluid out. After these procedures, if the baby still isn't breathing well on his own, the health professional will stimulate him to breathe by slapping his foot or firmly rubbing his back. The baby is likely to respond to this extra stimulation and start breathing and crying well on his own.

FACT

Not all babies cry a lot after they are born. Parents often listen for the sound of loud crying to signal that their baby is healthy. If your baby stops crying after a few cries but is awake and alert, pink and breathing well, then she is likely to be healthy and doing fine.

First Feeding

After the resuscitation, your baby will be wrapped in a blanket and handed back to either mom or dad. You may not be thinking about feeding your baby at this time, but if your baby's mother plans on breastfeeding, now would be a good time to start if she is feeling up to it. This is especially important, because after being awake and alert for an hour or two, your baby is likely to sleep most of the rest of his first day and will be harder to wake up for breastfeeding. Even if you aren't breastfeeding, you both should spend the first hour after delivery holding and bonding with your new baby if he is healthy and doesn't have to be taken immediately to the nursery.

The Nursery

Whether your baby is sick or well, he will eventually be taken to the nursery. Once there, he will be weighed, measured, and observed to make sure that no problems develop. Other routine procedures will include:

- A sponge bath
- A vitamin K shot
- Eye drops or ointment to prevent infection
- Observation to make sure he can maintain a normal body temperature
- Observation for difficulty breathing, heart murmurs, and color changes
- A first feeding of sugar water if you aren't breastfeeding

At-risk babies might also have blood sugar testing if they are very small or very large. Babies whose mothers have a positive Group B Strep test might have additional testing and antibiotics for a few days.

Rooming-In

Once it has been determined that your baby is healthy and his temperature doesn't drop when he isn't under a warmer, he probably will be able to leave the nursery and go visit his mother and other family members. At this point, you can usually decide to either have the baby stay in your room for all or most of the time, which is called rooming-in, or continue to have him go back and forth from the nursery.

ALERT!

Nursery workers often assume that sleeping mothers don't want to be awakened for nighttime breastfeedings. If you and your partner don't want your baby to get formula and she isn't rooming-in, be sure everyone knows to wake mom up for feedings and to not give a bottle unless your pediatrician says that it is medically necessary. You should also alert the nursery that you do not want them to use a pacifier, because that can often interfere with effective breastfeeding.

Rooming-in with your baby can make breastfeeding on demand easier for the mother and give her more time to bond with and understand your baby before going home, but it may make it harder for her to get much rest. Rooming-in is also a good idea for dad, so that he can also bond with the baby and help the mother get some rest.

Preemies and Sick Babies

After so many months of expecting that you are going to have a healthy baby, realizing that something might be wrong can be difficult. You will sometimes have some warning—for instance, if a problem was detected on a prenatal sonogram, or if your partner's OB/GYN predicted that she wouldn't be able to carry your baby to term—but most other times it is a complete surprise.

While seeing all of the things that happen to a normal baby can be confusing for many new parents, watching the doctors and nurses surrounding your sick baby can be really overwhelming. X-rays, blood tests, ventilators, and IVs all are things you might see if your baby is sick.

The NICU

If your baby is just a few weeks early or isn't very sick, she might be able to stay in a regular nursery. Sicker babies or preemies born before 35 weeks will likely need to be transferred to a Neonatal Intensive Care Unit or NICU. If there is a NICU in the hospital where your baby was born, the transfer will be easy, but it is possible that the baby will have to be transferred to a larger hospital with more advanced facilities.

A transfer can be especially hard because the mother won't be able to see her baby until she is discharged herself. She should be able to see her baby briefly before the transfer, though, and will get frequent updates over the phone or from you after you visit the NICU.

Premature Babies

Although it's common to hear of full-term babies being born at 38 to 42 weeks, only babies born before 35 weeks are usually considered to be premature. Older preterm babies, like those born between 35 and 37 weeks, usually do just as well as those born full-term.

If your baby is a preemie or gets sick shortly after being born and his mother is still recovering herself, a good job for dad is to gather as much information as he can about what is going on with his baby. Doctors should be able to give quick, regular updates about what is going on.

Your premature baby will likely need to spend some time in an NICU. How long mostly depends on how early your baby was and what complications she has. A good rule of thumb is that your baby probably will be discharged from the NICU close to her expected due date. So your 34-week preemie might spend just a few weeks in the NICU, while a baby born at 25 weeks is likely to be in the hospital for at least three months.

Sick Babies

Being "sick" typically means that your baby is having difficulty breathing or is showing some other signs of an infection. Standard procedures in situations like this usually involve your pediatrician examining your baby, ordering a blood count and blood cultures to look for an infection, and starting intravenous fluids and antibiotics for a few days. If all testing is normal and your child quickly recovers, the antibiotics are often stopped after forty-eight hours. Other testing might include a chest x-ray to look for pneumonia or other lung problems, and blood sugar monitoring.

Babies who still aren't breathing after the normal resuscitation procedure described above will need help to breathe with a respiratory bag and a mask placed over the mouth. In many cases, babies respond to fifteen or thirty seconds of "bagging," but if your child doesn't and she has a low heart rate, the resuscitation person might have to start doing chest compressions to get the baby's heart beating. Last, your baby might be intubated, or have a tube placed in her mouth and down to her lungs to help her breathe. In extreme cases, your baby will have to be given medications to help with the resuscitation.

Birth Defects

Babies born with birth defects might also need specialty care in a NICU, especially for congenital heart defects and conditions like spina bifida. Other common birth defects include hypospadias (a defect in the position in the opening of the urethra on a boy's penis), Down syndrome, club foot, and cleft lip and palate. These conditions can often be managed by your pediatrician in the nursery, with later specialty care after discharge.

If you are having trouble coping with the fact that your baby has a birth defect, talk to your pediatrician and/or look for a local support group for more help. Your baby doesn't have to be "physically perfect" to be perfect.

Hearing Screening

It is estimated that 3 out of every 1,000 children are born with a permanent hearing loss. In the past, hearing loss wasn't detected until the children affected were toddlers and already had speech and communication delays. A new emphasis on early detection of hearing loss and other developmental delays means that you should know very early if your child is born with a hearing loss.

In fact, the recent increase in universal hearing screening of newborns means that your baby is likely to have a hearing test even before leaving the hospital. This early detection can lead to early intervention and help your child learn to communicate well.

FACT

Unfortunately, not all states have laws that mandate hearing tests for newborns. If your baby's hearing isn't tested at the hospital, you can still ask your pediatrician to schedule a hearing test sometime in your baby's first few months.

As with any screening test, there will be some false positive test results. This means that some newborns who are tested will "fail" the test, but not actually have any hearing loss. Although this can be scary for parents, you really shouldn't think of this as failing the test. It instead simply means that more testing needs to be done in a few weeks. This is not uncommon, and most babies pass the second hearing test.

It is also possible to pass this test and still have a hearing loss. Although much less common than false positive tests, these false negative results are more serious. This means that it is very important to talk to your pediatrician if you think that your baby doesn't hear you, even if she had already passed a hearing test when she was born.

Bringing Baby Home

The timing of your baby's discharge from the hospital depends on many things, including how your baby was delivered. Although families often want to leave early (before forty-eight hours), that likely won't be possible if your baby was born by caesarean section. After a C-section, most mothers have to stay in the hospital for at least three to four days, if not longer.

Discharge Criteria

How well your baby is doing also will be a big factor in the decision as to whether or not she can go home early. Using criteria from the American Academy of Pediatrics, your baby should only be discharged early if she was born full-term, had a normal physical examination, and is maintaining a stable body temperature for at least six to twelve hours.

ALERT!

Don't accept an early discharge from the hospital, which usually means leaving less than forty-eight hours after your baby is born, unless your partner feels comfortable going home. She should be able to stay for at least two full days if she wants to.

Before going home, your baby will also have to be either breastfeeding or taking formula well. If your baby isn't latching on, isn't sucking well, or is taking less than an ounce of formula at a time, then she likely will need to spend a little time in the hospital nursery.

Your baby also probably won't be able to go home early if she is much smaller or bigger than the average baby, is having problems with her blood sugar, develops jaundice early, shows any signs of illness, or if the mother had a positive Group B Strep test.

Before You Go Home

Even if your baby is doing well, you shouldn't go home until you and her mother are ready. The hospital can be a great resource for you both to learn about breastfeeding, changing diapers, taking a temperature, and so on. Before discharge you also should try to take any parenting classes that the hospital offers.

You likely won't be able to learn everything you want to know about your baby in one or two short days in the hospital, but you should be able to learn the basics. It can be especially helpful for a new dad to perform as much of his baby's care in the hospital as he can. That means changing clothes and diapers, wrapping your baby in a blanket, picking him up, and holding and carrying him. Getting comfortable with these very basic procedures, with a nurse ready to step in if you are really doing something wrong, is a great way to learn.

Baby Basics

The "basics" are going to mean different things to different people. For a new dad who has had his first baby and was never really around a lot of babies before, simply holding your baby is something that will have to be learned. Dads with more experience may just need to brush up on other basics, like feedings, changing diapers, and dressing the baby. Learning to take a rectal temperature is another good skill to learn before you go home.

See One, Do One

Reading long, detailed instructions isn't the best way for most new dads to learn about changing diapers or dressing a baby. Unless you have seen or done these things before, even the best instructions are going to seem like they are written in a foreign language.

If you don't feel comfortable doing something, whether it is changing a diaper, feeding your baby, or simply picking him up, then ask someone to help you. New dads are much less likely to want to help out if they feel that they don't know what they are doing.

A much better approach is the basic "see one, do one" technique of learning baby basics. That means that you watch an experienced person perform each task, and then try it yourself. You'll feel more comfortable doing these things with someone watching, especially if that person can point out things you may be doing wrong.

Basics to Learn

These are some of the more important things that you should know how to do before discharge, so that you will feel more confident and will be able to be more helpful at home.

- ❒ Recognize proper breastfeeding techniques, including positioning, latching-on, and sucking
- ❒ Prepare your baby's formula and bottles (if using formula)
- ❒ Burp your baby
- ❒ Change a diaper
- ❒ Dress and undress your baby
- ❒ Pick up, carry, and hold your baby
- ❒ Take a rectal temperature
- ❒ Swaddle your baby by snugly wrapping him in a blanket
- ❒ Put your baby to sleep on his back to prevent SIDS
- ❒ If necessary, care for a circumcised penis

Early Health Problems

Your baby should do fine after he goes home if he got a clean bill of health in the hospital. Most of the more common problems that can affect a newborn are going to be easy to uncover while he is still in the hospital, including severe infections, pneumonia, respiratory distress syndrome, and major heart defects.

Still, especially with early discharges, your baby could be born with a problem and not start to show symptoms until after you get home. And then there are problems that don't even begin until after a few days of life. Knowing what to look for should ease your worries and help you recognize when your baby might be having a problem that requires a visit to your pediatrician.

Breastfeeding Problems

The first few weeks of breastfeeding can be difficult, especially for new parents. Afterwards, once a mom has a good milk supply and the baby has learned to latch on and suck well, things go much more smoothly.

During those first few days and weeks, though, moms might struggle with nipple soreness, a baby who doesn't latch on well or who has a poor suck, and other problems. At these times, instead of just giving a bottle of formula, you should get help.

FACT

Not all pediatricians are very supportive of breastfeeding or know how to help resolve breastfeeding problems. If you need extra help, be sure to find a lactation consultant in your area. These experts in breastfeeding can give you the support and information you're looking for.

Getting help is easy if you have friends or family members who have breastfed successfully before. If not, look to your pediatrician or a lactation consultant for some expert advice. It may not be easy, but most breastfeeding problems can be overcome with the right help. It's likely that after you receive help, your baby will soon be breastfeeding without further problems.

Signs that your baby is not breastfeeding well might include:

- Wanting to breastfeed fewer than eight to twelve times in a twenty-four-hour period
- Having fewer than two yellow-green stools by day three or four of life (these follow the black, tarry meconium stools he will have the first two days) or fewer than three to four loose yellow stools by day five to seven
- Having fewer than six full, wet diapers by day five to seven, although urinating less frequently is common until mom's milk comes in
- Losing more than 5 to 10 percent of his birth weight that first week
- Persistent nipple or breast pain for the mother

Remember that letting your baby breastfeed frequently, at least eight to twelve times a day, is the best way to help mom establish a good milk supply and encourage effective breastfeeding.

Problems with Formula

Although we often think of feeding problems as being limited to those babies who are breastfeeding, formula-fed babies can have problems too. One of the biggest problems is simply not tolerating the formula, which might lead to your having to change to a different type. This means if you are giving your baby a cow's-milk-based formula, you might have to switch to a soy or elemental formula.

Many of the things that parents interpret as problems with food are really normal reactions, such as the baby having gas, spitting up frequently, or having loose stools. Although changing the kind of formula your baby drinks is not usually harmful, it can cost you money and lead to increased anxiety if you think something is wrong. That is why it is usually a good idea to talk to your pediatrician before changing formula.

Another problem that formula-fed babies can have is simply not eating enough or being slow feeders. After the first few days of life, most babies will drink about 2 to 3 ounces of formula every three to four hours. Talk to your pediatrician if your baby is drinking much less than that or regularly going longer than three to four hours without wanting to eat.

Because the different brands of the same variety of formula, such as Enfamil Lipil with Iron and Similac Advance with Iron, have the same protein (cow's milk) and sugar (lactose), changing from one to another is usually not helpful when your baby has a real formula intolerance.

Poor Weight Gain

It is expected that a baby will lose weight during his first week of life. This upsets many parents who were happy with their healthy 7- or 8-pound baby and who don't like to see them drop even an ounce. However, your baby will almost certainly lose at least 5 to 10 percent of his birth weight during that first week. This weight loss is mostly because newborns lose excessive fluid they are born with and because at first they can't eat enough to keep up with their caloric needs.

Any more weight loss can be a problem, though. Or it might indicate a problem if your baby loses weight too rapidly. If your baby is already down 5 or 7 percent after just one or two days, then by the end of the week it might be well over 10 percent. These babies should be closely monitored every day or two to make sure that they don't continue to lose weight.

After the weight loss of the first week, your baby should start to gain some weight. You can expect a baby who is feeding well to gain at least ½ to 1 ounce each day, so that by the two-week checkup, the baby is back up to his birth weight. Continuing to lose weight or not getting back up to birth weight by two weeks can indicate a problem, especially with feeding, and should be investigated by your pediatrician.

Jaundice

Developing jaundice, which is a yellowish discoloration to the skin, is very common in newborns. This jaundice typically develops on the baby's second or third day, so it may not be seen in the hospital. Jaundice that develops within twenty-four hours of your baby's birth, or which rapidly gets worse, can be a sign of a more serious problem than the typical "physiological jaundice" that most other babies have.

FACT

Babies who have very high levels of jaundice can develop kernicterus, a form of brain damage. Although rare, the effects of kernicterus can be severe, with mental retardation, cerebral palsy, and hearing loss.

Jaundice usually starts on your baby's face and in her eyes and then spreads down her body as it gets worse. You should notify your pediatrician if the jaundice seems to be spreading quickly or has already reached your baby's arms and legs. Although many babies with jaundice are simply observed or are placed in indirect sunlight, some babies require blood testing and treatment with phototherapy and special lights. Because so many people are aware of this problem, jaundice rarely gets to a high enough level to cause serious or permanent problems anymore.

Other Symptoms

Although sickness in babies is usually discovered because they are having trouble feeding, other signs to look for include rapid breathing, excessive crying, a swollen abdomen, fever, excessive sleepiness, and persistent vomiting. However, occasional crying, vomiting, and even short periods of rapid breathing, called periodic breathing, can be normal.

One problem is recognizing whether or not something is excessive. If your new baby is sleeping for sixteen and a half hours a day, is that excessive? It sounds like a lot, but is actually average for a baby in the first week of life.

It can be hard to recognize when young infants are sick, so if you think there is something wrong with your baby, be sure to call your pediatrician. When your child's health is at stake, it's always better to be safe than sorry.

Caring for Siblings

In some ways, already having children can make having a new baby easy. After all, you are likely to already feel comfortable holding a small baby and may already know how to change a diaper. You may also already have a lot of the clothing and other baby accessories you will need, such as a crib, changing table, and infant carrier. And your baby's mother might already be a pro at breastfeeding.

Younger children, especially toddlers, generally have a harder time adjusting to a new baby arriving at home than an older sibling might. This is one reason that some parents choose to space children at least three or four years apart when planning their family.

Having other kids at home can also make things much more difficult. New dads might not be able to stay at the hospital as much as they would like with the new baby because they have to rush home and take care of the other kids. And once you bring the baby home, caring for your other children will leave both mom and dad with less time to spend with the new baby.

Another big problem with siblings is the development of jealousy toward the new baby. There are several things you can do to help prevent this kind of jealousy. These include:

- Preparing siblings for the arrival of the new baby throughout the pregnancy
- Making sure they are being cared for by someone they are comfortable with while you are in the hospital
- Having them at the hospital or at least visiting when the baby is born
- Asking other family members to pay a lot of attention to your other children after you bring your baby home
- Having older siblings help you with simple tasks, such as bringing you a diaper or baby wipe
- Spending "special time" alone with your other children each day, even for just a short time

You should also prepare for and accept regressions in your other children's behavior, although things like tantrums or hitting shouldn't be encouraged, even if your children are upset about the new baby. To be safe, you also shouldn't leave your new baby alone with a younger toddler or pre-school-age child.

Supporting a New Mom

Once she gets home with her baby, a new mother is likely to be both excited and exhausted. So many things go on in the hospital that it is often hard to fully recover before being discharged. That is one reason why it is important for mom to rest as much as she can while she is in the hospital and make sure she is ready when she does go home.

During those first few days after you bring your baby home from the hospital, it is going to be especially important for you to help out. What you actually do to help is going to vary depending on your situation. If your partner had a long or tough delivery or a C-section and is still recovering, then you may have to do a lot more than you ever expected.

Even with a quick recovery, you should still help, although that doesn't always mean taking care of the baby. It can sometimes be even more helpful to let the baby's mother spend most of her time bonding with the baby and just take over other household chores yourself. You might care for your other children, do the shopping, clean the house, etc. Helping doesn't always have to mean helping with the baby, unless that is what mom needs.

QUESTION?

How much is a new dad going to have to help?
You should want to help out as much as you can, but how much you have to do is also going to depend on how many kids you have. If you already have two or three kids at home or you have just had twins or triplets, you can expect to have to help out more than you ever imagined you would have to.

If you are still overwhelmed with all that is going on, try to arrange for extra help in the house from other family members or friends. You can ask friends to baby-sit your other kids, or maybe bring over ready-to-eat meals at least a few times each week. (Just remember to return the favor when they have a new baby!)

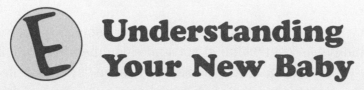

Chapter 4

Understanding Your New Baby

The first few days and weeks can be overwhelming for new parents. Especially if this is your first child, there are a lot of things that will be new to you. You may understand that your baby needs to eat, sleep, and have his diaper changed regularly, but what about all of the other things that are going on with him and his body? Learning to understand your new baby should help you to feel more comfortable caring for him.

Your Baby's Temperament

Understanding your baby's temperament can help you to understand why he does the things he does. Does he cry every time you change his diaper or when it is time to go to sleep? Is he fussy a lot or slow to adapt to changes in his routine? Or is he the model "easy" baby who rarely cries and always seems happy?

Basically, you can think of your baby's temperament as his personality. It is something he is born with and not something that is easily changed. Instead of trying to change it, you should try to understand your baby's temperament and adapt to it. Is he easily overstimulated or bothered by loud noises? Then try to keep things calm and quiet around him. Does he adapt poorly to changes in his regular routine? Then try to keep things on as much of a schedule as possible.

Responding to your baby's temperament is harder if your baby is very unpredictable. Fortunately, your baby's early temperament does not always predict how he will be later. Many infants who are difficult early on seem to outgrow this behavior and become more easy and outgoing later in infancy.

Can You Spoil a Baby?

Instinctively, parents often pick up their baby when he is crying, but should you? It depends on who you ask, but the advice to not pick up or hold your baby very often is now considered rather old-fashioned. Realizing this will help you to respond to family members or friends who incorrectly tell you not to hold your baby so much.

So how much holding is too much? Really, no amount of time is too much. Parents who practice "attachment parenting" even advocate that your baby be in close contact with you for most of the time. Instead of worrying about whether or not you will spoil your baby, you should trust your instincts as a new father and pick him up when it seems right.

What Your Baby's Cries Mean

Babies cry for a lot of different reasons. They may cry when they are wet, hungry, or sleepy. Babies also often cry when they are bored or just because they want to cry. Crying is the way babies communicate their needs, so it is easy to understand why they cry so much.

Once you understand that you can't spoil your baby by holding her a lot or carrying her around, you may be wondering how you can hold your baby all day and still get anything else done. One simple solution is to carry her in a baby sling or wrap. This will keep your baby snug, cozy, and close to you, and still keep your hands free.

Can you tell what your baby needs just by listening to him cry? Probably. But it likely isn't from the *sound* of his cry. At first, you will do better trying to understand your baby's cries in the context of what else is going on. Has it been two or three hours from his last feeding? Then he is likely hungry. Did you just notice him straining, like he was having a bowel movement? Then his crying probably means that he wants his diaper changed. Or if he has already been awake for several hours, then maybe he just needs to sleep.

Playtime with an Infant

While you should begin playing with your baby now, it is not what you would usually think of as formal play. Your baby is too young to grab things at this age and can't bat at a hanging mobile or other toy. Instead, he will mainly enjoy hearing and seeing things. They can't be just any things, though, because toys that are too loud or that move too quickly will probably upset your baby.

More simple toys, like a face drawn on a paper plate, a black-and-white mobile, or some other figure with highly contrasting bright colors, might hold his attention briefly. The best way to "play," though, might be just holding your baby close and letting him see his new daddy's face and listen to your voice.

Your Baby's Body

Getting to know and understand your baby's body can help you to feel more comfortable holding, handling, and carrying him. Can you hurt your baby if you are too rough? Of course you can, but babies aren't easily "breakable" if you do things in a gentle and caring manner.

Floppy Heads

Knowing that your baby has a floppy head is probably one of the most important things to understand about his little body. If you don't support his head and neck when lifting, carrying, or turning your baby over, you could very easily hurt him. His poor head control and lack of strong neck muscles can cause his head to quickly fall or flop backwards. You should continue to use one hand to support your baby's head and neck until he develops better head control in later months.

The Soft Spot

Your baby's soft spot, or fontanel, is one area of his body that you might be trying to avoid. Many new parents worry that if they touch their baby's head, they might push all the way through the soft spot. Although this part of his head isn't protected by bone, it is still fairly tough and is not easy to push through during the regular day-to-day tasks that you do to take care of your baby. So don't become overly worried about the soft spot when you put on your baby's hat, brush or wash his hair, or simply pat his head. Still, there is no reason to directly try to push on his soft spot.

Your baby's soft spot has a very important function. It is where the different plates of your baby's skull come together. Without this type of system, your baby's head would not be able to mold as it comes through the vaginal canal, and his brain would not be able to grow so quickly during his first few years.

Your baby's soft spot can also alert you to when he is sick. A sunken fontanel can be a sign of dehydration, and would be something to worry about if your baby also is vomiting, has diarrhea, or isn't eating well. On the other hand, a bulging fontanel can be a sign of raised pressure inside your baby's head. Babies with a bulging fontanel also are likely to be fussy or have a fever. Without any other symptoms, small changes in the fontanel may be normal. It is also normal if you sometimes see the fontanel pulsate in rhythm with your baby's heartbeat.

Umbilical Cord Stump

Your baby's umbilical cord stump is probably going to be another part of his body that you try to avoid. Until it completely falls off by two to three weeks, it might look strange, could smell or bleed, or even have some discharge. A little care and attention is important though, and can help to prevent any more serious problems from developing.

ALERT!

Your baby's umbilical cord stump needs some type of treatment to prevent it from getting infected. Whether it is having triple dye applied to it in the nursery and/or daily use of alcohol at home, something should be done to reduce the number of bacteria on the cord and prevent infections. Without some type of care, your baby could get tetanus or another infection. Follow your pediatrician's instructions carefully.

First, remember to keep his cord dry. That means no real baths until it falls off. Until then, just continue to give him sponge baths when necessary. It can also help if you leave his cord exposed to the air by not letting it be covered by his diaper or clothes. Last, many doctors will advise you to apply rubbing alcohol to the base of his cord with gauze or a cotton swab, as long as you don't overdo it.

Advice on cord care is surprisingly controversial. Some experts advocate "dry cord care," or basically doing nothing at all and simply watching for signs of an infection. Others recommend applying alcohol with each diaper change, which might be ten to twelve times each day if you are breastfeeding. (However, some studies have shown that applying alcohol too frequently, meaning more than two or three times a day, can make it take longer for the cord to come off.) Whatever method you choose, call your pediatrician if your child does develop an infection of the umbilical cord stump, known as omphalitis. Signs can include a persistent, foul-smelling discharge and redness around his belly button.

Your Baby's Body in Motion

You might be surprised by the way your baby moves during his first few weeks. Instead of smooth, purposeful movements, your baby will normally make quick, jerking movements. Chin quivering and occasional trembling of his hands are also normal.

One sign that a baby's movements are not normal is if he is not moving both of his arms and legs equally. For example, if he consistently doesn't move one arm, that could be a sign of nerve damage or a fractured clavicle (collarbone). Rhythmic movements, like jerking his arm or leg once every second, can be a sign of a seizure. You should call your pediatrician if you notice either of these patterns of movement or if you have any other concerns about the way that your baby moves his body.

Are Girls Different?

Sure they are, but most of the ways that they are different won't become important until much later. When your daughter gets older, you may have to worry about girl clothes, girl issues, and of course, puberty. In early infancy, those changes aren't as important.

There are a few things that you should be aware of, though, when caring for a baby girl. The first is that it isn't unusual for a newborn baby girl to have a little vaginal discharge. This discharge will be clear or white, will not have a foul odor, and can simply be wiped away. Keep in mind that the discharge can be a little blood-tinged, and that can still be normal. This discharge is caused by the effects of the hormone estrogen that the baby gets from her mother before being born, and the effect usually wears off by the time she is about two weeks old.

FACT

Estrogen from your baby's mother can cause swollen breasts in baby girls (and boys) and skin tags on a girl's hymen. It can also cause the outside of a baby girl's vagina to appear swollen when she is born.

The other big thing that you should understand about your little girl is how to clean and change her. When changing diapers, use a fresh diaper wipe or washcloth to also wipe your baby's vaginal area from front to back. That means going from the top of the vaginal area down toward her bottom. If you go the other away, then you may push up bacteria from her bottom into her vaginal area, leading to infections.

And Those Boys . . .

Dads usually have an easier time understanding a baby boy's body, because they are familiar with all of the anatomy. There are a few things that you might find surprising or different, though. One of the most common is that one or both of your baby's testicles might be undescended in early infancy. They usually descend later on their own, although sometimes surgery is required to treat this condition. Be sure to alert your pediatrician if you think your baby's testicles are undescended.

A circumcised dad might also be a little confused if his son is left intact, just as an uncircumcised father can be confused about a circumcised son. Either way, your baby's penis will not need any special care in early infancy, and you can just wash it like you do the rest of his body when you give him a bath.

Infant Reflexes

New fathers are often more familiar with their baby's reflexes than they think. Although you may not officially be aware of what they are, or know the names of them, these reflexes involve things you probably notice your baby doing every day. For example, you observe the rooting reflex when your baby looks for the breast or a bottle when he is ready to eat and his cheek is stroked.

Why does your baby tightly grab your finger when you put it into his hand? That's the palmar grasp reflex. The plantar grasp reflex causes the same thing to happen on his foot. In addition to being the easiest to recognize, these grasping reflexes also are often the last to disappear. The palmar grasp reflex doesn't usually go away until your baby is five to six months old. And the plantar grasp won't disappear until even later, when your baby is nine to twelve months old.

Infants are born with reflexes that help protect them in their environment. For example, the Moro or startle reflex might protect your baby if something covers her face all of a sudden. The parachute reflex, in which the arms extend if your baby falls forward, can protect her as she learns to walk. And the rooting and sucking reflex can help her to eat.

Observing these reflexes and the time at which they go away can help to make sure that your baby is growing and developing normally. The average dad doesn't need to be testing these reflexes on a regular basis, though. For most dads, it is just a fun thing to notice. Your pediatrician will be checking all of your baby's reflexes at his well-baby exams, and will pay special attention to them if you have any concerns about your baby's development. There are several other reflexes your pediatrician will check that you may also notice as you watch your baby.

Moro or Startle Reflex

This reflex is one of the easiest for parents to recognize. After your pediatrician stimulates this reflex, your baby should throw his arms and legs outward, cry, and then draw them back in. The Moro reflex also can occur if your baby is surprised or startled by a loud noise or if you quickly change his position.

If your baby doesn't have a Moro reflex or only responds with one side of his body or one arm, it can indicate a problem that your pediatrician will want to investigate. The Moro reflex is present at birth and usually goes away by two months.

Tonic Neck Reflex

This is an interesting reflex when you see it. In response to turning his head to one side, this reflex causes a relaxed baby to straighten his arm on that side and bend his other arm. If you then turn his head to the other side, he will reverse the positioning of his hands. The tonic neck reflex usually goes away by five to six months. This is one of the harder reflexes to see, so don't be surprised if you never see your baby getting into this "fencing position."

Early Sleeping Patterns

Although your baby is likely to do a lot of crying and eating, the one thing that he should be doing even more of is sleeping. Babies sleep about sixteen and a half hours a day during the first week of life, and may sleep even more during the first few days.

QUESTION?

Can my baby sleep too much?
Your baby may be sleeping too much if he is missing feedings, is difficult to wake up for feedings, or if he isn't awake at least briefly for some part of the day. Very young infants would not be able to get enough to eat if they didn't continue feeding through the night.

To help your baby sleep, you can try swaddling him, or wrapping him snugly in a blanket. And always put him to sleep on his back to help reduce the risk of Sudden Infant Death Syndrome (SIDS). Remember that it will be a few weeks or months before your baby gets into a regular pattern of sleeping more at night. Until then, he probably will sleep and eat on regular two-to four-hour cycles.

Understanding Baby Clothes

For a first-time father, a baby opens up a whole new world of things to understand. In addition to learning about your baby, you may be learning about all of the things you will use to help care for your baby. Most of the things you will use, such as formula or a car seat, come with an instruction label, but what about all of those clothes? Although many of the clothes that your baby will wear are easy to recognize—like undershirts, bibs, and hats—others can be more confusing. New dads probably won't know the difference between a jumper and a sleeper, or what a receiving blanket is. These definitions will help new dads understand the clothing that babies wear:

- **Onesie**—a one-piece, short-sleeved outfit without legs that snaps in the crotch area and is usually worn under other clothing
- **Shortall**—like overalls, but with short pant legs; this outfit snaps in the crotch and usually is worn over an undershirt or onesie
- **Romper**—a one-piece outfit with short legs that snaps on one shoulder and in the crotch and inner legs
- **Jumper**—a sleeveless, one-piece outfit with long pant legs; usually worn over an undershirt or onesie
- **Coverall**—a one-piece outfit with long pant legs and either short or long sleeves; may be footed and have snaps that either go all the way down from the neckline or just from the crotch to the feet
- **Nightgown**—a one-piece outfit with an elasticized bottom for newborns to sleep in
- **Sleeper**—a footed, one-piece, full-body outfit with a zipper or snaps that extend from the neckline to one pant leg
- **Receiving blanket**—a light blanket used to swaddle a baby
- **Bunting**—a baby blanket that can be snapped together so that your baby can "wear" it

The other big thing to understand about your baby's clothes is that he will outgrow them quickly. This makes it important to buy them a little bigger than necessary so that they last more than just a few weeks.

Realizing You're a Dad

When should it hit you that you're a dad? For some new fathers it is while they are still expecting the baby. For others, it happens quickly once the baby is born or when they first hold the baby. But sometimes it doesn't happen until later, and that's okay too.

With all that is going on those first few days, you might not realize that you're a dad until the first time your baby grasps your finger or the first time he smiles at you. For some dads it may not even happen until the first time your baby says "dada." If you are not feeling like a dad, you likely need to spend more time bonding with your baby.

The New Dad's Role

Knowing what role to take that first month after his baby is born can be difficult for a new dad. The role of the new mom is well defined, but dads don't always know what's expected of them. And different families will have different needs and expectations, which can make things even more confusing.

When you're trying to determine your role, it can help to simply have a talk with the new mom to figure out what your family needs from you. Should you try to stay home from work for a few weeks? Should you help care for the baby—for example, taking over some feedings and changing diapers—or should you just help around the house?

If mom wants to spend most of her time bonding with her baby, having dad take over some extra household chores can be extremely helpful. So you might do the laundry, cook the meals, or buy groceries, if those aren't things that you already are doing. For a new mom who just needs to catch up on sleep, it could be most helpful to take over with the baby for a while and give mom a break.

Dealing with Negative Emotions

A dad's role also can be shaped by his feelings toward his new baby. Although you might expect that all fathers would feel love, pride, and joy toward their baby, some instead feel resentment and jealousy, because they may no longer have their partner's full attention. If you find yourself having any of these feelings, do what you can to help overcome them before they harm your relationship with your child. You can either find someone else to watch the baby so you do have some special time alone with your partner, or you can make an effort to get more involved and do more things together with her and your baby.

Chapter 5

The First Four Weeks

Having survived the first few days, you can expect more of the same for the rest of this month, including a regular cycle of feeding and changing diapers, while your baby keeps up a cycle of crying and sleeping. As you are learning to do more with your baby, remember that while you do have to be gentle, babies are not as fragile as you might think.

Breastfeeding Essentials

Most parents have heard more than once that breastmilk is the best option for babies. When you think about all of the possible benefits for your baby, including improved development, fewer infections, and a lower risk of asthma, allergies, and obesity, you can see how important breastfeeding is. Breastfeeding can also benefit mothers by lowering their risk of breast cancer and helping them lose weight. In addition, you avoid the expense of having to buy formula. However, while many new moms start out and leave the hospital breastfeeding, far fewer are still breastfeeding after a few months.

A mom shouldn't feel guilty if she doesn't want to breastfeed, but if she simply feels that she *can't* breastfeed, she should understand that there are many places to go to get help anytime she starts having problems, including friends and family members, your pediatrician, or a lactation consultant.

Breastfeeding Goals

Many families start out with good intentions, and plan to breastfeed their baby. In the United States, almost 70 percent of babies start out breastfeeding. Many of them stop well before the American Academy of Pediatrics recommendation of breastfeeding for at least twelve months, though. In fact, by five to six months, only 30 percent of babies are still being breastfed. This is also well short of the goals set by the Healthy People 2010 target: that 75 percent of babies start breastfeeding, 50 percent are still breastfeeding at six months, and 25 percent make it to at least a year.

QUESTION?

Why don't more mothers breastfeed for at least a year, as the AAP recommends?
Mostly it is because of a lack of support. Many mothers simply don't know anyone else who has breastfed a baby, or they don't have friends, family members, or a doctor who will encourage and help them.

To help ensure that your baby is breastfed as long as both he and your partner want, it can help to set a goal for how long mom wants to breastfeed.

Will it just be six weeks, until she goes back to work? Or does she want to breastfeed for at least a year?

If you have a goal you both understand and are working toward, it may help so that she doesn't stop before she is really ready. If your goal is twelve months, and your baby isn't breastfeeding well at four or six months, then you will know you should get help for your partner to help her continue to breastfeed and still reach her goal. With a goal or target to shoot for, you may find it easier to work through any problems that occur.

Being Supportive of Breastfeeding

It may seem like a silly idea that dads learn how to breastfeed, but unless you understand some of the basics, it is hard to be helpful or supportive. Among the things that you should observe and learn include:

- The different methods of holding a baby while breastfeeding, such as the cradle, crossover, and football holds
- The rooting reflex and helping your baby latch on well (and not just to the nipple)
- Observing proper sucking and swallowing while breastfeeding
- How to release a baby from the breast

You also need to understand some of the specifics about how and when the breasts make milk. For example, it's important to know that:

- A mother's milk doesn't normally come in until a baby is three to five days old
- Infants should breastfeed every two to three hours for up to ten to fifteen minutes on each breast or thirty minutes on only one breast, or until the breast is soft and empty of milk
- If a baby only feeds well on one breast during a feeding, then he should alternate which breast he starts from the next time, so that each breast is fully stimulated to make milk

Breastfeeding can be stressful for a new mom. Learning as much as you can about breastfeeding, not pushing your baby to take a bottle of formula if breastfeeding isn't going well, and quickly getting help if there are problems all can help to ensure effective results for your partner and your baby.

The Facts about Formula

If the baby isn't breastfeeding, most dads will have a much more active role in feeding. If this describes you, you should learn how to prepare your baby's formula, how to hold your baby during feedings, and how to burp him afterward, among other things.

Formula Brands and Types

Considering the many different types and brands of formula, choosing which one to feed your baby can be confusing if you think about it. In reality, most parents probably just continue using whatever formula they were started on in the hospital. You should understand the different types, though, in case your baby is having problems, or you simply want to switch.

Although there are different brands, including Enfamil from Mead Johnson, Similac from Ross Pharmaceuticals, Carnation Good Start, and the many store-brand formulas, each brand offers most of the basic varieties of formula, including basic cow's milk, lactose-free, and soy-based. There also are hypoallergenic or elemental formulas, which are broken down into their most basic particles, preemie formulas, and other specialty formulas for infants with special dietary needs.

FACT

In addition to all of the choices among types and brands of formula, you also will have to decide whether you want a formula that is supplemented with DHA and ARA, fatty acids that are supposed to make formula more like breastmilk and enhance your baby's development.

Unless there is a family history of food or formula allergies, most babies who aren't breastfeeding should be started on a basic cow's-milk-based, iron-fortified formula. Many infants are changed to other formulas because of mild problems, such as loose stools, gas, or spitting up. This change is often unnecessary, so talk to your pediatrician before you change your baby's formula.

There are no formal recommendations on which brand to choose, although you should always choose a formula that is iron-fortified. All infant formulas meet the requirements of the Food and Drug Administration and so are safe and will meet your baby's nutritional needs. Many parents don't feel comfortable choosing the cheapest formula they can find, but you should feel confident that your baby will do just fine if you don't choose a "name brand" formula. And you should usually choose a powdered formula, because they are the least expensive.

Preparing Your Baby's Formula

The formula you buy will include instructions on how to prepare it, whether it is ready-to-feed, concentrated, or powder, and you should review and follow those instructions closely. Not preparing your baby's formula correctly can lead to your baby not getting enough calories if you make it too diluted, or not tolerating it if you make it too concentrated.

Once you know how to make the formula, you should decide how much to make. Because you can't reuse any leftover formula, you should try to make just the amount that your baby will take in one sitting, which will be about 2 to 3 ounces this first month.

Although it is often recommended that you boil water before using it to make formula, you may not have to do this if you are sure that your water supply is safe.

Feeding Your Baby

Just as with breastfeeding, there are different positions that you can use to feed your baby a bottle of formula. Most parents choose to place their baby in a reclining position in one arm and hold the bottle in the other. You could also choose to sit her up in a more upright position. Try both positions to see which is more comfortable for you and your baby. The one position to avoid is feeding your baby while she is lying down flat.

On Demand or On a Schedule?

Whether or not to feed your baby on demand or on a schedule is a confusing and somewhat controversial topic. Critics of on-demand feeding say that it can lead to irregular schedules and spoiling your baby. Because you've already learned that you really can't spoil a baby, it's easier to dismiss these so-called experts.

The main problem with on-demand feeding is that it is often misunderstood. Feeding your baby on demand doesn't mean that you feed your baby each time he cries. It simply means feeding him every time that he shows signs of being hungry. These signs or signals might be cries, or it might be that he begins rooting or sucking on his hands. Actually, crying is often a late sign of hunger.

ALERT!

Putting your baby on a schedule for her feedings early on can cause serious problems. Making a baby wait three or four hours for each feeding, especially if she is breastfed, can lead to your baby not getting enough to eat and becoming dehydrated.

With on-demand feeding, you feed your baby when he needs or demands to be fed, instead of waiting until a schedule says to feed him. This will likely work out to a "schedule" of breastfeeding every one and a half to three hours, or formula feeding every two to three hours. If you are feeding your baby much more often than that, you may be misinterpreting when he is really hungry, although he may eat more often during a growth spurt. Eating less often than that also can be a problem. If it has been more than two to three hours since his last feeding, you probably should feed your baby even if he doesn't show any hunger signs.

Diapering Essentials

It used to be that you didn't have a choice in what type of diaper to use, because everyone used cloth diapers. Then everyone started using disposable diapers, and using cloth diapers wasn't a popular option anymore. But now, even though most people use disposables, you have a choice of which type of diaper to use, especially if you live in a bigger city that has a diaper service so that you don't have to wash them yourself.

Disposables or Cloth?

Both disposable and cloth diapers have improved to the point that either could be used for the average baby. The main benefits of using cloth diapers are that they can be less expensive if you clean them yourself and they don't end up in a landfill like disposables do. The downside is that they don't always absorb wetness as well as disposables do, and you can sometimes have more leakage of urine and stool from them. On the other hand, some parents report fewer diaper rashes from cloth diapers. Just determine which type fits better into your overall lifestyle and needs, and understand that either can work for your baby.

It's Changing Time

When your baby needs a diaper change, get all of your supplies together. This will include a clean diaper, diaper wipes (or a wet washcloth if your baby's skin is too sensitive for wipes), and any diaper rash creams, ointments, or powders you might need.

If you are sent out to buy diapers or anything else, write down the brand name, the type you need, the size you are supposed to get, and about how much it will cost. This will help to keep you from buying the wrong thing and having to make another trip back to the store.

Diapers that are only wet are easy to change. Simply remove the wet diaper, clean your baby gently with the wipes or washcloth, and then put a clean diaper on the baby. If your baby had a bowel movement, things will be a little more complicated, as you quickly try to get the diaper changed without making a mess all over your baby and yourself. Instead of taking the diaper off all of the way, it can be better to undo it, and then use the top half of the diaper to wipe the bowel movement into the bottom half. There will be much less of the bowel movement left over to clean with the wipes if you do it this way.

If your baby boy was circumcised, be sure to follow any instructions you were given about the care of his circumcised penis when changing his diaper. For girls, remember to always wipe from front to back, so that you don't push any stool into the vaginal area, which can cause irritation and infections.

More Baby Basics

It might seem that feeding and diapering your baby are what you are going to spend most of your time doing, but there are a few other day-to-day tasks that you should be familiar and comfortable with. Sticking to the "see one, do one" technique that you learned in Chapter 3 and getting lots of practice will make you a pro in no time.

Burping

Burping the baby is one of the easier things that dads learn. After all, it isn't that complicated. However, there are several methods that can be used, and you should learn each to see which works best for your baby.

It is okay if your baby doesn't burp after each and every feeding, as long as it seems that she is otherwise doing well. However, if your baby seems more fussy or spits up more after feedings when she doesn't burp, you should keep trying.

The most common way to burp a baby is to simply place your baby against your shoulder and gently pat his back until he burps. Be sure to place a burp rag on your shoulder or you might get covered in spitup, which leads some dads to move to the next method, which is burping your baby as he sits on your lap. With this method, you lean the baby slightly forward and support the front of his chest, neck, and head with one hand while you pat his back with the other. If neither of these positions work for you, you could also burp him on your lap while he is lying on his stomach.

If you aren't able to get a burp, you might change positions and try again. You should also try to figure out if it works better to burp your baby at the end of the feeding, or to take a break to do it after several minutes of feeding.

Dressing Your Baby

After diaper changes, dressing the baby is one of the more challenging things that a new dad has to do. And undressing him isn't much easier.

Most of the difficulty probably results from the fear of hurting your baby, as you pull a shirt over his head or guide his arms through the sleeves. It can be a little intimidating to watch someone with more experience quickly and effortlessly undress and dress your baby, but that is the best way to learn. Then try it a few times yourself until you get the hang of it.

To make sure that everyone is comfortable in your home, set your thermostat to the temperature at which everyone is most comfortable, and then dress your baby accordingly, usually adding one more layer for your baby than you do for yourself.

Bathing

Bath time is easy for most of the first month until your baby's umbilical cord comes off, because she will only need a sponge bath a few times a week. You can expect that she won't like these early baths, though.

To get started with a sponge bath, get everything ready beforehand. You will need a basin filled with warm water and a mild soap, a washcloth, a cup of warm water for rinsing, and a soft surface to place your baby on, such as the bed or kitchen counter with another towel on it. Once you're ready, undress your baby and wrap her in a towel. Place her on the soft surface you have chosen and gently wash each part of her body with the washcloth you have dipped in the basin of soapy water. Rinse her off when you're done and wrap her in another towel to get dry. Last, use a moisturizer if her skin appears dry and get her dressed again.

Once the umbilical cord comes off, you can give your baby a regular bath. These are still different from the baths you may be used to, though, because you won't be submerging your baby in the water. Instead, you will support her head and neck and hold most of her body just above the small amount of soapy water that you put in the sink or small tub you are bathing her in. You will then wash and rinse each part of her body with a washcloth and warm water.

When bathing your baby, be sure that the water isn't too hot, that your baby isn't submerged in the water, and that you always keep at least one hand supporting her head and neck.

Growth and Development

It might not seem that a lot happens in your baby's growth and development this first month. After all, babies at this age don't pick up any big milestones, such as sitting up, rolling over, or walking. And instead of doubling or tripling their birth weight, as they will later this year, they actually lose weight that first week!

Among the things you can expect are that your baby:

❏ Regains his birth weight by about two weeks of age
❏ Continues to gain about ½ to 1 ounce each day
❏ Grows about 1½ inches in length
❏ Briefly focuses on your face or other objects that are about 8 to 12 inches away from him
❏ Follows objects moved in front of his face, from the side toward his nose
❏ Moves his arms and legs equally well, although his movements will likely be quite jerky
❏ Lifts his head briefly
❏ Responds to a bell or loud noise and recognizes and turns toward some familiar sounds

❐ Makes a variety of noises, including cries and grunts

❐ Has a variety of reflexes, including the Moro (startle reflex), stepping (a reflexive up and down movement of a baby's legs), rooting, and grasp reflex (see Chapter 4)

Keep in mind that there is usually a range of weeks to months for the average baby to reach his milestones, so try not to compare babies of the same age. Do talk to your pediatrician if you are concerned that your baby isn't meeting his milestones, though.

FACT

The highest risk period for Sudden Infant Death Syndrome (SIDS) isn't until an infant is about two to four months old, but it is never too early to begin protecting your baby. The biggest thing you can do to reduce his risk of SIDS is to always put him to sleep on his back. (See Chapter 6 for other ways to protect your baby.)

Health Problems

In addition to the regular conditions that can affect children of all ages, such as colds, stomach viruses, and ear infections, there are also some problems that are more common during a baby's first few weeks and months. Watching out for these symptoms and problems can help you recognize them early and prevent serious problems from occurring.

Allergic Colitis

Although this condition is not usually serious, babies with allergic colitis often give their parents quite a scare, mostly because the main symptom is having bloody stools. The blood makes parents think that something life-threatening is affecting their baby, but it usually just indicates a simple milk allergy. Most infant formulas are based on cow's milk, and those milk proteins can trigger the allergy. Soy formulas aren't always tolerated well by these babies either, so switching to an elemental formula is usually the best option to treat these infants.

Even though allergic colitis is usually caused by cow's milk proteins, that doesn't mean that breastfed infants can't be affected too. If a mother is drinking milk or eating foods that have milk as an ingredient, the milk proteins can pass into her breastmilk and cause problems for her baby. Simply avoiding milk products and continuing to breastfeed can usually prevent further symptoms.

Birthmarks and Rashes

Birthmarks are not usually a problem, but they are something to be familiar with. The more obvious ones are flat red or pink marks that can be found on your baby's eyelids, forehead, or on the back of his neck. With an official name of salmon patches, more people know them by their more descriptive names, such as stork bites or angel kisses. Unlike many other types of birthmarks, these usually fade by the time an infant is eighteen months old.

Early on, another type of birthmark can look similar to salmon patches. This birthmark is called a hemangioma or "strawberry." It can start as a flat red mark, but then is likely to grow until your baby is about eighteen months old. After it stops growing, it should then slowly begin getting smaller over the next three to four years. Occasionally hemangiomas require early treatment if they are located on a lip, where they can interfere with your baby's drinking and eating, or in a spot that hinders eyesight.

ALERT!

If your baby's hemangioma begins bleeding, gets big very quickly, or is located somewhere that you think might cause a problem, be sure to see your pediatrician right away. Early treatment with steroids can help them to stop growing.

Newborns rarely have good skin. In addition to the well-known neonatal or baby acne, your baby might have other types of rashes, including:

- **Heat rashes or prickly heat**—small bumps, most commonly on a baby's neck, chest, upper back, and any other areas covered by clothing

- **Erythema toxicum**—blotchy, red areas that may show up in a baby's first few days
- **Acrocyanosis**—bluish color on a baby's hands and feet
- **Epstein's pearls**—small, white bumps on the roof of your baby's mouth
- **Sebaceous gland hyperplasia**—tiny, yellow bumps on a baby's nose

Most of these rashes don't require treatment and go away on their own, but you should talk to your pediatrician if you think that they are severe or aren't going away.

Fever

Infants normally have higher temperatures than older kids and adults, but a real fever is never normal. Although many experts don't consider a baby to have a fever until the temperature is 100.4° Fahrenheit or higher, a temperature above 100° might indicate a problem in the first few weeks, especially if your baby is very fussy, isn't eating well, or has other symptoms. Because he may not have many other symptoms when he is sick, any newborn with a real fever should be considered to have a medical emergency and needs immediate care. You should talk to your pediatrician about what she considers to be a fever and always get the baby's rectal temperature if you suspect that his temperature is too high.

Having a fever is simply one symptom or sign that your baby is sick. It is possible to be deathly ill and not have a fever, so don't use your baby's temperature as your only way to judge whether your baby needs medical attention.

Jaundice

As you learned in Chapter 3, jaundice usually begins during day two to three of a baby's life, peaks by day four or five, and then gradually goes away by the end of the first week. Sometimes jaundice may not begin until later, in which case it is usually caused by breastmilk. With a much later peak, in a baby's second or third week, it may also linger much longer, sometimes as long as two to three months. If your baby is otherwise well, lingering jaundice is not usually a reason to stop breastfeeding, although you should keep in touch with your pediatrician.

Jaundice is not always normal, though. There are some conditions, including blood and liver disorders, that cannot always simply be observed until they go away. That is why it is a good idea to talk to your pediatrician when your baby is jaundiced, especially if he has other symptoms.

Pyloric Stenosis

Although most parents aren't familiar with the term "pyloric stenosis," they often do recognize that its main symptom, projectile vomiting, is something to worry about. While many babies have simple vomiting or spitting up, the baby with true projectile vomiting, which is often described as "going across the room," should see his pediatrician.

Infants with this condition have an enlargement of their pylorus, the muscle that controls the outflow of food from the stomach into the intestines. As it continues to enlarge, no formula or breastmilk is able to get through and it is vomited back up. Although in many cases infants vomit after each feeding in the beginning, the vomiting sometimes occurs after only one or a few feedings, delaying the diagnosis.

FACT

Reflux or spitting up is a common condition that many babies have. For most of them, spitting up, even when it is frequent, doesn't cause anything more than a mess. Signs that reflux might be more serious can be that your baby is very fussy, especially when eating; if he is coughing and choking when he spits up; or if it doesn't seem that he is gaining weight well.

Pyloric stenosis is more common in boys, seems to be genetic, peaks when infants are about three weeks old, and can be formally diagnosed with an ultrasound or upper GI test. The definitive treatment is surgery.

Umbilical Cord Problems

Parents usually get distressed when their baby's umbilical cord doesn't look quite right, and many don't like performing even basic cord care. The biggest problems occur when your baby's cord doesn't come off after three to four weeks, which can be caused by an umbilical granuloma, or if it gets infected. Keep in mind that a little odor or discharge can be normal. A cord is more likely to be infected if there is a lot of discharge or if the skin around the cord is red.

Umbilical hernias are also common and usually go away by the time your child is four to five years old. If your baby's cord is sticking out and seems painful, be sure to talk to your pediatrician.

Watching for Postpartum Depression

The tragic consequences of postpartum depression (PPD) have recently raised the awareness of this common disorder, which affects 10 to 15 percent of new mothers. Although we often think that mothers should be only happy and excited when they have a baby, giving birth can also trigger many unwanted negative feelings and emotions. These feelings of sadness and anxiety can lead to a mild case of the "baby blues" or to a more serious disorder, such as postpartum depression or postpartum psychosis.

Postpartum depression can affect almost any mother during the first year after her baby is born, whether or not it is her first baby. Changes in hormone levels may be the cause of PPD. It is also thought that feeling tired, stressed, and overwhelmed may contribute to this condition.

The consequences of depression being unrecognized and untreated can be tragic for the whole family. Be sure to get help for your baby's mother if you think she is having problems with postpartum depression.

New dads are often in a good position to recognize the early symptoms of postpartum depression and to offer a lot of help and support, so that a new mom doesn't get overwhelmed by all of the things that she is expected to do. Watch for the symptoms of PPD so you can get help for your partner if she needs it. Be aware of a mother who:

- Is crying a lot and feeling sad and depressed most of the time
- Is feeling irritable or restless
- Has no energy
- Is either not eating and is losing weight, or is overeating and gaining a lot of weight
- Has trouble focusing, making decisions, or remembering things
- Feels guilty or worthless
- Is not sleeping well or is overly tired
- Is complaining of a lot of physical symptoms, like headaches, chest pains, hyperventilation, or heart palpitations
- Is not interested in caring for her baby, or is overly worried that she will hurt the baby
- Has lost interest in her usual activities, or doesn't get any pleasure from them

Of course, after their baby is born, many new mothers and fathers can have some of these symptoms. They may be tired and not have much energy, just because there are so many things to do and a lot of sleepless nights. If a mother has a few of these symptoms but also is happy and excited to be caring for her baby and otherwise seems well, then she probably doesn't have PPD.

If you think your partner is showing signs of PPD, be sure to talk to a health professional and get some help before she harms herself or her baby. You should also be on the watch for postpartum psychosis, which is a much more serious disorder. A mother who has postpartum psychosis loses touch with reality and may have hallucinations and delusions.

Chapter 6

Your Baby's Second and Third Month

These early months are a fun time. Your baby isn't going to be sitting up or talking yet, but she will have more regular sleep and wake times than she did as a newborn. She will also be more alert and interactive, and is more likely to look at you and respond to things that you do, like singing lullabies. Add in regular smiles and laughs and it no longer seems that you have a baby who simply sleeps, eats, and cries.

Feeding Considerations

Your baby's diet isn't going to change much from what she's been eating so far. Babies at this age don't need a lot of variety. During these early months, it is still too early to start solid foods, even cereal. And babies who are only a few months old don't usually need water or juice yet. So your baby will just continue breastfeeding or drinking formula for now. She will likely be eating *more* at each feeding, though.

Breastfeeding

For many parents, the first few weeks of breastfeeding are the hardest. Fortunately, by two to three months, most mothers have overcome any difficulties and are breastfeeding well without any problems. In addition to mom now having a good and regular supply of breastmilk, most parents have gotten comfortable with the whole idea of breastfeeding. Even if new problems come up, by this time many parents have the confidence that they will be able to solve them and continue breastfeeding.

ALERT!

If mom's breastmilk supply has decreased, simply supplementing with formula is never a good answer. Although supplements may sometimes become necessary, the main goal should be to increase mom's milk supply, with extra breastfeedings, pumping after each feeding, and getting help from a lactation consultant. Herbs like fenugreek can also help to increase a mother's milk supply.

Breastfeeding can also be a little easier at this age because most babies are feeding a little less often. Instead of the eight to twelve feedings during the first few weeks, many babies are down to just seven or eight feedings by two months. Keep in mind that some babies continue to feed eight to twelve times a day and won't cut back on their feedings until three or four months. Signs that your baby is getting enough to eat, such as frequent wet diapers and regular bowel movements, being satisfied after feedings, and gaining weight, are often better ways to tell whether your baby is eating enough.

Some babies also cut back on how long they will breastfeed during each feeding. An effective or fast eater might be done in just ten minutes, while a slow feeder might take twenty to thirty minutes or more. Babies may also eat more or less often depending on whether or not they are going through or have just completed a growth spurt (see the section on growth spurts later in this chapter). Recognizing these situations can help to make sure that you understand what's normal and keep you from worrying unnecessarily.

Formula Feeding

Unless there has been a problem, your baby should still be on the same formula that she was drinking during her first month. If she is doing well, there is usually no reason to change the type of formula or brand that she is eating. Remember that changing formulas too often usually won't help vague symptoms, like occasional gas or loose stools, and it can cause its own problems. Some babies have trouble adjusting to the new formula and may eat less or get constipated.

The main change right now is going to be in the amount of formula that your baby is drinking. By two months, she should increase her intake to about 4 or 5 ounces at each feeding. And that will increase again to 5 to 6 ounces by three or four months, with most infants drinking a total of 24 to 32 ounces a day. Some bigger babies might be drinking up to 40 ounces a day, and others might be drinking less. Remember that how well your baby is growing is usually more important than the exact number of ounces that your baby drinks.

FACT

Remember that most babies aren't ready for solid baby foods at this age. Introducing solids is usually best delayed until your baby is four to six months old. See Chapter 11 if you are eager to start solid foods early, or talk to your pediatrician to get more help and advice.

Although she is eating more at each feeding, your baby may start eating less often by this age. She will likely go from six to eight feedings a day during her first month to only five or six feedings a day over the next few months. How often she eats is going to depend a lot on how much she eats at each feeding, how long she sleeps at night, and how long she can go without a meal. Some babies do better drinking 8 ounces four times a day, while others can't drink more than 3 or 4 ounces at a time, and so are still eating six to eight times a day. Your baby will probably be on a fairly regular schedule for meals now, but that doesn't mean that it has to be like every other baby's feeding schedule. Instead, figure out what works best for you, your baby, and her mother, and talk to your pediatrician if you think your baby is eating too much or too little or isn't gaining weight well.

Sleeping Patterns

Babies usually aren't sleeping through the night at this age. They will likely be sleeping for longer and longer stretches of time, though, and they will probably be awake more during the day.

If it still seems that your baby is sleeping most of the time, that is because he really is.

On average, in his second month, a baby is sleeping about fifteen and a half hours a day. And while there may be one stretch of sleep at night that is four to five hours long, many babies are just sleeping for two to three hours at a time and then wanting to eat.

If your baby wakes himself frequently when he moves his arms or hands, you might try swaddling him snugly in a light blanket. If you don't feel comfortable firmly folding a blanket around your baby or can't get the swaddling just right, you might buy special swaddling blankets, which are easy to use.

Although the goal for most parents is to help their babies fall asleep on their own and sleep through the night, that isn't going to happen at this age. After six to eight weeks you can start putting your baby down to sleep while he is drowsy but awake, but in these early months, you might have to rock him to sleep or let him fall asleep breastfeeding. The main early goal is simply to help your baby get into a regular routine of sleeping, ideally with more sleep at night and longer periods of being awake during the day.

Early Development

Your baby's early milestones might not sound as important as her later ones, when she will be walking, running, and talking. But these early milestones, like the first smile and first laugh, can be so much more exciting than the ones that happen later. These moments can be especially emotional for new fathers who haven't been through the experience before. In fact, for some new dads, this is the time when they might get that feeling of "hey, I'm a dad!"

Two- and Three-Month Milestones

The milestones that your infant is likely to reach at this age include:

- ❑ Smiling by two months
- ❑ Looking at or regarding her own hand
- ❑ Following objects past the midline of her face
- ❑ Laughing, squealing, and saying "ooh" and "aah"
- ❑ Being able to hold her head up at a 45° and then 90° angle
- ❑ Being able to sit with support and hold her head fairly steady by four months

By the time she reaches the end of her third month, your baby also may be able to bear weight on her legs, roll over, lift herself up on her arms while lying on her chest, grasp a rattle, and hold her hands together. Remember that not all children reach these milestones at the same age, so being a little late can be normal. If your baby is delayed and not catching up after a few weeks or months, or is delayed in more than one area, be sure to talk to your pediatrician.

Growth Spurts and Slowdowns

In a baby's first month, growth is fairly predictable. As you've learned, babies usually lose weight that first week and then slowly start gaining weight until they again reach their birth weight by the time they are two weeks old. For the rest of that first month, most babies continue to gain ½ to 1 ounce each day.

In their second and third month, healthy babies continue to steadily gain weight. But unlike the gradual 1 ounce a day that they gained in the first month, further growth can be a little bit more unpredictable. So they may gain a lot of weight one week and almost none the next, although they will still average about 1 ounce a day and about 5 pounds between one and four months.

It may not seem important to understand these growth spurts and slow-downs, because you won't be weighing your baby that often, but it can help you to understand any increases or decreases in her feedings. During a growth spurt, your baby will likely want to breastfeed more often or drink more formula. Likewise, during a slowdown, she may not want to eat as much. Be sure to see your pediatrician if your baby isn't eating well for more than a few days or if she has a lot of other symptoms, like fever, vomiting, or fussiness.

FACT

Growth spurts are an important way that mothers are "told" to increase their supply of breastmilk. As a baby wants to eat more and breastfeeds more during a growth spurt, it signals a mother's body to produce more milk, based on the simple principle of supply and demand.

Medical Problems

Many of the problems that your child was at risk for as a newborn can still occur in these first few months. This includes pyloric stenosis (with projectile vomiting) and the colds, coughs, and stomach viruses that all infants can get. At this age, fever is still a big concern, so you should still call your pediatrician right away if your baby has a temperature at or above 100.4° Fahrenheit.

There also are other problems that don't start or aren't noticeable until a baby's second or third month of life, such as plagiocephaly (otherwise known as a flat head) and eczema. In addition to watching for these issues, be sure to take your baby to your pediatrician for his two-month checkup to get an official word on how well he is doing. (See Chapter 15 for more information on regular checkups.)

Flat Head

In recent years, more and more babies are developing a flattening to one side of the back of their head. In the extreme form, the child's ear and forehead can be pushed forward, so that his head is obviously misshapen.

Unlike many other medical conditions that are discovered, the cause of these babies' flat heads is fairly obvious. With the recommendation that infants should sleep on their backs to prevent SIDS came the unintended consequence that babies spend much less time on their stomachs and more time on their backs. The pressure from being on their back for so much of the day causes these children to have flat heads, which has the medical name of "positional plagiocephaly."

Fortunately, most infants will later have a normally shaped head, if it's possible to vary the position that they stay in most of the time. This can mean rotating which side of your baby's head he sleeps on and keeping him on his stomach more when he is awake. Remember that with the risk of SIDS, even a flat head isn't a good reason to put your infant to sleep on his stomach.

ALERT!

A misshapen head also can be caused by more serious conditions, such as craniosynostosis. Although additional testing is sometimes necessary, your doctor should be able to tell by the pattern of your baby's head shape if the problem is just from positioning or from craniosynostosis, in which the bones of a baby's skull fuse together prematurely.

For babies who continue to worsen or who don't improve at all with positioning changes, a referral to a specialist for an evaluation can be a good idea. Treatment with a molding helmet or band can also be helpful in more extreme cases.

Eczema

Parents often give up on the idea of beautiful baby skin and get used to their baby's bad skin and various rashes during the first few weeks. Once those rashes improve, some babies develop another kind of rash called eczema.

Eczema typically begins after a baby is two months old, at which time he can develop dry, red, rough, and itchy patches on his skin. Although almost any part of your baby's skin can be affected, their cheeks and the creases of the elbows and knees are the most common areas where the rash starts.

FACT

Eczema, like hay fever and asthma, is a type of allergic disorder. If your child suffers from any allergy problems, you should try to figure out whether there are any special things that seem to trigger your child's reaction. You can then learn to avoid those triggers.

Eczema can be difficult to treat, but flare-ups usually can be brought under control with frequent use of moisturizers and a topical steroid cream. Moisturizers, especially right after baths, can also help to prevent new flares. Still, eczema does commonly come and go, which can be frustrating as you try to figure out what triggers the rash and how to keep it from returning. Talk to your pediatrician if you are having a hard time controlling and treating your child's eczema.

Reflux

Spitting up is so common that it is almost expected in a baby's first few weeks of life. But by two or three months, many parents expect it to have gone away or at least improved. Unfortunately, that usually isn't the case, and most infants don't get over their reflux until they are six to nine months old or even later.

If you remember the warning signs of reflux, including poor weight gain, your infant choking as he spits up, or pain and fussiness, you will know when your child needs more help, and when you simply need to keep your clothes and other things protected from your baby's normal spitup.

Avoiding Infections

After your baby's first month, when she is awake for longer periods of time and getting bigger, it can be tempting to want to take her out and show her off. While fun, this still puts her at risk of getting infections. That doesn't mean that you have to live in a bubble, but you should avoid unnecessarily exposing your infant to people who may be sick. This is especially important during the winter cold and flu season. It is also a good idea to delay the start of day care until your infant is at least two to three months old.

Until your baby is two to three months old, your pediatrician will likely be fairly aggressive when your baby gets a fever. At this age, infants with a fever typically get a workup that includes a blood and urine culture and a spinal tap. Since even a simple cold can cause a fever, avoiding these tests is one good reason to avoid exposing your child to a lot of people until he is older.

Even if you don't take her out, your baby might still get sick if you have older children in school or day care who get sick and bring an illness home. Frequent hand washing, encouraging your kids to cover their mouths when they cough and sneeze, and not sharing toys, bottles, and utensils can help to decrease this risk.

Remember that people are often most contagious the day or two before they actually start showing symptoms, so it is not always helpful to simply avoid people who seem sick. You should practice "universal precautions" as health professionals do, and consider just about any person that you and your baby have contact with to be a possible source of germs that can get your baby sick. Again, this doesn't mean that you have to be totally isolated with your baby, but use good judgment and understand that the more people your baby is around, the higher the chance that she will get sick.

Safety Alerts

If you have gotten your home babyproofed, your baby should be safe at this age. (See Chapter 13 for more information on childproofing.) He isn't going to be crawling or walking yet, so can't get into too much trouble. However, there are some specific things you should watch out for. Some early milestones, namely rolling over and grasping things, can put your baby at risk of injuries from falls and choking if you aren't careful. Also, your baby is now entering the prime risk period for Sudden Infant Death Syndrome (SIDS).

Falls

Before a baby becomes mobile, if you put her down in a safe place, you can usually assume that she will stay safe. Everything changes once she begins rolling around, though, and this often starts well before parents expect it. Parents who wait until they actually see their baby roll over before they start being careful to not leave her alone on a bed, changing table, or the couch are likely to see the baby suffer at least one fall. Keep in mind that the first time your baby rolls over might also be the first time that she rolls off of your bed.

Babies typically begin rolling over between two and six months, but because those are averages and some babies roll over even earlier, it is a good idea to never leave your baby alone in any place where she can roll off and fall.

Choking

Because your baby is only going to be eating breastmilk and formula at this age, you don't have to worry about him choking on any solid foods. However, rolling over does put your baby at risk for choking if he can get to something and put it in his mouth. These choking hazards can include small pieces of candy, coins, buttons, marbles, and any other small items. Be sure to keep small objects out of your baby's reach at all times.

SIDS

Parents are usually well aware of the tragedy of infants who die of Sudden Infant Death Syndrome (SIDS). And most know how to avoid SIDS, especially that they should put their baby to sleep on his back and not on his stomach. The following are less well-known tips to help reduce your baby's risk of SIDS:

- Avoid side sleeping, which is better than letting your baby sleep on his stomach, but not as safe as back sleeping (side-sleepers may roll onto their backs)
- Make sure that all caregivers know to put your baby to sleep on his back
- Don't let your baby get overheated when he is sleeping
- Don't let anyone smoke around your baby

A safe crib, in addition to helpinsg avoid injuries, can also help avoid SIDS. Features of a safe crib include a firm mattress with a tight-fitting crib sheet, slats that are not more than 2⅜ inches apart, and no soft objects, such as fluffy blankets, comforters, pillows, or toys.

QUESTION?

When can I move my baby to a crib in his own room?
In the first few months, many parents have their baby sleep in a bassinet near their bed to make getting up for frequent feedings easier. You can either do this and wait until the baby is sleeping for 4–6 hour stretches before moving him to a separate room, or you can start him off there as soon as he comes home from the hospital.

If you are using a blanket instead of a sleeper, tuck it under the mattress so that it only covers your baby up to his chest. Then place your baby to sleep with his feet near the end that has the blanket tucked under it. This will help to make sure that the blanket can't cover your baby's face.

Lullabies and Early Playtime

Changing diapers, feeding your baby, and getting her to sleep are often seen as essential duties. Playtime is important too, both to stimulate her development and to encourage strong bonding. It is often overlooked though, since many people consider playing to involve things a baby at this age can't do yet, like learning to ride a bike, playing catch, or even something as simple as playing peek-a-boo and hide-and-seek.

When thinking about what kinds of games to play with your younger infant, it can help to consider what she can do. At this age, your baby can see simple faces and high-contrast patterns and has begun to track objects, but she probably isn't grasping things yet. So black-and-white baby toys, a face or bull's-eye drawn on a paper plate, a mirror, and simple mobiles can be fun for your younger infant to play with. Still, holding your baby close to your own face, talking quietly, and responding to her responses can be the best toy at this age. Other great ways to bond include massaging or singing to your baby.

Baby Massage

Just about everyone loves a good massage, and that is especially true for babies. In addition to promoting bonding, a massage can be soothing for your baby. If you still feel that your baby is "breakable," a regular massage can help you to become more comfortable touching and holding him.

Although there are books and classes that you can take, you can start with some basic techniques. Try undressing your baby, placing him on a towel, and then gently but firmly massaging different areas of his body. For example, you might start with his hands, wrists, and arms, and then move to his legs, or rub his abdomen. If your baby cries too much, end the session, and try again later.

Singing Lullabies

An old-fashioned lullaby can be a fun way to play with and bond with your baby. Knowing a few lullabies, like Brahms' "Lullaby," "Rock-a-Bye Baby," and "Hush, Little Baby," can help you feel more comfortable singing to your baby.

Don't worry if you don't remember all of the words. Your baby won't mind. The sound of your voice and expressions on your face are often more important than the actual lyrics. You can simply make up your own words to finish the lullaby. Or you could also sing any of your favorite songs, even something like Bruce Springsteen's "Born to Run," in a lullaby type of tone. Or just make up your own lullabies. As long as some of the words rhyme, your baby will likely love it.

Going Back to Work

By three months, many parents who had planned to go back to work already have. Even if they qualify for twelve weeks of leave under The Family and Medical Leave Act, many parents can't stay out of work for that long because that leave is usually unpaid. Most try to make it at least six weeks, though.

ALERT!

Going back to work and separating from their baby can be stressful for many new mothers and fathers. That makes it important to watch out for, and get help dealing with, increased stress and frustration at this time. Dads should also review the signs of postpartum depression, which might be triggered or worsened when a mother goes back to work.

Whenever you go back to work, try to plan things in advance. If neither you nor your partner will be staying home during the day, are you comfortable with the arrangements you have made for a caregiver? Will there be enough help at home to get everything done and still have enough time to get some rest so that you can function at work? If your baby's mother is the one going back to work, be as supportive as you can, and help her to make the necessary plans. Will she be able to pump during the day if she is breastfeeding?

If you or your partner are not ready to go back to work, look at all of your options to see if it would be possible to stay home a little longer. Maybe you could use up some sick leave or come to some other agreement with your employer. Or perhaps you could just go back part-time. Be realistic about your family's needs, both emotional and financial.

Chapter 7

Months Four Through Seven

These middle months of your baby's first year are an especially fun and exciting time. All of a sudden your baby will be sitting up, reaching for things, and talking more. In addition to the jump in your child's development, during this time your baby will have doubled his birth weight, started solid foods, and is likely to be sleeping through at least a good part of the night.

Feeding Considerations

Because you are going to start solid foods at some point during this time in your baby's life, you can expect mealtimes to become a little more interesting. It can also be fun to watch your baby's face as you introduce new foods, tastes, and textures. Even though she begins to eat some solid foods, don't expect your baby to cut back very much on breast or formula feeding just yet. The bulk of her calories and nutrition will still be from breastmilk or formula.

Continuing to Breastfeed

Although many mothers start out with a plan to breastfeed until their baby is at least a year old, many stop breastfeeding around this time. Reasons for stopping can include that they are having problems, they are getting pressure to stop from other family members or friends, or simply because they think that they went long enough.

Just because your baby is getting a tooth or has started biting, that isn't a reason for his mother to stop breastfeeding. Babies can be discouraged from biting by stopping the feeding after they bite and saying "No" firmly or by gently pushing them into the breast for a few seconds.

Before stopping, moms should consider if the baby is really ready to stop. If they are both enjoying breastfeeding, there may be no reason to stop yet. Remember that the American Academy of Pediatrics guidelines recommend going to at least a year. This is a good time for you to offer some support and encouragement for mom to continue to breastfeed as long as she and your baby want. And you can get help from a lactation consultant if she is stopping before she wants to because of problems.

One simple reason to continue to breastfeed at this age is that both mom and baby still get all of the benefits that breastfeeding provides. Also consider that if breastfeeding has been going well up to this point, then it should continue to go well with few problems. And your baby will probably cut back on some feedings soon and may be down to just five to seven feedings a day by six months.

Continuing Formula

At this age, your baby is likely to still be taking 5 to 6 ounces of formula four to six times a day. Although she may be eating more at each feeding and feeding fewer times a day, the total daily formula intake will still be about 24 to 32 ounces. Don't expect any big changes in formula feeding until later, when your baby is eating a good two or three meals of solid foods each day.

Special formula for older infants is available, but it is not something that you necessarily need to change to. The regular infant formulas, plus the solid foods that she will be eating, provide all of the nutrition that your baby will need until she is twelve months old.

Starting Solids

You can start solid foods at some point during these months of your baby's life. As long as you don't start too early or before your baby is ready, she should do well with solids. A reflex called the tongue thrust reflex is most likely going to be the limiting factor in starting solids. This reflex causes a baby to use her tongue to push nonliquids out of her mouth, which is useful to avoid choking on things. Because this reflex usually goes away at about four months, most infants aren't ready to start solids before then.

ALERT!

Even if you think that your baby is ready for solids, that doesn't mean that she will want to eat them. If your baby isn't ready for solids, then wait before offering them. Don't try to rush things by putting solid foods in a bottle or infant feeder before she is ready.

Some signs of readiness include that your baby:

- Has doubled her birth weight
- Is at least four months old

- Has lost her tongue thrust reflex
- Has no risks for developing food allergies (risks include having other food allergies, eczema, or asthma, or having other family members with these problems)

The first solid to try is an iron-fortified rice cereal. You can slowly work your way up from there. If you start the cereal early, such as right at four months, you can probably wait another month or two to start vegetables or fruits. Parents who start a little later can go a little quicker, although it is still a very good idea to wait two to three days between introducing new foods so that you can watch for a reaction. (See Chapter 11 for more information on infant nutrition.)

Sleeping and Naps

These months of big changes in your baby's growth and development also include changes in his sleep patterns. While younger babies often continue to get up every two or three hours for feedings, by four to five months most infants are going much longer without waking up. And it is during these months that you can begin to work on your baby's sleep routines, deal with sleep problems, and help teach him to fall asleep on his own.

Sleeping All Night

Getting the baby to sleep all night is an important early goal for most parents. And that's understandable, because if you are up for most of the night with a crying baby, it can be hard to get through the next day. Night-time sleep for parents becomes especially important as your baby is more awake and alert during the day and can require more of your attention.

Fortunately, by four to seven months, the majority of infants are sleeping through most of the night. Even if they are waking up one or two times for a feeding, there is often at least one long stretch of five to six hours that they are sleeping. If your baby is still waking up frequently at this age, it can be a good time to review how he goes to sleep and what you do when he wakes up.

If your breastfeeding baby had been sleeping well but begins waking up during the night to feed a lot more, make sure that he is getting enough to eat during the day. If you recently dropped a feeding, it may be that he is trying to make up for it.

Regular Daytime Naps

Although babies sleep more at night at this age, they still sleep a lot during the day too. By six months, in addition to ten or eleven hours of night-time sleep, most infants are sleeping for three or four hours during the day. This is often divided into two naps, including an early morning and early afternoon nap. Younger infants are probably still taking three naps.

If your baby isn't taking regular naps at this age, you should try to figure out why. Is it because his daytime routine is very unpredictable, so he doesn't really know when it is naptime? If so, then try to plan your day around your baby's naps.

Teething and Tooth Care

Surprisingly, teething is one of the more misunderstood topics in early childhood, and different parents often have very different ideas about teething. Do you think that teething can cause fever, diarrhea, or a runny nose? Do you know when to expect your baby's first tooth?

The First Tooth

The average infant gets his first tooth at about six months, but the timing of this event varies quite a bit. Some babies get a tooth earlier or later and some are even born with a natal tooth. You can usually expect that your baby will get his first tooth sometime between three and fifteen months.

Because the timing of teething is largely genetic, you can sometimes predict when your baby's first tooth will erupt if you know when other family members got their first teeth. If a baby's parents or siblings didn't get their first teeth until eleven or twelve months, then you can expect that your baby won't get his first tooth until later too. If everyone was teething early, then he might too.

The timing of when a child gets his first tooth can be very variable. You usually don't have to worry even if your baby doesn't have any teeth after he is twelve or fifteen months old. Talk to your pediatrician if you are concerned, though, especially if your baby has any other medical problems.

Teething Symptoms

Most parents suspect that their baby is teething at around three or four months when he starts drooling a lot and wants to chew on things. While it is possible for a baby to get his first tooth that early, in most cases those aren't signs of teething. Instead, those are normal physical and developmental milestones that most children begin at this age, whether or not they are teething.

Still, your baby may start drooling more and want to chew on things when he really does start teething. The key to figuring out whether or not he is teething is to look for other signs and symptoms. Is he a little fussier than usual? Can you see or feel his first tooth coming through? Do his gums look red or swollen? All of those things can be associated with teething, which typically begins as the bottom two middle teeth, the central incisors, erupt.

After your baby gets his first tooth, he will usually continue to get three or four more teeth every three or four months. This will continue until he gets all twenty of his baby teeth at around age two and a half years.

Brushing Baby Teeth

You don't necessarily need to brush these first teeth, but you do need to clean them. A moist washcloth or a piece of soft gauze can be used to wipe them clean before bed each night. Once your child gets several more teeth, you can begin using a soft infant's toothbrush instead.

You probably don't have to start using toothpaste until your baby gets a few more teeth either. And once you do, be sure to use a non-fluoride toothpaste until your child is old enough to spit out the toothpaste.

Swallowing too much of a fluoride toothpaste can cause fluorosis and staining on his teeth.

Going to the Dentist

The timing of the first visit to the dentist is controversial. The American Academy of Pediatric Dentists recommends a visit once your baby gets his first tooth. And that's not a bad idea. An early visit to the dentist can help to identify problems and educate parents in proper tooth care to avoid later problems. Such an early visit is not always practical, though, since many people don't have access to a pediatric dentist.

FACT

Dental caries (cavities) are the most common disease caused by bacteria in early childhood, with 40 percent of children having tooth decay by the time they go to kindergarten. This makes taking care of your infant's teeth important. Don't neglect them just because they are "baby" teeth.

The American Academy of Pediatrics (AAP) used to recommend a later visit, around age three. It now recommends an earlier visit, especially if your child has any risk factors for developing problems with his teeth, such as frequent nighttime feedings. Infants who already have cavities should also see a pediatric dentist. Whether or not you see a dentist, your pediatrician can examine and review your child's oral health at each well-child visit, which is also recommended by the AAP.

Normal Development

There are big changes in store for your baby at this age, all of which will help him to become a little more independent. Instead of just lying in one position, he will now be able to roll over and sit up to observe and interact with the world around him. From four to seven months, the milestones that your child is likely to achieve include:

❏ Passing a block from one hand to the other
❏ Reaching for things
❏ Looking for objects that you drop
❏ Imitating many speech sounds
❏ Turning toward a voice
❏ Talking in single syllables
❏ Rolling over
❏ Sitting without support

He also probably will be able to hold his head steady if you try to pull on his arms to get him up to a sitting position. And he may be able to stand by holding on to things, put syllables together, and say dada and mama, although those words won't be used as a label for you or his mother.

Medical Problems

There aren't too many medical problems that begin exclusively during this time period, but one of them, intussusception, can be especially dangerous. As you start solids and vary your child's diet, constipation often becomes a problem. Developmental delays become a little more apparent at this age, when it is more obvious that your child isn't meeting milestones, such as sitting up or rolling over.

QUESTION?

Do I still have to worry about fever at this age?
Though it's still concerning, a fever in an infant more than three months old is usually not considered to be a medical emergency as it is in younger infants. You should still call your pediatrician, though, especially if your baby seems sick and is very fussy, isn't eating, or is having trouble breathing.

And your baby will still be at risk for general childhood problems and infections, including eczema, reflux, diarrhea, and colds and coughs. If your child has reflux, it may continue to be just as bad at this age. For many infants, it does begin to improve now though, as your baby is sitting up more and eating more solid foods.

In addition to watching for problems, don't forget your baby's four- and six-month well-child visits to your pediatrician to review your baby's growth and development and to get her vaccines.

Intussusception

Intussusception, which is a form of intestinal blockage that has some characteristic symptoms, can begin when an infant is three to four months old. Like babies with other forms of blockage, these infants have a lot of vomiting, which may be dark green, or bilious. They also go through periods of pain and decreased activity or lethargy, both of which alternate with other times when they seem just fine. Bloody, jellylike stools are a late symptom of this condition.

You should call your pediatrician right away or go to an emergency room if you think that your baby might have intussusception. Diagnosis and treatment is commonly with an air enema, which will tell you if the child has an intussusception and in many cases will reduce it. Less commonly, surgery has to be done to reduce the blockage.

Intussusception is more common in boys and often occurs before a baby is two years old. However, it can occur in children up to about age six.

Constipation

Once you start solid foods, constipation can become a big problem. Even breastfeeding infants, who rarely get constipated, can begin to have hard stools when they start cereal. To help treat constipation, you can begin to offer a few extra ounces of water or diluted apple juice. Or simply offer cereals that have some fiber in them, such as barley or oatmeal. Although rice cereal is well tolerated by most infants, it doesn't have any fiber, so it can cause constipation.

Developmental Delays

Severe developmental delays are often obvious at any age. Most parents can recognize a problem if their two-month-old isn't making any noises or isn't looking at them at all. Motor delays, especially when they are mild, can often be harder to spot. You likely wouldn't notice or worry if your four-month-old wasn't holding his head up at a 90° angle, but you probably would start to worry if your seven-month-old wasn't rolling over or wasn't holding his head steady as he sat with support. Many parents anticipate the bigger milestones, such as sitting up and rolling over, so this time period is often when more developmental delays are noticed. Be sure to let your pediatrician know if there is anything that doesn't seem normal about your baby's development.

Infant Safety Alerts

The fact that your baby is getting a little more mobile means that it is important to review all of the childproofing that you have done to make sure that your home is safe. You will also want to consider whether or not you are going to use a mobile baby walker. Remember that your big goal is to provide a safe place where your infant can explore and have fun, and where you don't have to worry about him falling, choking, or getting hurt in any way. If your baby has grown a lot, you should also make sure that he still fits in his car seat or consider a larger alternative that is still rear-facing.

ALERT!

Don't leave your baby unsupervised, even if your home is well childproofed. You won't be in a position to save your child in unpredictable circumstances, like a highchair tipping over or someone leaving a gate open, if you aren't around to notice these potential dangers.

Highchairs

Once your baby can sit without much support and has good head control, you can consider using a highchair or feeding chair during his meals. This is mostly for feeding solids, though; you should still hold your baby when you feed him a bottle. The main safety factors to keep in mind when using any type of highchair are that you secure your baby in the chair with its harness straps and that you always supervise him when he is sitting in the chair.

Rolling Over and SIDS

Infants at this age are still at big risk for SIDS and so should still be put to sleep on their backs. The big concern is, what do you do once your baby begins rolling over? Do you stay up all night rolling him back off of his stomach? In addition to being impractical, doing something like that isn't usually necessary. Once your baby is rolling over well, he should be at less risk of SIDS. You should still keep his crib safe and make sure that he doesn't get overheated, though, to keep his risk of SIDS even lower.

Sun Exposure

Although you can start using sunscreen at age six months, that doesn't mean that you should put your baby in direct sunlight very much. Younger infants are still at big risk of getting overheated and likely won't tolerate the sun for very long, even if they don't get a sunburn. Staying in the shade or under a cover or wearing clothing that covers the skin are better alternatives than being in the sun. And remember that you can use sunscreen on even younger infants if it is really necessary and if you just put it on small areas of exposed skin.

Playing with Your Baby

As you probably have discovered these last few months, playing with your baby is fun, both for you and for her. How can you play now? Singing lullabies and massaging your baby will still be good things to do. Your baby will likely enjoy it if you read simple books, too.

New activities might involve toys that she can easily manipulate, like plastic rings that interlock, rattles, squeeze toys, soft blocks, and other simple, handheld toys. She will also enjoy looking at herself in a mirror, listening to music boxes, and interacting with a soft puppet on your hand.

Tummy Time

The important advice to put an infant to sleep on her back means that she is on her stomach for only short periods of time or sometimes not at all. In addition to causing a flat head, this can cause an infant to be delayed in reaching some of her milestones, such as rolling over and crawling. Although even a baby who is hardly ever on her stomach will eventually reach these milestones, daily tummy time can help ensure that she won't be late.

FACT

Although studies have shown that some infants do have delayed development if they sleep only on their back, it is not a permanent effect. And while they may pick up milestones later than infants who sleep on their stomach, they still reach those milestones at what is considered to be a normal time.

In practicing daily tummy time, you simply put your baby on her stomach for short periods of time when she is awake. To make this more enjoyable, you can get down on the floor with your baby, or use some tummy-time toys, such as a playmat or gym. If your baby cries the whole time that she is on her tummy, limit each time to just a few minutes or wait a few weeks and then try again.

Playing on the Go

At this age your baby is likely to enjoy getting out more, especially once she has good head control and can sit up fairly well. You can take your baby out in a baby jogger or sports stroller, an infant carrier or sling, or just a regular stroller, to allow her to explore the world as you do things and get around too. Of course, you could simply carry her, but if you are going to be out for a while or if you are going on a long walk, a carrier or stroller will be more comfortable.

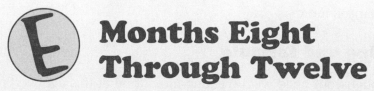

Chapter 8

Months Eight Through Twelve

While some things are getting easier at this age, such as diaper changes and baths, other things become more challenging. Instead of just drinking formula or breastmilk, your baby is now eating baby food, finger foods, and maybe even table foods. And instead of just lying or rolling around, she is taking her first steps and interacting with her environment much more.

Feeding Your Older Infant

Your child's diet is going to change quite a bit during these months. In addition to continuing on breastmilk or formula, your child will be eating a lot more baby food at this age. You will be able to start introducing finger foods and table foods, which your baby is sure to enjoy. Your baby also will start feeding himself more.

Breastfeeding and Formula

Although your child will be eating more food at this age, he probably will still be breastfeeding four or five times a day. If you and your partner had the goal of letting your baby breastfeed until twelve months, don't let little problems stop you now. One of the biggest mistakes to avoid is thinking that a temporary nursing strike means that your baby is ready to stop breastfeeding. Even if he loses interest for a while and doesn't want to breastfeed, he will likely get back to breastfeeding in just a few days. In the meantime, your partner may have to pump to keep her milk supply up.

QUESTION?

How can I tell the difference between a nursing strike and my baby wanting to wean?
Most babies wean slowly, dropping one feeding every few days or weeks. If your baby refuses most or all of her feedings all of a sudden, then it is more likely to be a nursing strike than weaning, which means that she should be able to continue breastfeeding once she gets over whatever is bothering her.

By this age, your baby may have cut his intake of formula down to just three or four feedings a day. This isn't the time to totally stop formula though. You may be eager to switch to regular milk, but there is no need to make that change before he is a year old. Instead of a gradual change to milk at this age, wait until he is twelve months old. Then you can either switch to milk "cold turkey," or start the gradual change at that point.

Baby Food

In addition to single-ingredient cereals, fruits, and vegetables, there will be a lot more variety in your baby's diet at this age. You can now start more multi-ingredient or mixed foods such as rice cereal with applesauce, mixed vegetables, and vegetable beef dinners. Just be sure that your infant has eaten and tolerated all of the ingredients in a multi-ingredient food. For example, if your baby didn't tolerate bananas, then don't give a banana-apple dessert.

Finger Foods

Your baby should be ready for finger foods once he is sitting up well on his own and is able to pick up things with his thumb and finger and bring them to his mouth. This usually happens at about eight to nine months, although some infants aren't interested in finger foods until a little later. The first finger foods are usually offered as a snack and can include dry cereals like Cheerios, baby cookies and crackers, and plain wafer cookies. Be sure to always supervise your baby when he is eating and don't offer foods he can choke on, such as whole grapes or raw vegetables. Remember that you don't have to wait until your baby has teeth to start safe types of regular food. As long as you choose foods that are soft and well cooked or that can easily break down in his mouth, he should be able to eat them without teeth.

ALERT!

Most parents know not to give honey to their baby in the first year, but it is also important to avoid foods made with honey. This includes honey cereals and honey graham crackers, a popular finger food among some parents. If a food has honey in it, and it is not pasteurized, then you should avoid it until your baby is older so that you don't risk his getting botulism.

Table Food

Once your baby is doing well with textured baby food and finger foods, you can start to offer more regular food that you are eating. You still want to avoid foods that your baby can choke on. Also, don't add a lot of salt or other seasonings to the food. If you do add a lot of seasonings, separate the food that you are going to give your baby from the food that the rest of the family will eat. Table foods that your baby should do well with include cut-up meats, well-cooked vegetables and pasta, and small pieces of cheese and ripe fruits.

Weaning Your Baby

Weaning actually has a few different meanings. For breastfeeding babies, it usually means the time when they gradually cut back on breastfeeding with the idea of soon stopping. For bottle babies, weaning is the process of going from a bottle to a cup.

If weaning from breastfeeding, first make sure that both your partner and your baby are ready. And remember that the American Academy of Pediatrics (AAP) recommendation to breastfeed until twelve months is a minimum and not a limit on how long to breastfeed. If mom and baby both want to, your baby can continue to breastfeed after his first birthday. Once your baby does start weaning, try to let him do it gradually, eliminating one feeding every few days or weeks. Or, even better, wait until your baby starts to give up these feedings on his own.

You should usually wean from a bottle just as slowly. You can make it easier if you offer juice and water in a cup only. That way, when you switch from formula to cow's milk when your baby is a year old and make the transition to using a cup, he will already be used to it.

This is a good age to introduce the sippie cup. The easiest way to do this is to offer him water and 100 percent fruit juice in a cup only; you can also offer formula or expressed breastmilk in a cup. If your breastfeeding baby who has never had a bottle weans before a year of age, consider offering formula in a cup only, so that you don't have to worry about bottle weaning.

First Steps

Your baby's first steps are one of the bigger milestones that most dads anticipate. Sure, it's exciting when your baby first rolls over or sits up, but beginning to walk is even more exciting. Few other milestones provoke calls to the grandparents and a rush to get the movie camera.

Cruising

Before your baby learns to walk, she will begin cruising around, or walking while holding on to things. This usually begins at around nine or ten months, once your baby is able to get to a sitting and then standing position by herself. She will quickly become more adventurous, walking while holding furniture, your hand, or her push toys.

Provide a safe environment for your child to walk around in. That means no sharp corners on furniture, no heavy objects or breakables that she can grab from tables that she pulls up on, and no stairs that she can fall down. Your child becomes much faster and mobile as she learns to walk, so make sure that you keep her safe.

Once your baby is cruising around effortlessly, you might think that she will quickly be walking. For some infants that's true, but for others it can take four or five months for them to walk well. On average, babies are walking on their own by ten to fifteen months. Talk to your pediatrician if your baby isn't walking by that time.

Baby Shoes

Many parents rush to get their kids into shoes once they are cruising or walking. After all, that's what shoes are for, right? Well, not really. Shoes are meant to protect your feet, and your baby doesn't really need to wear shoes until she is walking outside. She can wear them inside too, but not until she is walking well on her own. It is much harder to learn to walk with shoes on, especially hard-soled shoes.

Older Infant Development

Learning to walk is just one of the big milestones that infants pick up at this age. Your baby will soon seem all grown up as she begins talking, playing, and exploring the world around her.

Baby Talk

Although your baby probably won't pick up more than a few words by twelve months, you will begin to hear what sounds like a whole new language. After mastering single syllables, she will quickly begin putting syllables together and jabbering away. She will also begin saying mama and dada between six and nine months, although it won't be specifically to call you or her mom until she is about fourteen months old.

FACT

Having a hearing loss is one of the most common birth defects, affecting three out of every thousand children, and causing speech and communication delays. An early hearing test can help to identify whether or not your child has a hearing loss, and it's also a good idea for most young children with speech delays.

Next, she will begin saying a few other words, like ball or cat. Some babies don't say their first word, other than mama and dada, until about fifteen to eighteen months. If you are concerned about your baby's language development, be sure to talk to your pediatrician to find out if she needs to have her hearing checked or needs an early childhood intervention referral.

Other Milestones

Your child's development does seem to explode at this age. While she was only rolling around just a few months ago, interested only in mouth toys, she is now developing complex behaviors to explore her world. These include the concept of object permanence, which is the idea that things still exist even if you can't see them anymore. She will also be developing object mastery, as she learns to operate and play with more complicated toys with buttons, levers, and doors. The milestones that will help her develop these new patterns of behavior include:

❏ Beginning to wave "bye-bye" by seven months (although some kids don't do this until fourteen months)

❒ Letting you know what she wants sometimes without simply crying, like by pointing to things

❒ Picking up things with her finger and thumb in a pincer grasp

❒ Putting things that she picks up into her mouth

❒ Banging objects together

❒ Being able to pull up to a standing position and get to a sitting position by ten months

❒ Responding to simple one-step commands and the word "no" when she wants to by eleven or twelve months

❒ Looking for things that move out of her sight by eleven months

She also may begin to imitate things that you are doing and will soon be able to scribble on paper, use a spoon and fork to eat, stack blocks on top of each other, walk backwards, and run. With your twelve-month well-child visit coming up at the end of this time period, now is a good time to list any concerns you have about your child's development. That way you will be prepared to discuss them with your pediatrician and get some help if it is needed.

Separation and Stranger Anxiety

Parents are often surprised when their baby starts to show anxiety toward new people and new situations. Even the most outgoing child who was easy to leave with other caregivers might become a little anxious at times by eight to nine months. Understanding these common emotional reactions will help you learn how to help your child cope if you have to leave her with something that she isn't familiar with. It also helps to understand that many kids outgrow these types of anxiety by about eighteen months.

Separation Anxiety

When most people think of separation anxiety, they picture a child crying as he is left at day care. Some kids do only have problems with longer separations, which also include a parent leaving to go to work, or a sitter taking over for an evening. For other children, even shorter separations can be difficult. Your baby may cry if you put him down, walk out of the room, or if you simply aren't paying attention to him in the same room. There are several things you can try to ease separation anxiety:

- Practice short separations and quickly come back to help your baby get used to being away from you
- Stay calm when you leave your baby and don't get overly anxious about her crying
- Have someone distract her with a favorite toy when you leave
- Don't leave her when she is overly tired or hungry and is likely to be fussy anyway

Having separation or stranger anxiety doesn't mean that your child is spoiled or "too bonded" to his parents. Instead, it is a normal part of development and usually happens in children who have a healthy attachment to their caregivers. The lack of anxiety about strangers or separation can also be normal too.

Separation anxiety can be even more stressful if an infant has a strong preference for one parent and cries when that parent leaves the room. Although classically seen as happening to dads, with the baby having a preference for mom, it usually depends on who is the primary caregiver. If dad stays home and mom works outside the home, the preference will likely be for dad. Either way, if you are concerned because there is a strong preference for one parent, the other parent probably needs to spend more time with the baby. And the "preferred" parent shouldn't be too quick to rescue a baby who is crying with the other parent.

Stranger Anxiety

Anxiety about strange people and new situations begins at about the same time as separation anxiety, and both can exist together if you try to leave your baby with a new caregiver, such as a new baby sitter or new person at day care. This is a good reason not to start a new day care at this age.

More commonly, your baby will just seem a little shy or anxious when she encounters someone new while you are still with her. This may be a family member or friend who doesn't come over very often, or someone she has never met before. If you stay calm and try to slowly introduce her to these new people, she will likely get used to them too.

Playing with Your Older Infant

As your baby is getting more interested in things and becoming more social, he also is more fun to play with. You likely always had fun playing with him when he was younger, but you often just got to see the reaction he had to what you were doing. Maybe you made him laugh, smile, or reach for things, but he didn't really participate very much.

Now you can expect your child to really play more. He should be able to roll a ball back to you and push toy cars around. He will also begin to enjoy simple cloth and cardboard books and being read to as you hold him on your lap. Other fun games can include peek-a-boo, and he will likely enjoy stacking ring cones and nesting cups.

Discipline and Temper Tantrums

Your baby is too young to be punished, but it's never too early for a little discipline. What's the difference? True discipline involves teaching your child, to encourage good behavior and eliminate bad behaviors. Trying to stop behaviors that you think are bad doesn't mean that you will punish your baby, though. Instead of a time-out or taking away a toy for the rest of the day, as you might do with an older child, you can simply say "no" firmly and remove your child from the situation, whether he is hitting or biting another child or pulling all of the leaves off of your houseplants.

If you have childproofed your home well, your child shouldn't be able to get into too much trouble at this age. If your child does start having temper tantrums at this age, it is important to simply not give in to them. If you do, you will reinforce crying or having a tantrum as the right way to get something he wants. If you don't give in to tantrums, your child will sooner or later learn that they don't work.

Although you can discipline your infant at this age, you shouldn't spank or punish your child. What you consider misbehavior at this age is really just your child exploring his world and seeing what kind of reaction he can get from you. It is normal behavior for older infants to look at you and then do something that you have told them not to do.

The First Birthday Party

Like many of your baby's other firsts, the first birthday party can be the most exciting one. Your baby may or may not understand that the party is for him, but either way, the first birthday is a happy celebration for parents, friends, and other family members.

One fun trend in infant birthday parties is for your baby to have a small, separate, baby-safe cake. While you will neatly cut another cake for guests, this cake can be just for your baby, who can make a mess and simply eat it with his hands. Or maybe he will just get his face and mouth right into the cake.

While letting your baby eat his first birthday cake can be fun, make sure that you only give him a baby-safe cake. That means no ingredients that he might have problems with, like nuts or other choking hazards.

These parties can be fun, even if your baby doesn't know that it's his birthday. You don't have to spend a lot of money on it by renting a Bounce House or hiring a clown. A simple, informal party can be just as much fun, especially if your baby is very shy or anxious around crowds. Try to schedule it between nap and meal times to avoid dealing with a guest of honor who is already not in the best mood because he is tired or hungry.

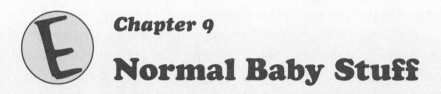

Chapter 9

Normal Baby Stuff

New parents almost always try to do what's best for their baby. Unfortunately, they can sometimes misunderstand many of the normal things that babies do, thinking that those things are a problem. This can lead to unnecessary treatments, dietary changes, and worry, which themselves can cause something that is normal to become a real problem. Reviewing these normal things that babies do can help you to keep with the basic principle of "do no harm," just as your pediatrician does.

Crying

Instinctively, parents think that crying is always a sign of some kind of distress in their baby. And it often is. It's normal for a baby to cry when he is hungry, cold, or needs to have a diaper changed. He may also cry when he is bored and just wants to be picked up. So babies cry a lot. In fact, it is now estimated that the average baby cries for two to four hours a day.

Remember that crying isn't always normal, though. Crying can be a sign of an illness or that your baby is in pain. Signs of "normal" crying usually include that your baby is eating and growing well and has no other symptoms, such as fever, vomiting, or trouble breathing. If your baby's cries seem excessive, see Chapter 10 for tips. Call your pediatrician if you still need help or think there may be a serious underlying problem.

Spitting Up

Most babies normally spit up at least some of the time. It may be when they eat a little too much, don't burp well, or get too excited after a meal. Other babies spit up after most or all of their feedings. Aside from cleaning up the messes these babies cause, there usually is nothing to worry about. Signs that your baby's spitting up is a problem can include that he is fussy for most of the day or night, seems to be choking or having trouble breathing when he spits up, or isn't gaining weight well.

QUESTION?

When will my baby stop spitting up?
Many babies stop spitting up when they are around six to nine months old, or once they are sitting up well and eating more solid foods. Other babies don't stop until much later, when they are twelve to eighteen months old. Talk to your pediatrician if your baby's reflux (spitting up) isn't getting better over time, or begins causing problems.

For normal spitting up, you often don't have to do anything except for keeping burp rags handy to minimize messes. Changing your baby's formula isn't usually helpful, although thickened formulas sometimes decrease the amount of spitting up. Other nonmedical interventions might include feeding your baby smaller amounts more frequently if the spitting up seems to be related to the amount he drinks at one time, or burping your baby more often during each feeding. You might also hold your baby upright after feedings and try to reduce how much stimulation he gets after his feedings. Talk to your pediatrician if your baby's spitting up seems to be a problem. Also remember that if it isn't bothering your baby, you don't have to do anything.

Hiccups and Gas

Hiccups and gas are other normal things that parents worry about and often overtreat. Neither usually requires any treatment or change in diet at all. Hiccups are hardly ever a sign of a problem, although gas can be if it is associated with other symptoms, such as diarrhea or excessive crying.

The big problem occurs when you have a baby who cries a lot while having hiccups or gas. Is your baby just swallowing a lot of air when he is crying, which causes hiccups and gas? Or is he crying *because* of the hiccups and gas? In situations like this, seeing your pediatrician is usually best to try to sort things out. You should avoid giving your baby a lot of gas drops or making dietary changes on your own, because they are often unnecessary.

Bowel Movements

Parents are often concerned about their baby's bowel movements. Is she having too many or too few? Should they be green or smell so much? Why does she always cry when she has a bowel movement?

It is easy to see why parents get so worried, because a baby's bowel movements change so much during her first year. They go from the thick, black, tarry meconium stools of the first few days to the yellow, seedy, breast-milk stools. Formula-fed babies' stools will change too, and will usually be a little firmer than breastfed babies.

Although frequent at first, how often your baby has bowel movements will also change over time. By two to three months, some breastfed babies might only have a bowel movement once a week. Even formula-fed babies might not have bowel movements every day. Keep in mind that if your baby has true constipation, in addition to having infrequent stools, the ones that she does have will be large and firm or small hard balls. If they are soft, then your baby likely isn't really constipated.

For younger infants, especially in their first few weeks of life, not having regular bowel movements can be a sign of a serious problem. Especially for breastfed babies, constipation may indicate that your baby isn't getting enough to eat.

Your baby's stools might also change in response to new foods that you introduce into his diet. This commonly occurs when you start a baby on cereal for the first time, or change his formula. Stools might also change if your baby has an intolerance or reaction to other foods that you introduce, and this is a good reason to start new foods slowly. That way, you can easily identify which food is causing the problem. Even if you aren't giving new foods to your baby directly, breastfed babies can react to foods in their mother's diet and have changes in their bowel movements.

Recognizing the many normal changes that your baby's bowel movements might have is important. If you think every green or loose stool is a problem, then you might make unnecessary changes to her diet or eliminate important foods. If your baby's stools are worrying you, talk to your pediatrician before you change formulas or make any other changes. This is especially important before you begin any medications or treatments for constipation in a younger infant, or if a nursing mother starts eliminating a lot of foods from her diet.

Infant Growth Patterns

When a baby is healthy and is eating and sleeping well, many dads next focus on how well their baby is growing. Is he keeping up with other kids his age? What are his percentiles on the growth charts? Is he too big or too small? For kids with medical problems, the concerns about growth can be even stronger.

Normal Growth Expectations

No matter how big or small a baby is at birth, most dads expect that he will quickly grow into a big, bouncing, bundle of joy. But how big will he get? And how quickly will he get there? Although growth patterns vary from child to child, you can expect that your infant will:

- Regain his birth weight by two weeks and then gain 1½ to 2 pounds a month
- Gain about 1 pound a month beginning at three months
- Double his birth weight by five months
- Triple his birth weight by twelve months
- Grow about 10 inches in his first year, although he won't double his birth height until he is three to four years old

Infants can grow normally in many different ways. A baby's growth can be normal at either the 5th percentile or 95th percentile. It can even be normal if your child is changing percentiles early on. Failing to gain weight or to grow taller are more reliable indicators of poor growth in early infancy than which percentile your baby is at.

And you can expect that a baby's head will grow about 4 inches in his first year. However, keep in mind that your baby may grow a little slower or faster than these averages. Your baby's weight at birth and his very early growth both usually represent conditions during your partner's pregnancy. After a few months, genetics often take over. At this time, a big baby born to small parents will often slow down in his growth, while a small baby born to big parents might grow more quickly and move up on his growth charts.

Growth Charts and Percentiles

An important part of your baby's well-child visits to his pediatrician is recording his height, weight, and head circumference on a growth chart. It's common for parents to get confused trying to understand these growth charts. Keep in mind that the 50th percentile represents the average child. But whether they are above or below the 50th percentile does not indicate how well or poorly they are growing. By definition, one-half of kids are below that percentile, and one-half are above it. So kids at the 5th, 25th, and 95th percentile can all be growing normally. What do those numbers mean then? Well, a child at the 5th percentile is bigger than 5 percent of kids at the same age. Likewise, a child at the 95th percentile is bigger than 95 percent of kids.

Parents are often more concerned about percentiles than pediatricians are. Since the percentile doesn't really indicate whether a child is growing normally, pediatricians look more to the fact that a child is staying at the same percentile or growth curve. Steady growth along a growth curve is usually the best indication that a child is growing normally.

Milestones of Development

In addition to how well their baby is growing, parents often are concerned about her development. Is your baby meeting her developmental milestones on time? Is she rolling over and sitting up when she should? Is she keeping up with other kids that you know who are the same age?

FACT

The best way for your pediatrician to track your infant's development, especially if you are concerned about delays, is to use a formal tool or test. The Denver II Test is one of the most commonly used developmental assessment forms. It includes a set of thirty questions and observations about your child to determine whether she is delayed. It can be used for newborns and children up to age six years.

While sometimes there may be a problem if your child isn't keeping up with another child of the same age, this can also be normal. Keep in mind that there are very wide age ranges for when children reach each milestone. For example, most infants will be rolling over sometime between two and five months—quite a wide range of normal! The range is even larger if you also consider that some infants are rolling over before two months and others aren't rolling until after five months. And all of the kids might be developing normally.

Of course, you should talk to your pediatrician if you think your baby isn't developing on time. Some warning signs about your child's development to look for include that she:

- Seems to have a hand preference early on
- Is delayed on many or all of her milestones and doesn't seem to be catching up
- Doesn't look at you or follow things by six weeks, which can be a sign of blindness
- Doesn't startle at loud noises, which can be a sign of a hearing loss
- Seems floppy or has poor muscle tone
- Seems rigid, with increased muscle tone

If you are concerned that your baby hasn't reached a milestone, well-child visits are a good time to talk about this and also for your pediatrician to observe which milestones your baby has reached since the last visit. In considering your child's development, your pediatrician probably will ask about her social or personal development, language, and fine and gross motor skills.

"Normal" Health Problems

There are many health problems that affect children and require treatment, such as eczema, urinary tract infections, and asthma. In addition, there are other conditions that often go away without treatment. These include things like blocked tear ducts, cradle cap, hair loss, acrocyanosis, and umbilical hernia. Although these problems are "normal," they sometimes may require treatment, so you should talk to your pediatrician when they occur.

Blocked Tear Ducts

Tears drain from the inner corner of the eye to the nose through the nasolacrimal ducts. In some infants, this duct is blocked, so tears can't drain to the nose. Instead, the eye tears a lot. Other symptoms can include some redness around the eye and a yellowish discharge from the affected eye.

In most cases, the tear duct will open up on its own by the time your baby is a year old. This can be helped by massaging the side of the nose where the tear duct is. If the tear duct doesn't eventually open up on its own, or if your child's tear duct gets frequently infected, then your pediatrician can use a probe to open it up.

ALERT!

Each of these "normal" conditions can be confused with a more serious condition or can become serious themselves. For example, instead of cradle cap, thick scale on your baby's head could be a sign of a fungal infection. Talk to your pediatrician before deciding that these things really are normal.

Cradle Cap

Cradle cap is often more distressing for parents than for the babies who have it. The thick, yellow scale or flaky, dry skin that accompanies cradle cap doesn't look normal, but it usually is not as bad as it looks. Most babies don't develop any symptoms, the cradle cap doesn't bother them, and it eventually goes away on its own.

If it does bother you or your child, though, you can treat it. The most common treatment involves simply massaging baby oil into the affected areas and then using a soft brush to loosen and remove the scales. More persistent cases might respond to a medicated shampoo, like Selsun Blue or Nizoral AD, used a few times a week. Talk to your pediatrician if the rash seems very itchy or if your baby also has an itchy rash all over the rest of his body.

Hair Loss

There are different types of hair loss, or alopecia, that can affect your baby. One of the most common is traction alopecia, which results from the back of your baby's head rubbing against surfaces he lies on. The hair in this area will eventually grow back once your baby is sitting up more and rolling over.

Another type of normal hair loss that affects infants is called telogen effluvium, and involves the process by which baby hairs fall out. These hairs are eventually replaced by mature hairs after a few months.

Acrocyanosis

Parents expect their baby's skin to have a nice pink color. After all, pink is a sign of health and that your baby is getting enough oxygen. Many babies can normally have blue hands and feet at times, though. This is a sign of an immature circulatory system and is different from the central cyanosis that can accompany heart and breathing problems. It is not normal if your baby's chest, lips, or tongue also look blue.

Umbilical Hernia

When an infant has an umbilical hernia, his belly button will protrude out at times. It often becomes worse when he strains or cries, and then goes back in if you push on it or when he relaxes. Although impressive looking, especially when they are large, umbilical hernias almost always go away on their own, though sometimes not until your child is four or five years old.

Folk remedies, such as taping a coin to hold the hernia in, aren't helpful and should be avoided. If the hernia is very large or isn't improving at all over time, surgical correction might be done earlier than age five years. You should also call your pediatrician if the hernia seems stuck out or is painful.

How Tall Will Your Baby Be?

Once they understand that the baby is growing well and is healthy, many dads turn to wondering how big the child will be when he grows up. Will he be short? Will he be tall? Is there a star basketball player in your family's future? While it really isn't that important, trying to predict your baby's future height can be a fun thing to do.

There are many tools on the Internet to help you automate the process of trying to predict your baby's height. ✎*Pediatrics.about.com* includes both of the methods described in this section as well as links to other ways to help you figure out how tall your baby will be.

Two Years Times Two Method

One of the most common methods to figure out how tall a child will be is to consider how tall she is once she turns two years old. You can predict your child's future height by simply doubling her height at age two years. So if your two-year-old is 3 feet tall already, she should be about 6 feet tall as an adult. A small two-year-old who is only 32 inches tall will likely be about 64 inches tall when she grows up, or 5 feet 4 inches tall.

Keep in mind that many other things can factor into what your child's future height will be, including chronic medical problems, genetics, and nutrition. This general method can give you a fairly good idea of how tall she will be, though.

Mid-Parental Height and Genetics

The two years times two method is easy to use, but it doesn't help you much in your baby's first year. And there isn't a similar method for younger kids. Simply multiplying your baby's height at birth by a number won't work, because your baby's growth patterns are likely to change during his first year. So even if he is at the top of the growth charts at birth, he could easily move down to being average later on.

Because genetics are a key factor in determining a child's future height, you can often predict how tall a baby will be by considering what his parents' heights are. Most people understand that tall parents have tall kids and short parents have short kids, but this method can give you a more specific height to expect.

Using the mid-parental height method, you first average your height with mom's height. If you are 6 feet tall and mom is 5 feet tall, the average of your heights would be 5 feet 6 inches. Next, you add 2½ inches to this average if you have a boy, or subtract 2½ inches if you have a girl. Using this same example, you would then expect a boy to be 5 feet 8½ inches and a girl to be 5 feet 3½ inches tall. Of course, this is just an estimate and not some magical formula. Your child may be a little taller or shorter than that, although there is a 68 percent chance that a child would be within 2 inches of that prediction.

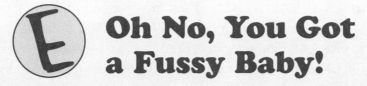

Chapter 10

Oh No, You Got a Fussy Baby!

After coming home with a happy and healthy baby, nothing can be more difficult than hearing that baby cry most or all of the time. This crying often adds to the new-parent anxiety and causes many new dads to question whether they are doing something wrong. Like most other parenting issues, you will be better prepared if you understand what to expect and learn some strategies for dealing with fussiness in advance.

What's Normal?

Some crying is normal and is to be expected from the average baby. If you are thinking that your baby is going to be all smiles and happiness all of the time, then you probably are going to be disappointed. In between the daily routine of eating and sleeping, there will be times when your baby cries.

This "normal" crying is not what upsets most parents. It is when the crying becomes inconsolable and goes on for hours and hours that parents begin to have problems dealing with it. Even this can be normal, though. As you learned in Chapter 9, many experts believe that the average baby cries for a total of two to four hours a day.

QUESTION?

Why do babies cry so much?
It is easy to understand why babies cry if you consider that it is really the only way they can communicate their needs. They cry when they are hungry, wet, or tired. And they may cry when they are overstimulated or simply bored. No one really knows why some babies cry so much more than others, though.

Your baby might start being more fussy at around two or three weeks of age. To get ready for this time, you might learn about different soothing techniques and try to get some extra help at home. In anticipation of this time, you should also not make any big changes in your baby's routine, such as by changing what he is eating or going on a trip.

Fathers should be especially careful not to blame their partner for doing something wrong and causing the crying. Although it may not always be known what is causing your baby to cry, it likely isn't because he is breastfeeding wrong, being spoiled, or because mom is doing something else wrong. Instead of placing blame, do what you can to help. One great way to do this is by giving mom a break from her crying baby.

Your pediatrician should be your first and best resource for getting help for your baby if she is crying more than the normal few hours. With a complete physical exam, a review of your baby's weight gain, and a thorough discussion of your baby's symptoms, you and your pediatrician should be able to get a better understanding of why your baby is crying so much. In addition to ruling out feeding problems and reflux as the cause of your baby's crying, your pediatrician can look for other less common medical causes of crying, such as infantile glaucoma, infections, or raised intracranial pressure.

Understanding Colic

Crying babies often just get labeled as having colic or being colicky. So what exactly is colic? It is usually described as a daily period of crying for one to three hours in the early evening, although it may occur at other times or even throughout the day, in an otherwise healthy baby. After starting at about two to three weeks of age, it usually reaches its peak at six weeks and then gradually improves over the next month or two.

Colic is very common, but nobody really knows what causes it. The many theories about it include the possibility that these babies have immature nervous systems or immature gastrointestinal systems. Other people believe that babies with colic have food sensitivities, are simply overstimulated and are crying to let off steam, or have anxious parents.

Most babies who cry will pull up their legs, and their stomachs will get hard. This usually doesn't mean that they have a stomachache though, even if they have a lot of gas at these times. It is just the typical reaction to crying that most babies go through.

While the cause isn't known, it is well accepted that colicky babies usually outgrow their crying by about three months of age. Because there are other medical causes of crying, you shouldn't just dismiss your baby's crying as colic. If you do, a serious medical problem might be overlooked. At the same time, you also don't want to put your baby through a lot of unnecessary tests or treatments. By the time you get through three or four formula changes, two or three medicines for reflux, and an upper GI, your baby with colic will probably already have reached his peak time of crying and will be getting better on his own. Whether or not there is a medical cause for your baby's crying that needs to be treated, try different ways to soothe your baby and ease his crying.

Reflux: Serious or Not?

Spitting up or having gastroesophageal reflux is common in younger infants, affecting about half of all babies. It occurs when formula, breastmilk, or other food comes back up and out of your baby's stomach, so that your baby spits up or vomits. Simple reflux usually doesn't cause problems though, except for being a little messy.

Spitting up is more of a problem when it is associated with gastroesophageal reflux disease (GERD). Although most infants with reflux don't actually have GERD, those who do can have poor weight gain in addition to spitting up, or they may aspirate and cough, choke, or have difficulty breathing. Crying, refusing to eat, and being irritable for all or most of the day are other symptoms of GERD.

Since reflux is so common, knowing if a child's crying and spitting up are related can be difficult. Some clues to look for that indicate reflux is *not* causing your baby's crying can include that he is eager to eat and doesn't cry during, or just after, his feedings. If you and your doctor aren't sure one way or another, you may decide to try an intervention, such as thickening his feedings, or trying an acid-reducing medication.

FACT

Babies spit up so easily because the muscle that usually prevents stomach contents from refluxing backward is immature and not working properly. It is estimated that almost half of babies spit up twice a day. Most don't have any symptoms of a more serious problem, though, and are called "happy spitters."

Many infants also are tested for reflux. However, the use of additional testing, such as an upper GI test, is not usually helpful in this situation. If your baby is spitting up, then you already know that he has reflux, which will likely show up on the upper GI. And a positive upper GI doesn't mean that your baby is refluxing acid, which is what would be making the reflux painful. However, undergoing an upper GI can be helpful for those babies who are fussy a lot but who aren't spitting up, because the test might detect "silent" reflux.

Breastfeeding Problems

Fussiness is especially worrisome for parents who have a breastfeeding baby. The first thoughts are often that something is wrong with his breastfeeding, usually that he isn't getting enough to eat, and that he should change to formula. This is almost never helpful. Talk to your pediatrician or a lactation consultant before your fussy baby stops breastfeeding.

A baby who isn't getting enough to eat likely will be fussy. However, in addition to his crying a lot, you should notice other signs and symptoms too. He may not be having regular wet diapers or bowel movements, and he probably won't be gaining weight well.

Mom's Diet

What a breastfeeding mother is eating also often gets the blame for a baby being fussy. This is actually less of a problem than most parents believe. While many things a mother eats and drinks do pass into her breastmilk, most wouldn't be responsible for a baby being fussy.

Eliminating some of the most common culprits from a breastfeeding mother's diet can be something that is easy to try if you think that might be the problem. You might start by first eliminating dairy products and caffeine and then observing for a decline in crying. If that wasn't helpful, you might try eliminating a few other foods and keeping a diary to see if the crying improves. Be careful that your partner doesn't limit her diet too much, because proper nutrition is an essential part of effective breastfeeding.

Some of the foods that can cause problems for breastfeeding babies include:

- Chocolate
- Citrus fruits and citrus juices

- Vegetables; especially bell peppers, broccoli, Brussels sprouts, cabbage, cauliflower, onions, and tomatoes
- "Allergic" foods, such as eggs, soy, wheat, and peanuts
- Foods with added spices, such as garlic and curry

If after several days of eliminating a lot of these foods you don't notice any improvement in the crying, your partner can then start to slowly reintroduce them into her diet.

You should also remember that milk is a common ingredient in many foods, including yogurt, bread, cheese, sour cream, ice cream, and cottage cheese. If your partner simply stops drinking milk, but still eats all of these other foods, then milk proteins might still be irritating your baby.

Too Much or Not Enough?

Milk that comes out of the breast too quickly, known as overactive letdown, can cause your baby to cough and choke when he is eating. This may lead to his being fussy, but probably just during feedings. If this seems to be the reason for your baby's fussiness, your partner can trying pumping for a few minutes until the flow slows down a little or just wait until your baby gets used to the quick flow of breastmilk. If your baby isn't getting enough to eat because of an overactive letdown, he may be fussy all of the time just because he is hungry.

The way that your baby breastfeeds can also cause him to become fussy. Some babies who feed very often and don't fully empty a breast at each feeding may be getting too much of the sugary foremilk. This low-fat milk is less filling than the high-fat hindmilk, and can lead to gas and crying. If you think that this may be your baby's problem, your partner should make sure that your baby finishes feeding from one breast before switching him to the other. Or she can just alternate which breast he starts eating from for each feeding.

Formula Problems

When faced with a fussy, crying baby, many parents often first turn to changing the formula that their baby is drinking. Unfortunately, this usually doesn't work to reduce the baby's crying. Whether you simply try another brand of formula or a totally different type, like a soy or elemental formula, changing formula isn't necessary for most fussy babies without other symptoms. Since it is so easy to do, though, some parents go through two or three different formulas before they even see their pediatrician.

That is not to say that crying babies can't have formula problems. It is just that when they do, they usually have many other symptoms. In addition to crying, infants with formula allergies or intolerances usually also have diarrhea and excessive gas. They may also be poor eaters and may not gain weight well.

A crying baby who has these symptoms may indeed have a formula intolerance, and in that case you may need to change to a different formula. You should still talk to your pediatrician to help you choose the right formula, though. If it turns out that the problem isn't your infant's formula, you might also consider changing to a different nipple or type of bottle.

Fussy-Baby Experts

As with most parenting issues, there are many experts whose books you can read for help in getting your baby to sleep well. Each offers suggestions and tips to avoid bad sleep habits and help your baby sleep all night. Although each expert's advice is likely to work for most parents and their babies, you should choose the one that fits best with your own parenting style and way of doing things.

The advice from all of the experts is more similar than it is different, though each offers his or her own theories about why babies cry so much along with tips to help soothe and settle a crying baby.

Dr. Ferber's Method

If you don't like to let your baby cry, then one of the most popular sleep experts, Dr. Richard Ferber, probably isn't for you. His book *Solve Your*

Child's Sleep Problems often gets a bad rap as advocating a simple "cry it out" method of getting babies to sleep. Actually, he emphasizes the need for proper sleep associations and offers a gradual or progressive approach to teaching your child to fall asleep and stay in his bed. This method does involve crying, but it is not a cold-turkey, cry-all-night-until-you-fall-asleep way of getting your baby to sleep. Instead, Dr. Ferber recommends that once your baby is five to six months old and not sleeping well, you teach him to fall asleep on his own and let him cry for progressively longer periods of time before briefly checking on him.

QUESTION?

Is one sleep expert better than all of the others?
Not necessarily. There isn't one absolute right or wrong way to get your baby to sleep all night, so you should use the method that you feel most comfortable with. Keep in mind that if your baby is waking up a lot, there will be some crying no matter which method you choose.

If you don't feel comfortable with the Ferber method, there are many other experts and books to give you more detailed advice. The experts include Dr. T. Berry Brazelton, Dr. Harvey Karp, Dr. William Sears, and Dr. Marc Weissbluth. Another popular book is *The No-Cry Sleep Solution* by Elizabeth Pantley.

The Brazelton Way

Dr. T. Berry Brazelton is a popular pediatrician and is considered to be an expert on many parenting topics, including sleep, discipline, potty training, and fussy babies. His book *Calming Your Fussy Baby* offers a simple, easy-to-read overview of why infants cry and how to cope with a fussy baby. Instead of trying to "cure" crying as some authors do, Dr. Brazelton offers tips to make it more manageable. It may not be the right book for you if you are looking for a lot of details in using different soothing techniques.

If, like Dr. Brazelton, you believe that crying and colic serve a purpose, and that crying is just your baby's way of "letting off steam," then you probably agree with him that eliminating it altogether is not always a good idea.

Although seen as a "cry it out" method by some, he only recommends stopping the techniques you are using to try to soothe your baby when they are not working or are making your baby fussier.

Dr. Harvey Karp

The Happiest Baby on the Block is without a doubt the most popular book about crying babies right now. Its author, Dr. Harvey Karp, offers a "new way to calm crying and help your newborn baby sleep longer." Part of the book's popularity is that it offers specific and easy-to-try techniques that do soothe and calm many babies.

Most of those techniques, summarized by the "5 S's," are things that everyone tries almost instinctively and understands. Most parents try to **swaddle** their baby, let them **suck** on a pacifier, **swing** or use rhythmic motions, and use a "**shhhing**" **sound** to comfort their baby. But when these techniques aren't working for you, Dr. Karp offers tips for using them in the right way and in the right order. If you don't want to read the whole book or still find Dr. Karp's techniques hard to understand, video and DVD versions are also available so that you can directly see his methods.

Although most parents who try the 5 S's like them, one common complaint is that some babies get "spoiled" and become dependent on swaddling to get to sleep. Parents then have a new problem when they later have to wean their baby from swaddling and get him to sleep on his own.

ALERT!

If you have a baby who cries excessively, see your pediatrician for an evaluation before you simply decide that you have a fussy baby. Although there's usually nothing to worry about, medical conditions that lead to such excessive crying can be serious and are important to discover.

William and Martha Sears

William and Martha Sears are often seen as advocates of "attachment parenting." Their *The Fussy Baby Book* offers help for all parents. The chapter titled "Creative Ways to Soothe a Fussy Baby" offers many tips, some of which will likely work for you. Of all the books about fussy babies, this one offers the most ideas and soothing techniques, including different ways to hold, carry, and calm your baby.

Dr. Marc Weissbluth

Dr. Weissbluth's first book helped many parents get their children to sleep through the night. Because crying babies and sleep problems are often seen as being related, it should come as no surprise that he has now written a book to help you soothe *Your Fussy Baby*.

Although his book is similar to others about fussy babies in that it offers soothing and calming techniques, such as swaddling, rocking, massage, and singing lullabies, Dr. Weissbluth is probably the most honest fussy-baby expert. Instead of pushing his own theory of why babies cry, he discusses all of the theories and then simply concludes that no one knows the real answer. Many parents also will appreciate the long chapter on preventing sleep problems.

Shaken Baby Syndrome

One consequence of having a baby who cries inconsolably is that it can lead some inexperienced parents to harm their baby. The baby might be forcibly shaken to the point that she develops bleeding in and around her brain, which can cause either permanent brain damage or death. Even a brief episode of shaking, for five or ten seconds, or a single blow against the floor, bed, or another surface, can cause brain damage.

To prevent shaken baby syndrome, simply remember to never shake your baby. If your baby's crying is getting you to the point that you're so frustrated you think you might shake your baby, get help right away, either from a family member, friend, or by calling 911 if no one else is available to help you before you might harm your child.

Pacifiers and Thumb-Sucking

Dads often think that a baby doesn't need a pacifier, but using a pacifier or sucking on her thumb or fingers isn't necessarily a bad habit for a baby. Many younger infants actually enjoy the security they get from this type of non-nutritive sucking, and it can be something that is healthy and normal and encouraged. It also can provide a calming or soothing effect for many infants.

The problem lies more with prolonged thumb-sucking or pacifier use. If a child continues to use a pacifier or suck her thumb past age three to five years, then it can affect her teeth and speech and language development.

ALERT!

Recent reports have linked pacifier use with stopping breastfeeding early and with infants getting a lot of ear infections, in addition to the negative effects on your child's teeth and his speech. Don't let your infant use a pacifier too much or for too long.

Fortunately, most infants give up these habits well before they become a problem, often by age six to nine months. To help keep this healthy habit from turning into a bad habit, you might try one of the following strategies:

- Avoid the types of pacifiers that clip on your baby's clothes, which makes it always available
- Avoid giving the pacifier at bedtime, or quickly take it out of the baby's mouth once she falls asleep
- Avoid letting your baby have a pacifier all day long
- Make the pacifier less available once your baby begins to lose interest in it
- Get your older infant attached to another type of security object, like a small blanket, instead of the pacifier
- Don't be so quick to put the pacifier back in her mouth each time it comes out

If trying to break your child's pacifier habit is too stressful for her, it's okay to let her continue to have one. Since there likely won't be any damage to your baby's teeth unless she continues to use a pacifier after she is two to four years old, you don't have to be too aggressive at this age unless you begin noticing problems, such as a speech delay or tooth deformities.

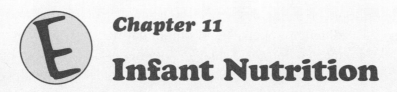

Chapter 11

Infant Nutrition

What and how much to feed their baby is one of the things that many parents have trouble with, especially if they are getting a lot of differing advice on when to start solids, how long to breastfeed, or what foods to avoid. Being familiar with your baby's nutritional requirements and needs can help so that you have one less thing to worry about this year.

The Nutrition Rules

Parents often want detailed rules for how much to feed their baby. How many ounces does he need each day or during each feeding? How often should he eat? What should they be feeding him?

Unfortunately, there aren't any formal "rules" that specify what each and every child should be eating. Just as kids come in different shapes and sizes, they also have different appetites and nutritional needs. One baby might only drink 24 ounces of formula, while another needs 32 or even 40 ounces a day. Or one six-month-old might be eating two meals a day, with cereal, vegetables, and fruits, while another is just barely starting cereal. And all of these kids, with their very different diets, could be growing and developing just fine. So instead of looking for strict rules, parents should follow more general guidelines, and simply make sure that their baby is satisfied and growing well.

Among the foods that you should avoid during your baby's first year include honey, because of the risk of botulism; egg whites and peanut butter, because of the risk of food allergies; and any foods that your baby might choke on. Many parents also avoid citrus juices, but that is more often because it isn't well tolerated and not because it is dangerous.

Breastfeeding Basics

It can help your baby to breastfeed effectively if you understand some of the basics of breastfeeding. This includes how to use pumped breastmilk and how to help increase your partner's milk supply if it begins to decrease.

Pumping and Storing Breastmilk

There are many reasons why your partner may want to pump and store her breastmilk for use later on. Some of these reasons include that she may be at work and unable to breastfeed all of the time, or she may have to go on a trip without her baby and isn't ready to wean. Some babies are also fed pumped breastmilk if dad wants to be able to feed his exclusively breastfed baby some of the time or if you get your milk from a human breastmilk bank.

There are many different types of breast pumps available for your partner, from manually operated hand pumps to hospital-grade electric pumps. There is even a hands-free pump that operates on batteries. Any of these can get the job done, but if your partner is going to be pumping a lot or is pumping to build up her milk supply, you should try to get a hospital-grade pump. These are more expensive, but they often can be rented from a lactation consultant.

The following guidelines from the American Academy of Pediatrics and La Leche League International will help you decide how long you can store pumped breastmilk. According to these guidelines, stored milk can be kept:

- At room temperature for four hours
- In a small refrigerator or cooler at work until you get home to store it in your refrigerator or freezer
- Unfrozen in a refrigerator for three to eight days
- In a freezer that is in the same compartment as the refrigerator for two weeks
- In a freezer with a separate door from the refrigerator for one to three or four months
- In a chest freezer for six months

Frozen breastmilk can be thawed by moving it into a refrigerator for up to twenty-four hours. Once you are ready to use it, refrigerated breastmilk should be warmed by running it under warm water, and then it should be shaken and put in a bottle or cup for your baby to drink. Like formula, expressed breastmilk should not be heated in a microwave oven.

Increasing Breastmilk Supply

Although there are other reasons to have a poor milk supply, the amount of breastmilk a mother has usually is based on basic supply and demand. As a mother's breasts are emptied of milk, it signals her body to make more. If a baby isn't breastfeeding often enough or doesn't latch on and suck well, then that signal to make more milk is not there and her supply probably will decrease.

How long should my baby breastfeed?
A good general answer is the longer the better, with two months being better than no breastfeeding at all and six months being better than two or four months. Ideally, your baby should breastfeed until he is at least twelve months old. Keep in mind that this is really a minimum recommendation, and that your baby can continue to breastfeed after he is a year old if he and mom want to.

If a mother has a low supply of milk, giving the baby formula and hoping her supply eventually increases is not the answer. Instead, make sure that your baby is latching on and sucking well and is eating at least every two or three hours. Extra pumping after each feeding with a hospital-grade breast pump can also help increase her supply.

It's also important to make sure that your baby's mother isn't overly stressed, anxious, or depressed and is getting enough to eat and drink. She might want to try one of the herbs that can help to increase a mother's supply of breastmilk, such as fenugreek and blessed thistle. These are available over-the-counter in capsule form and as dried herbs to make teas. However, she should be sure to consult with your pediatrician or her obstetrician before she takes a supplement while breastfeeding. Most important, you should consult a lactation consultant to help your partner get her milk supply back up so that your baby can be exclusively breastfed.

Formula Feeding

Feeding formula to your baby should go very smoothly once you decide on the type and brand of formula your baby is going to drink and you understand how much your baby will take at each feeding and throughout each day. Keep in mind that your baby isn't likely to cut back on his intake of formula until he is eating two to three meals of cereal and baby food a day.

Formula Guidelines

If not breastfeeding, babies usually drink formula throughout their first year. Once they reach their first birthday, they can then usually be switched to whole cow's milk, unless they have a milk allergy or intolerance. What some parents struggle with most is the amount of formula to give each day.

If you are still having trouble figuring out how much formula you should expect your baby to drink each day, you can use the American Academy of Pediatrics estimate of 2½ ounces of formula a day for each pound of body weight. So a 13-pound baby would probably drink about 32 ounces of formula in twenty-four hours.

Most babies start out drinking 2 to 3 ounces of formula during the first few weeks, with frequent feedings (every three to four hours). By two months, many have moved up to 5 to 6 ounces per feeding and have spaced their feedings so that they are only eating five to six times a day. Keep in mind that your baby may drink less more frequently or bigger bottles less often, but she probably will be averaging about 24 to 32 ounces a day after she is two months old.

While many babies will plateau and continue to drink 5 to 6 ounces at a time as they get older, some babies increase their intake to 6 or 7 ounces at each feeding once they are three to five months old. If your baby isn't consistently drinking much more than that, you might check with your pediatrician to make sure that you are not overfeeding your baby. Although it isn't usually easy to overfeed a baby, since most turn away or spit up if they get overfull, it can happen if you misinterpret when she is actually hungry and feed your baby each time she cries.

Infant Formula Alternatives

The only real alternatives to infant formulas are other infant formulas, such as a soy or elemental formula if your baby is having a problem with a cow's-milk-based formula. While formula is a "second best" alternative to breastmilk, by the time you begin having problems with formula feeding, it will likely be too late to breastfeed. If you do begin to have formula problems early on or while your baby is still breastfeeding a little, especially within the first week or so after being born, you might talk to a lactation consultant to help get your baby exclusively breastfeeding and avoid formula altogether.

Homemade infant formula, goat's milk, and cow's milk are poor alternatives to a commercially prepared iron-fortified infant formula and should be avoided. None of them offer any advantages over formula, and in fact can lead to vitamin and mineral deficiencies, gastrointestinal disturbances, and other problems.

Once your baby is doing well with a formula, you should usually stick to it for the rest of your baby's first year. Although formula for older infants is being marketed, most children don't need the extra calcium and other vitamins and minerals in these formulas, because they can get them from the baby foods they are eating. Talk to your pediatrician if you are considering changing to a different formula, because most changes are unnecessary.

Avoiding Food Allergies

It's no fun having a child with food allergies. In addition to the fear of serious, life-threatening reactions, it can be a struggle to simply know what is safe to feed him. Complicating matters is the fact that many foods that children commonly are allergic to, such as milk, eggs, soy, and wheat, can be "hidden" ingredients in many other foods.

ALERT!

Many foods that commonly cause allergies can pass into breastmilk, so your baby might develop a milk or peanut allergy and have allergy symptoms even though he has never eaten those foods directly. Eliminating foods your infant is allergic to from a breastfeeding mother's diet, and then later in his own diet, can help to avoid further symptoms.

To try to avoid food allergies, some parents delay giving certain foods that kids commonly are allergic to, such as peanut butter, cow's milk, and eggs. While those foods should usually be avoided during your baby's first year anyway, after that, it may not be necessary to avoid them if your baby doesn't have any risk factors for food allergies. Still, as long as your toddler has a well-balanced diet, delaying some foods isn't going to hurt him and it might be a good idea if you are really worried about food allergies.

If your baby does have risk factors for food allergies, such as having formula allergies, other types of allergic disorders like eczema or asthma, or has a family member with food allergies or other allergic disorders, you may be able to reduce his chance of developing a food allergy by making sure he:

- Breastfeeds exclusively for at least six months
- Continues to breastfeed until he is at least twelve months old
- Drinks a hypoallergenic formula if he is being supplemented or isn't breastfeeding
- Doesn't begin solid foods until six months
- Doesn't eat or drink any dairy products until he is twelve months old
- Doesn't eat eggs until he is two years old
- Doesn't eat peanuts or peanut butter, nuts, or fish until he is three years old

You can reduce your baby's risk even more if the mother doesn't eat nuts while breastfeeding. The need to eliminate other foods, such as cow's milk, eggs, and fish from a nursing mother's diet, is more controversial.

What's First? Cereal, Fruits, or Vegetables?

Most parents look forward to starting solid foods, because it is a fun thing to do for both them and their baby. For a dad with a breastfeeding baby, starting solids can be especially rewarding because it lets dad be a bigger part of his baby's feedings. Many parents start too early, though.

Although the general guidelines are that you can start solids anytime between four and six months, you can usually wait until six months. You may have a good reason to start early if your baby is no longer satisfied with just breastmilk or formula. Make sure, though, that you aren't confusing a growth spurt and a few days of increased feedings for a need to start solid foods. Other things to look for include that your baby has doubled her birth weight and is no longer trying to push solid foods out of her mouth with her tongue.

You don't want to start solid foods too early, but you also don't want to wait too long. If solids aren't started by the time your baby is seven to eight months old, she may be less likely to want to eat solid foods at all.

Once you know that your baby is ready for solid foods, knowing what to start with is easy. In almost all cases, the best first food to start with is an iron-fortified, single-grain rice cereal. Rice cereal is usually the best tolerated and the least likely to cause allergies or other problems.

The first time you start cereal, you probably will have to make it very thin, by mixing 1 teaspoon of cereal with 4 or 5 teaspoons of expressed breastmilk, formula, or water. And don't expect your baby to eat a lot of it. At first, she may eat just 1 or 2 teaspoons a day, and a lot of that might end up all over her face. If she doesn't want it at all, try again in a few days. It might also help to make sure she isn't overly hungry when you offer cereal, by giving it after a feeding or after at least a few minutes of breastfeeding or a few ounces of formula.

Once your baby is eating rice cereal well, you can either begin offering other cereals, such as oatmeal or barley, or just stick with rice. Some parents like to offer a variety of foods and flavors early, with the idea that it will encourage good eating habits later, while others are worried about triggering an allergic reaction if they offer too many different foods too early. Limiting your child to rice cereal is probably only necessary if your child is at risk for developing food allergies.

You can eventually mix your baby's cereal with less formula as she gets more used to the thicker texture, and work your way up to 3 to 5 tablespoons of cereal a day. Next, especially if your baby is already more than six months old, you can offer single-ingredient baby food, such as pureed vegetables and fruits. She will likely just start out with 1 or 2 tablespoons once or twice a day and then later move up to 2 to 3 table-spoons at a time.

Keep in mind that although portion sizes are usually presented in table-spoons, you will be using a smaller-sized baby spoon to feed your baby. And because the average jar of baby food is 2½ ounces or 5 tablespoons (15 tea-spoons), she may not finish the whole jar at one feeding.

Once you do start solid foods, your baby might become constipated, even if he is still breastfeeding. If this happens, you can usually give your baby a few ounces of water, diluted fruit juice, or switch to a cereal with more fiber, such as barley or oatmeal.

When to Feed Solids

Knowing when to feed solid foods can be confusing. Do you just do it in the morning? Or with the standard breakfast, lunch, and dinner? And do you feed the solids before or after your baby breastfeeds or drinks his formula?

This is another one of those questions that doesn't have a definite answer. Some babies do better eating solids before anything else, when they are the most hungry. Others get frustrated taking small amounts of food off of a spoon when they are so hungry, and they do better eating solids after breast-milk or formula or at a separate time altogether.

Introducing New Foods

In addition to starting too early, the other mistake some parents make when feeding solid foods is offering too many foods too quickly. If you do this, such as by introducing bananas one day and peaches the next, and your baby has a problem, it won't be easy to know which food is causing the problem. Instead, you should offer one new food every two to three days and don't offer combination foods or mixed cereals until your baby has had all of the ingredients separately.

What's Next?

Once your baby is eating two to three meals a day, consisting of 3 to 5 tablespoons of cereal and 2 to 3 tablespoons of vegetables and fruits, he will likely be ready for some meat and protein foods. This will usually occur when your baby is about eight months old. Remember that he will still have three to five feedings of breastmilk and formula in addition to the solid foods.

You don't have to wait until your baby has teeth to start finger foods or baby foods with more texture. It is more important that your baby is sitting up well, can begin to grasp small pieces of food with his fingers and bring them to his mouth, and doesn't choke when you give them to him.

By eight to nine months, or once your baby is sitting up well, he should be ready for some finger foods, like Cheerios, crackers, and arrowroot cookies. At this age he is also likely to be ready for foods with more texture, like Stage 3 baby foods.

Vitamins and Minerals

The need for infant vitamins is a confusing topic. Babies do need vitamins to grow well and to be healthy. They need them for strong bones, healthy teeth, and to build up their blood and prevent anemia. The confusing part is that most infants get all of the vitamins and minerals they need through the foods that they eat and drink, including vitamin A, calcium, zinc, and the vitamins and minerals discussed in this section. So while they do need vitamins and minerals, they don't always need a supplement each day, unless they were born prematurely or have some other health problem.

Iron

Iron is one of the more important minerals your baby needs. The effects of a diet poor in iron, which can lead to iron deficiency anemia, are well known. These include learning problems, developmental delays, and behavioral problems.

However, your infant, unless he was born premature, should be able to get all of the iron he needs from breastmilk or an iron-fortified formula during his first four to six months. After that time he does need extra iron, but you can usually provide it from the baby foods that he is beginning to eat, such as an iron-fortified infant rice cereal, in addition to continuing to feed him his breastmilk or formula.

QUESTION?

Will iron cause my baby to have any medical problems?
No. Iron is essential for your baby's growth and development and it does not cause colic, constipation, or any other problems. Infants who drink a low-iron formula or plain cow's milk are likely to develop medical problems, though, including anemia.

If your baby is otherwise well, he probably won't develop an iron deficiency unless you switch him to cow's milk before his first birthday or you do not begin to give extra iron after he is six months old. Remember that premature babies often do need a vitamin supplement that has iron in it.

Fluoride

Newborns don't need fluoride, but once your infant is about six months old and begins getting teeth, he will need fluoride to keep them strong and growing well. The main source of this fluoride isn't an extra vitamin though. You can instead provide it by offering your baby some fluoridated tap water each day.

Your baby may not be getting enough fluoride if he is drinking any of the following:

- Well water
- Tap water that is not fluoridated
- Bottled water that does not have added fluoride
- Water that is filtered of fluoride

- Breastmilk exclusively
- Ready-to-feed formula exclusively

You can start your baby on fluoride supplements, but getting too much fluoride can easily lead to fluorosis or staining of their teeth, so it is usually best to try to give your baby fluoridated water. If you are exclusively breastfeeding, offering some extra water with fluoride once your baby is six months old is the best way to avoid problems. Talk to your pediatrician to get a prescription for a fluoride supplement if your baby has no way of getting fluoride from the water he is drinking.

Vitamin D

Not getting enough vitamin D can cause a baby to get a bone disorder called rickets. Because infant formula is fortified with vitamin D, infants drinking at least 17 ounces of formula each day do not need any extra vitamin D.

FACT

Rickets, caused by a deficiency of vitamin D, is a serious disorder that causes skeletal deformities and poor growth. Although not as common as it used to be, it does still affect some children, especially those who are very dark-skinned, don't get any or little sun exposure, and are exclusively breastfed.

Unlike formula, breastmilk does not contain enough vitamin D for babies, but that wasn't thought to be a problem because it was believed that exclusively breastfed infants got enough vitamin D from sunlight exposure. However, now that the effects of excessive sun exposure are known and sunscreen is being used more often, it is thought that exposure to the sun is not enough for breastfed babies. The American Academy of Pediatrics now recommends that breastfed babies receive a vitamin D supplement beginning in the first two months of life. The need for vitamin D supplements is a controversial topic though, especially for light-skinned infants in sunny climates, so you might talk to your pediatrician about whether this is necessary for your baby.

Feeding Problems

Feeding your baby will probably be fun, as long as everything goes smoothly. The biggest problems usually include food intolerances, not wanting to eat solid foods, and not growing well, although that isn't always because of feeding problems. Infants grow quickly during their first year, so any big slowdowns or periods of real weight loss can be very concerning. Not growing well or having failure to thrive requires a thorough evaluation by your pediatrician. Remember that some kids do move down on their growth charts between six and eighteen months and it can be normal if they are otherwise well and still gaining some weight.

Homemade baby food doesn't mean giving food to your baby right off of your plate. It involves preparing your own baby food as an alternative to commercially prepared baby foods. Use a food processor or blender to create a mushy consistency, don't add salt or other spices to the baby foods you prepare, and avoid beets, carrots, collard greens, spinach, and turnips, which can be high in naturally occurring nitrates.

Food Allergies and Intolerances

Many symptoms are blamed on food allergies and intolerances, including diarrhea, gas, crying, rashes, spitting up, and runny noses. And while these symptoms really might indicate a feeding problem, they can have many other causes if they only happen occasionally. Even if your baby develops a symptom right after you start a new food, it could still be just a coincidence, so talk to your pediatrician if you think your baby is developing a food allergy or intolerance. This is especially important before you make big changes to his diet or begin restricting a lot of different foods.

Refusing to Eat

Babies who refuse to eat can be frustrating to take care of, especially if they don't want to drink their breastmilk or formula. If your baby had previously been eating well and all of a sudden decides not to eat as much, he may just be at the end of a growth spurt or is having a short "strike." Other causes for a baby not wanting to eat can include gastro-esophageal reflux (see Chapter 10) and a food aversion, which often affects older infants who won't eat solid foods.

This situation is more concerning if the food refusal lasts more than a few days or if your baby has other symptoms, such as increased fussiness or fever. If there are any other symptoms or if the food refusal lingers, a trip to your pediatrician is a good idea.

Avoiding Bad Habits

What your baby doesn't eat can be just as important as what he does eat. And during his first year, he won't be the one making most of those choices. As you make choices for your child, avoid giving him too much juice or junk food, and be careful not to create a picky eater.

Too Much Juice

Most kids like drinking juice. Whether they are thirsty, hungry, or simply crying because they are angry, infants rarely turn away a bottle of juice when it is offered to them. This can lead some parents to start using juice as a pacifier, creating a bad habit that is very hard to break.

There are actually strict recommendations for how much juice infants should drink.

To avoid negative health effects, like becoming overweight or getting cavities, you should follow these recommendations from the American Academy of Pediatrics:

- Don't give juice to infants under six months old
- Limit juice intake to 4 to 6 ounces a day
- Only give pasteurized 100 percent fruit juices (instead of fruit drinks)
- Don't give juice in a bottle

You might also dilute the juice with water when you do give it to your older infant and avoid giving infants juice at bedtime or in the middle of the night. And it can be helpful to have designated times, either at meals or snacks, for your child to have juice. That way he isn't walking around with a cup of juice all day. If he is really thirsty at other times, offer some water instead.

QUESTION?

Can I make my own fruit juice?
Sure. The American Academy of Pediatrics recommendation to avoid unpasteurized fruit juices really only applies to commercial sources of juices, which might contain harmful bacteria if not pasteurized. Making your own juice using fresh fruit can be a healthful alternative to other drinks.

Junk-Food Junkies

Early infancy is probably the time when you have the most control over what your child eats. After all, a nine-month-old can't go to the pantry to get a cookie or to the refrigerator to get a soda. Sure, she might cry if she doesn't get what she wants, but you still have control over what you give her to eat.

In addition to too much juice, one of the biggest sources of junk food in an infant's diet is the type of finger foods you give her to snack on. Foods to avoid include sugary cereal and other typical junk foods, such sugary cookies, chips, or doughnuts. Soft, small pieces of fruits and vegetables, plain wafer cookies, and low-sugar cereals are better options.

Once you let your baby start eating table foods, your own choices, if they are unhealthy, can begin to affect your child's diet. Choosing healthy finger foods, not giving too much juice, and offering a variety of healthful foods at meals can help you avoid creating a junk-food junkie.

Obesity levels are rising to epidemic levels in children and adults. Although you shouldn't limit your child's calories or intake of fat, it is never too early to start offering nutritious choices and a diet that's healthful overall.

Creating a Picky Eater

Parents usually worry when their kids don't eat well. Often, though, if your child is growing and developing normally and is active, being picky is not as big a problem as most parents believe.

Kids can be picky eaters because they are drinking too much formula or juice or eating a lot of junk food, and then simply aren't hungry when it's time for dinner. On the other hand, some picky eaters just don't want to eat a variety of foods. A child who is really just a "natural" picky eater—one who eats small amounts of food or has little variety in her diet but has no bad habits—probably is normal, especially if she is gaining weight normally and is physically active. It can still be frustrating when your child refuses to eat most of the things that you offer her, though, so you should try to avoid actually creating a picky eater.

Picky eaters who are truly "created" are more likely to live in homes where other family members also aren't good eaters. Most older infants welcome a variety of foods and they are eager to eat new things from the plates of other family members. The family of a picky eater may not eat many fruits and vegetables or may not like to try new foods, leaving little variety at each meal. In addition to offering your child a variety of healthful foods, including fruits and vegetables, it is important that other family members also eat and enjoy a variety of foods in order to avoid creating a picky eater.

Chapter 12

Sleep Schedules

With all of the other things to be concerned about during your baby's first year—including her overall health, safety, growth, and development—whether or not she is sleeping well may seem like a small problem. However, the parent who is getting by on little or no sleep each night will understand how important it can be to have a baby who is sleeping well.

Sleep Basics

Your baby will sleep a lot his first year. This starts with about sixteen or seventeen hours a day during his first month, and gradually decreases to about fourteen hours by his first birthday. So even when he is a year old, your baby will likely be spending more than half of each day sleeping.

Not all of that sleeping will be at night, though. Early on, instead of long stretches of sleep, your newborn will probably have regular cycles of eating, sleeping, and waking each day. Although there may be one longer stretch of four or five hours, most of these cycles will be just two or three hours. Over the next three or four months, your baby's sleep patterns should become more organized. He will still be sleeping a lot (about fifteen hours at four months) but there will be more sleep at night, longer periods of wakefulness during the day, and more regular nap times.

Parents often over- and underestimate how much their baby is sleeping. To get a better idea of how much sleep your baby is getting, it can help to keep a diary or log of your baby's naps and overnight sleep times. That can also help you to find your baby's natural sleep schedule.

Just as your baby's sleep patterns change over this first year, sleep advice also changes. It is important to realize that much of the advice for older children—letting them fall asleep on their own, not letting them fall asleep while feeding, and perhaps letting them cry it out—doesn't apply to your newborn or younger infant. Your newborn probably will fall asleep breastfeeding or drinking a bottle or may need to be rocked to sleep. Helping your child get to sleep in these first few months doesn't mean that you are creating problems for later.

As your baby gets older, you may have to work a little more at preventing and fixing sleep problems that develop, so that all family members can get a healthful amount of sleep. However, for many babies, whether or not they sleep well is just part of who they are naturally. It is possible to create good and bad sleepers, but sometimes you just have to wait and adjust to your child's natural sleep schedule until things work themselves out as the child gets older.

Night Feedings

In early infancy, nighttime feedings are to be expected. Your newborn will likely continue to eat every two to three hours at night, just as he does during the day. He may go for one long stretch of four to five hours without eating, but in general, he will eat two or three times at night, during the time when you would usually be asleep.

FACT

If your baby had been sleeping well at night and is now waking up more to eat, you should make sure that he is getting enough to eat during the day. This commonly happens when parents try to stretch their baby's daytime feedings past three or four hours. Adding an extra feeding back to your baby's daytime schedule will usually get him back to sleeping well again.

Once he is gaining weight well, it is fine if your baby wants to go even longer between feedings at night. Still, you usually shouldn't expect your baby to go all night without waking up for a feeding until he is four to six months old. Talk to your pediatrician if you think your baby is going too long at night without eating.

Also, six months is not a magic age at which all children stop needing to eat at night. Some older infants still need one or two feedings at night, although others aren't really hungry and are just used to eating to help them fall asleep. If you think that's the case, you can gradually decrease how many minutes your baby is breastfed at each nighttime feeding or put less formula in his bottle. You may have to go back to his customary feedings if he isn't satisfied with the decreased feedings or seems to wake up more afterward.

Where Will Your Baby Sleep?

Even if you have a well-designed nursery and a beautiful crib, it can be tough to decide where your baby will sleep. Should you put her in her crib right away or use a bassinet or side sleeper to keep her close? Or do you plan on letting your baby sleep with you in your bed? Although you will have to decide what is best for your baby, you should avoid letting your baby get used to sleeping in a bouncy chair, moving swing, or car seat. Although all of these can be acceptable options, especially if it is hard to get your baby to sleep any other way, your baby may become dependent on them, and have a hard time moving to a crib later on.

Bassinet or Crib?

Your baby can start off in a crib, or you can first use a bassinet and then have her graduate to a crib once she outgrows her bassinet or is sleeping for longer stretches at a time. In the first few weeks and months it can be easiest to keep your baby nearby in a bassinet, because she frequently wakes up to eat. That way, you can wake up, get her fed, and then put her right back to sleep. Even if your baby wakes up frequently, this can help everyone quickly get back to sleep and still get some rest through the night.

In addition to figuring whether to use a crib or bassinet, parents of multiples also must decide if they want to let their babies sleep separately or together. Many opt to let their multiples sleep together in a bassinet or crib for at least their first few months and then separate them later on.

The main downside to having your baby nearby is that it may cause you to wake up every time that she stirs or wakes up briefly, even if it isn't a full awakening that requires your attention. That closeness does offer some reassurance, though, for many parents who worry about their younger baby through the night.

A bassinet is also a lot cozier than a crib will be for your newborn baby.

On the other hand, starting her off in a crib does save you the expense of buying a bassinet, and if swaddled, she will likely feel just as cozy and comfortable in a crib.

The Family Bed

Having your baby sleep in bed with you is a controversial way to put your baby to sleep. Although advocates praise the benefits of a family bed, other people question how safe it is and say that it may increase the risk of Sudden Infant Death Syndrome (SIDS). While the American Academy of Pediatrics and the Consumer Product Safety Commission are against co-sleeping, there are many other experts who highly recommend the practice. Most notable of these experts is the respected pediatrician and author Dr. William Sears. (See his Web site, listed in Appendix C, for more information.)

If you do choose to share your bed with your baby, be sure to keep the bed safe, so that your baby can't roll off or get smothered by pillows and soft bedding and can't get trapped between the bed and a wall or headboard. Safer co-sleeping means using bedding that fits tightly on the mattress, avoiding pillows and soft blankets, and making sure that there is no room between the bed and the wall. A bedside sleeper or co-sleeper right next to your bed can be a safe way to get all of the benefits of having your baby sleep very close to you.

Sleeping Through the Night

For most parents, this is the ultimate goal: having a baby who sleeps well all night long. After all, if your baby is sleeping well, then that probably means you are sleeping well too. If you are expecting your baby to come home from the hospital and go straight to sleeping through the night, though, you are in for a big disappointment.

So when will your baby start sleeping through the night? That really depends on what you mean by "sleeping through the night." Some parents consider that to mean a good ten- or eleven-hour stretch without waking up. Most other parents are satisfied with six or eight hours and consider that to be sleeping through the night, because that means that they are getting a nice long stretch of uninterrupted sleep.

When to Expect It

Although you sometimes hear of some infants sleeping through the night at two months, the average infant doesn't begin to sleep all night until four to six months. It doesn't necessarily mean that you are doing something wrong if your younger infant isn't sleeping well or that other parents have a magic way to put their baby to sleep. Again, some babies are just naturally better sleepers than others.

FACT

It can be hard to live in a sleep-deprived state for much of your infant's first few months. In addition to mom and dad taking turns caring for their baby at night, you can consider hiring a night nanny. Although not inexpensive, they can provide total care overnight or simply bring your baby to mom for breastfeedings, allowing parents to get a good night's rest.

If your baby isn't sleeping well by four to six months, or is waking up very frequently before that, you should look for things that may be interfering with your baby's sleep. Is he falling asleep while feeding or being rocked, then waking up every hour, and needing that same routine to get back to sleep? Then you may have created poor sleep associations and need to adjust your bedtime routine to help him fall asleep on his own.

Another common issue is what to do about the baby who was previously sleeping all night and then begins waking up a lot when he gets older. This can occur when your child is sick, after he has just gotten over an illness, or as he goes through a new developmental stage. With the onset of separation anxiety at about nine months, or when your child learns a new skill, such as sitting up or crawling, infants may begin waking up more. If you stick to your usual sleep routines, your baby should quickly begin to sleep well again. Try not to create any new sleep habits during these times, and see your pediatrician if the poor sleep lingers more than a few nights or your child is also fussier than usual or seems sick.

Bedtime Routines

Once your baby is two to three months old, you can begin to work on a regular bedtime routine to help him sleep through the night. That usually means putting him to sleep while he is drowsy, but still awake, so that he learns to fall asleep on his own. You can still get him ready for bed, perhaps give him a bath, read a story, or sing a lullaby. A last feeding will also be a part of his bedtime routine, but you should try to not let him fall asleep eating as he gets older. Also, your baby will not learn to fall asleep on his own if he falls asleep watching a moving mobile or listening to music.

ALERT!

Some babies need to cry a little as they go to sleep. If it is for only a very short time or if your baby cries even more if you try to pick her up and put her back to sleep, then consider letting her fuss herself to sleep. This crying, especially early on, shouldn't be a prolonged, very high-pitched or loud, screaming type of cry though; if it is, you should respond to your child instead of simply letting her cry.

If your baby cries after you try putting him down while still awake, you should check on him after a few minutes and try to soothe him to sleep. The eventual goal will be for him to fall asleep without much fussing after you put him down.

The idea behind teaching your baby to fall asleep by himself is that if he later wakes up, then he will be able to simply put himself back to sleep. Everyone goes through brief periods of light sleep as they drift through different sleep stages. Infants who don't know how to go to sleep on their own often wake up during these light sleep stages, while those who do and have good sleep associations continue to sleep and are likely to sleep all night.

Daytime Naps

Because babies need a lot of sleep and they don't get all of their sleep at night, regular naps are an important part of your baby's sleep schedule. In the first few weeks and months, as your baby is still in a regular sleeping, waking, and eating cycle, you don't have to think of daytime sleep as naps. They are just another part of your baby's overall need for sleep.

FACT

Regular long naps are much better than more frequent, short naps. If your baby is only napping for twenty or thirty minutes at a time, then it is unlikely that she will be as well rested as if she took a good sixty- or ninety-minute nap.

Later on, by three to four months, your baby's sleep will become more organized. You can then expect her to sleep more at night, and have three regular naps during the day. Although the length of naps varies, they are usually about one and a half hours each.

By six months, most infants are only requiring two daytime naps and they are sleeping even longer at night. This routine of an early morning and early afternoon nap will probably continue until your child is well into his toddler years. If your baby doesn't nap well, make sure that you are not waiting until she is overtired before putting her down, and that you have a regular and strict routine for naps. Your infant is less likely to take good naps if she sometimes takes a nap at home, sometimes in the car, and falls asleep in her stroller other times. Try to organize your daytime schedule around your baby's naps.

Avoiding Common Sleep Problems

In addition to frequently waking up, common sleep problems include having trouble falling asleep and simply not sleeping enough. They all can contribute to both you and your baby not getting enough sleep, leading to fussy and irritable babies and parents. The most common sleep problems include:

- Taking a long time to fall asleep
- Frequently waking up
- Waking up too early in the morning

- Not taking regular, long naps during the day
- Having a backward sleep schedule, sleeping a lot during the day and staying up most of the night

Most of these problems can be resolved by avoiding the bad habits mentioned earlier, sticking to a regular routine for naps and bedtime, and teaching your infant to fall asleep on her own with a good bedtime routine.

Swaddling in a blanket is a popular way to help babies sleep well. Being wrapped firmly in a blanket can help to prevent him from making jerking movements that can wake him up and will help him to sleep cozy and secure. You should stop swaddling your baby as he gets older, especially once he is able to roll over.

Is It a Problem?

Before you even begin to look for advice on "fixing" a sleep problem, you first have to decide whether you or your baby even has a problem. If your nine- or twelve-month-old is sleeping for four or five hours at a time, wakes up once or twice at night to feed, and you both quickly go back to sleep, then there may not really be a problem. Especially if everyone is well rested the next day, you may not want to adjust anything to eliminate those feedings or awakenings.

How about if your older infant continues to fall asleep breastfeeding or with a bottle or pacifier? Isn't that a problem? It can be if she hasn't learned to fall asleep on her own and is frequently waking up after falling asleep like that. However, if your bedtime routine works for you and your baby is sleeping well, then it isn't really a problem that needs to be fixed.

Mistakes and Misunderstandings

Many sleep problems can be avoided if you have realistic expectations and know the bad habits to avoid. If you expect your baby to sleep through the night at two or three weeks of age and you let her cry it out all night, then you will quickly have a very sick baby. Likewise, thinking that it is normal for a nine-month-old to feed every hour through the night will probably leave you both sleep-deprived. Some of the most common mistakes and misunderstandings to avoid include the following:

- Don't let your newborn skip meals because he is sleeping a lot. Although you don't have to wake up an older baby who is feeding and gaining weight well, in the first few weeks you should wake your baby up if he has gone more than four to six hours without eating.
- Don't start solid foods like cereal early in order to help your baby sleep longer—this probably won't work anyway.
- Don't wait until your baby is overtired to put him to sleep.
- Be careful not to skip naps because you are out and about and busy. Try to adjust your daily routine to your child's nap schedule.
- Don't put your younger infant to sleep with a security object, like a large stuffed animal or blanket, as it may raise the risk of SIDS.

One of the most important sleep habits to avoid is putting your baby to sleep on his stomach, even if you think it helps him to sleep better. The extra risk of SIDS isn't worth a little more sleep at night.

FACT

If your baby seems to be crying more than he is sleeping, maybe you need some advice from a fussy-baby expert. See Chapter 10 for information about some of the most popular experts and summaries of their advice.

Dad's Role and Sleep

As in all other aspects of parenting, a father should have an equal role with his partner when it comes to caring for their baby at night. This usually means taking turns attending to the baby each night or each time he wakes up. That way, both parents can get some sleep, especially during the first few months when nighttime awakenings are the most common.

A father can help with nighttime feedings even if his baby is exclusively breastfed. He can feed a bottle of pumped breastmilk or even simply bring the baby to mom to breastfeed and then return the baby to the bassinet or crib.

If you decide that one parent will take on the sole role of caring for the baby at night, then the other can make up for it by doing more at other times. This is a good compromise if, for example, one parent has a very hard time getting back to sleep after waking up at night. Good ways to make up for not getting up in the middle of the night can include taking over the first and last feedings of the day, so that your partner can go to sleep a little earlier and sleep in the next morning.

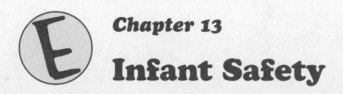

Chapter 13

Infant Safety

Babyproofing the house before your baby first comes home is fairly easy because newborn babies and even younger infants aren't very mobile and can't get into too much trouble. But once your baby starts crawling and walking, you have to be much more careful. In fact, you may have to begin babyproofing again, so your child isn't hurt in an avoidable injury or accident.

Infant Car Seats

Do you need a new car seat already? While any child under a year old definitely needs to stay in a car seat, the type of seat she sits in is going to depend a great deal on how tall she is and how much she weighs. A smaller baby might be able to stay in an infant-only seat until at least her one-year birthday, while a bigger baby might outgrow that type of seat before she is six to nine months old.

Although being twelve months and 20 pounds is usually the standard for when to switch a child to the forward-facing position, some people follow the advice that the rear-facing position is always safest, and continue to keep their older babies facing the rear for as long as they fit in the seat.

Which Type of Seat?

The average infant-only seat fits a child comfortably until he is about 20 to 22 pounds, so your baby can safely stay in this type of seat at least until he reaches that weight. If he doesn't reach 20 pounds by the time he is twelve months old, you should continue to use your infant-only seat in the rear-facing position until he reaches 20 pounds.

Babies who weigh more than 22 pounds or are too tall to fit in their infant-only seat need to be moved to a convertible car seat. This type of seat can be used in either the forward-facing or rear-facing position. It is safe to use as a rear-facing seat for children up to 30 to 35 pounds and 30 inches tall, and so will accommodate even the biggest of babies.

You should keep using your convertible seat in the rear-facing position until your baby is at least twelve months old. After that, providing he weighs more than 20 pounds, you can start to use it as a forward-facing car seat. Again, you can continue to keep your child in a rear-facing position until he reaches the seat's rear-facing weight limits. Many experts think this is still the safest position for your child.

Common Mistakes to Avoid

Even with all of the publicity about car seat safety, the detailed instructions included with each car seat, and the car seat safety checkups provided in most communities, people continue to make mistakes in how they put their kids in their car seat. Among the more common mistakes are:

- Putting the harness chest clip in the wrong position and not at armpit level
- Allowing the harness straps to become loose, twisted, or positioned too high above the infant's shoulders
- Placing a child in a forward-facing seat before he is 20 pounds and twelve months old
- Placing a child in a rear-facing car seat in the path of an air bag
- Putting a blanket or heavy jacket under the harness straps

Be sure you avoid these mistakes. You should also read the instructions when you install your child's car seat. If you still aren't sure that you are using it correctly, go to a car seat safety inspection station. You can find one in your area at the Web site *www.seatcheck.org.*

Childproofing the House

Even before your baby gets moving, it is time for you to get on all fours, crawl around the house, and make sure that everything is safe. Remember that your main goal in getting your house childproofed is creating a safe environment for your baby to explore and play in.

It is never too soon to childproof your house, but do it at least before your baby is six months old. If you wait much longer your infant may already be crawling, cruising, or walking, and you probably then won't discover hazards until they have already hurt your child.

THE EVERYTHING FATHER'S FIRST YEAR BOOK

General Tips

Although the kitchen and the bathroom can be especially hazardous, every room of the house that your baby can enter has to be safe. There are many basic safety measures to take care of in each room, including:

- Putting covers on unused electrical outlets (these can range from simple plastic plugs to more sophisticated covers that slide or pop off to make outlets easily accessible)
- Installing gates on stairs, both at the top and bottom of each staircase
- Either removing furniture with sharp edges or installing soft guards
- Removing breakables from low shelves and tables
- Placing nonskid backing on rugs that your child might slip or slide on
- Installing "no-tip" accessories or wall anchors for heavy furniture so it can't fall over on your child
- Placing finger guards on doors so they don't slam on your infant's fingers
- Keeping cords for window shades or blinds out of reach
- Placing window guards on upstairs windows so your kids won't fall through the screens if the window is open
- Securing electrical cords with cord holders and electrical outlet protectors
- Setting the temperature of hot water heaters to 120° Fahrenheit

You should also look carefully for hidden dangers and remove them. Things to watch for range from the little plastic caps on door stops, which kids can choke on, to heavy items on low carts or tables that can easily tip over, especially TVs.

The Kitchen

One of the biggest dangers in the kitchen is the stove. There are now many devices to make the stove safe, including locks for the knobs and adjustable covers or guards to keep your baby away from things cooking on the stovetop. You should also secure your other kitchen appliances. Even the dishwasher and refrigerator can be hazards, so place a locking strap on both to keep your kids out.

Instead of relying on latches and locks to keep your infant safe from poisons and other hazards in your cabinets, consider moving them to cabinets that are higher up and out of reach.

Kitchen cabinets are often harder to secure than you would think, and they contain many things that could be hazardous to a young child. There are many safety products to help childproof your cabinets. You can choose either a system that latches on to the outside of cabinet handles, which is simpler to install but easy to forget to put back on, or one that installs inside the cabinet as a latch. Or use a combination of the two, especially on the cabinets that contain cleaners, poisons, or breakables.

The Bathroom

As in the kitchen, you should secure the drawers and cabinets in your bathroom. Also consider installing toilet lid locks to prevent drowning, and keep hot appliances such as curling irons out of your infant's reach. A non-slip mat and a faucet cushion can help make the bathtub safe, too.

The Fireplace

While a warm fire is nice on a cold night, fireplaces are hard to keep childproofed. Among the dangers are the sharp edges around the hearth and the risk of getting burned when you have a fire going.

The easiest way to childproof a fireplace is to simply place a heat-resistant safety gate around the whole thing. That way you don't have to worry about your kids getting into the fireplace and playing with ashes, falling on the sharp corners of the hearth, or getting close to the flames. If your fireplace is fueled by natural gas, be sure to secure your gas key, place a cover on your gas valve cover, and install a carbon monoxide detector.

The Garage

Many people don't consider the garage as being really part of the house and so don't take steps to keep it childproofed. With all of the dangers that a garage may hold, including gardening products, insecticides, lawn equipment, and power tools, it is especially important to keep it safe in case your child does get inside by himself. In addition to securing these dangerous items, you should keep your car locked and your keys out of reach so your kids can't accidentally lock themselves inside.

FACT

No matter how safe your house is, it is going to be hard to keep your kids safe if they can easily get out of the house. To keep them inside the house and out of rooms in your house that aren't childproofed, install childproof doorknob covers.

Poison Control

If you do a good job of childproofing your house, your infant shouldn't be at too much risk of getting into any real poisons. If he does get into a poison, such as one of your own medicines, household cleaners, or something even more serious such as a pesticide, do you know what to do?

In Case of Emergency

The American Academy of Pediatrics no longer recommends that parents keep syrup of ipecac in their homes to induce vomiting. Instead, you should just call Poison Control. This used to mean remembering your local poison control number, but getting help got a lot easier a few years ago when the system was switched to a single nationwide toll-free number. To call your nearest poison control center from anywhere in the United States, you now simply dial ☎1-800-222-1222, and a poison safety expert will help you figure out what to do for your child.

To prevent poisonings, remember to use products with child-resistant caps, even vitamins and herbal supplements. Store your household cleaners, chemicals, and insecticides out of reach in a locked cabinet. Also keep all hazardous products in their original containers, instead of transferring them to a milk or soda bottle to use them.

Lead Poisoning

As your infant becomes more mobile, paint chips become a potential source of lead poisoning. If you live in a new house, your kids aren't at risk, but if you live in a house that was built before 1950, or that was built before 1978 and is now being remodeled, these paint chips can be a hazard to them. If you have an older home with deteriorating paint, be sure to have your home and your child tested for lead. You also can keep your kids safe from paint chips and dust contaminated with lead by washing their toys and pacifiers often and covering or sealing places that might be covered with lead paint. In addition, you may want to consider having the lead paint professionally removed from your home.

ALERT!

The U.S. Department of Housing and Urban Development estimates that 25 percent of houses still have "significant" amounts of lead-based paints. Most parents do a poor job of estimating how old their home is, potentially putting their children at risk.

If you have a job or hobby that involves working with lead, it is important to change your clothes before you go in the house, and to wash your clothing separately from your family's clothes.

Baby Walkers

Baby walkers are one product for infants that have always had a bad reputation. If you are considering buying or using a mobile baby walker, keep in mind that the American Academy of Pediatrics has actually called for a ban on their sale because they are associated with so many injuries, and they won't help your baby learn to walk any faster. Why are baby walkers so unsafe?

Well, they aren't. The problem with baby walkers, in particular mobile baby walkers, is that they make your baby mobile. And often they make your baby too mobile, allowing her to get into things that aren't safe. Still, if your house is well childproofed and your child is well supervised and kept away from stairs or other dangers, a mobile baby walker can be safe and fun for your baby to use.

An alternative to a mobile baby walker can be a stationary walker or activity center. These include lots of bells and whistles to keep your older infant entertained.

Choking Prevention

Parents often worry about their baby choking on food once he starts finger and table foods, but the average house has a lot of other choke hazards that put infants even more at risk. These hazards can range from large pieces of food to coins your baby may find on the floor to your older children's toys.

Younger children naturally put everything in their mouths. This is the way that they learn to explore the world around them, so it is impossible to "teach" them not to put things in their mouths. Instead, it is the parents' responsibility to keep the house free of choking hazards—which can be a daily chore.

First aid for a choking infant usually involves placing the child face down on your lap and giving five back blows with the heel of your hand to the area just between the infant's shoulder blades. If that doesn't work, the next step is placing the infant face up and giving five compressions to the infant's breastbone. A CPR class can teach you more first aid to help a choking infant.

The following tips can help keep your baby safe from choking:

- Once your infant is eight to nine months old and you start offering finger foods, cut them up into small, bite-size pieces

- Avoid giving "choke foods," such as grapes, peanuts, and chewing gum, to your infant or toddler
- Only let your infant play with age-appropriate toys (no parts smaller than 1¼ inch in diameter and 2½ inches long)
- If you have older kids, consider putting their toys, which often do have small parts, in a separate room that your infant can't enter
- Warn older children not to give their younger siblings foods or toys that they might choke on
- Let your younger infant play with Mylar balloons instead of rubber or latex balloons, which can be a choking hazard if they pop
- Look for and pick up small objects, like coins, pins, batteries, and buttons, each time you put your baby down on the floor

It is also important to learn CPR so that you know what to do if your baby is choking on something.

Recalls and Product Alerts

Although it seems that most child products, household products, and toys are being built to high safety standards, each year many children are hurt or killed by unsafe products that have already been recalled. Do you know whether any of the products in your home have been recalled?

A new Web site, *www.recalls.gov*, makes it easy to find all types of recalled products, including consumer products, motor vehicles (including cars and car seats), boats, food, medicine, cosmetics, and environmental products.

The Consumer Product Safety Commission issued more than 200 recalls in 2003, including recalls of toys, space heaters, playpens, and other baby equipment. Unfortunately, it is often up to parents to identify which products have been recalled, and then either repair these unsafe products or remove them from their homes. Even if you send in your product registration card, there is no guarantee that you will be notified if the product has been recalled, so regularly watch the news, magazines, and Web sites for recall alerts and information.

Even more of a concern is the rise in popularity of buying used products, some of which may have been recalled, from online auction sites. As long as you check to be sure a product hasn't been recalled, most used baby accessories can be safe. However, don't buy a used car seat on the Internet, since there is no way to make sure that it wasn't damaged in a car crash.

Sunscreen

Keeping your kids safe from the harmful effects of the sun is very important. Remember that most people get 80 percent of their lifetime exposure to the sun before age 18. Increased exposure means increased risk of skin cancer, so it is never too soon to start limiting that exposure.

In addition to using sunscreen, sun safety can include keeping your child covered up with light, loose-fitting clothing, a hat, and sunglasses. It's also best to avoid being outdoors during the hottest part of the day, between about 10 A.M. and 4 P.M.

When to Start Using Sunscreen

Younger children often are forgotten when the family puts on sunscreen, because the parents think it isn't necessary or just not appropriate for infants. In fact, the American Academy of Pediatrics recommends that you start using a sunscreen on your infant once she is six months old, and that you apply it at least thirty minutes before you take her outside. You should then reapply it about every two hours, or sooner if your child was in the water.

QUESTION?

How long can an infant stay in the sun?
The easy answer is "not long." A young child is not able to cool his body easily, so he can quickly get overheated. If your baby seems red, irritable, or sleepy after even a few minutes in the sun, move him into the shade.

The SPF, or sun protection factor, of sunscreen refers to how much protection it gives from the sun. The higher the SPF, the more protection the sunscreen offers. In general, you should use a sunscreen with an SPF of at least 15 on your infant.

What about Younger Infants?

Just because you don't start using sunscreen until age six months doesn't mean that protecting your younger infant isn't important. Sun exposure can be even more harmful for younger infants than for older ones, and the usual recommendation is to just keep them out of the sun. If you must have your younger infant out in the sun and can't keep him covered up, you can still apply sunscreen to his skin. Just limit yourself to using small amounts and only apply it to small areas that are exposed to the sun.

Insect Repellents

Insect bites used to be considered a simple nuisance. The biggest problem they caused was an itchy, or sometimes painful, red spot. The rise in West Nile disease and other insect-borne illnesses makes it even more important to keep your children safe from insects.

FACT

Alternatives to DEET include natural insect repellents, including those that contain citronella or soybean oil. They may not work as well as insect repellents with DEET, but they are a good alternative if you aren't convinced that DEET is safe to use on younger children.

The most commonly used insect repellents are those that are made with DEET, which can be safely used on infants as young as two months of age. Although you shouldn't put the insect repellent on your infant's hands or around her mouth or eyes, you can put it on other exposed areas of skin or clothing. Always be sure to wash it off once you get back inside.

Pool and Water Safety

Drowning is a leading cause of death for younger children, so it is important to keep your backyard pool safe. Even if your young children know how to swim, they should not be considered drown-proof and should always be supervised around the water. In addition to not leaving your children alone around a pool, you can keep your kids safe by:

- Putting a fence around your pool with a self-closing and self-latching gate
- Locking or childproofing all exits from your house that lead to the pool
- Leaving a telephone by the pool so that you can quickly call for help if you need it
- Keeping toys away from the sides of the pool so that you don't attract younger children, who might fall in
- Storing rescue equipment near the pool so you are ready in an emergency

Infant Swimming Lessons

Although the American Academy of Pediatrics doesn't recommend formal swimming lessons until age five, that doesn't mean that you can't take your infant in the water. Aquatic programs are also popular at this age, and although these are not really swimming lessons, they can help you get your baby used to being in the water. Just remember, whether as part of a class or in your pool at home, if your baby is in the water, keep your hands on her at all times.

Indoor Water Safety

Pools aren't the only drowning risk for younger children. A crawling baby can pull up on a bucket, fall in, and quickly drown. Other hazards include the bathtub, toilet, and any other container of water. Remember to never leave your infant alone near any water, not even for just a few seconds or minutes, which is more than enough time for your baby to drown. Don't assume that a bath ring or seat will be enough to keep your baby safe— these are meant to make bath time easier, not provide supervision.

Kids and Pets

Having a family pet is a popular tradition in many families. For your infant's safety, remember that no matter how kid-safe that you think your dog or cat is, you should never leave your baby unsupervised around an animal. Any pet, even one that is usually tame and playful, can bite or attack if it feels threatened by an aggressive infant who is pulling on its ears or invading its space.

Some families also enjoy having more exotic pets, like iguanas, turtles, snakes, and other reptiles. Because of the risk of salmonella to children who touch or handle these reptiles, which can cause fever, vomiting, and diarrhea, younger children shouldn't have any contact with these types of reptiles. You should even be careful to wash your hands and any surfaces that touch the reptile with soap and water so that you don't contaminate your younger children. Small baby turtles with a shell less than 4 inches in length are especially dangerous, because younger kids can put them in their mouths. In fact, sale of such turtles has been banned by the FDA.

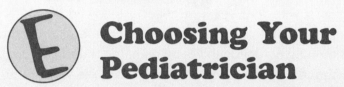

Chapter 14

Choosing Your Pediatrician

For many parents, their pediatrician is one of the people they have the most contact with outside the house during their baby's first year. That makes choosing a good one important. Having a pediatrician that you will be comfortable with will also help you feel confident that your child is growing and developing normally and that you are making the right choices about his care.

Training of Pediatricians

It can help you to understand your pediatrician and develop a better relationship if you realize how many years of training that he had to go through to learn how to take care of your child. Your child's doctor endured many years of school, training, and sleepless nights before becoming a pediatrician.

Training begins with four years of college, followed by four years of medical school, and then three years in a pediatric internship and residency program. Although there probably is no pediatric training during college and just a few months of it in medical school, the three years of residency are spent solely on learning to take care of children, including newborns, infants, preschool and school-age children, and teenagers. These eleven years of training leave most pediatricians well prepared to recognize and treat common pediatric problems as well as provide guidance to help you raise happy and healthy children.

As an alternative to a pediatrician, there are other health-care professionals who can provide your child's care. These include family practice doctors, nurse practitioners, pediatric nurse practitioners, and physician assistants. Just be sure to see a health-care provider who cares for a lot of kids on a regular basis.

In addition to graduating from each of these programs, your pediatrician had to pass three steps of the United States Medical Licensing Examination to get his medical license, and also had to pass an exam from the American Board of Pediatrics to become board certified in pediatrics.

A pediatrician's training doesn't end there. Even after eleven years of preparation and all of those exams, your pediatrician also has to complete training each year to get Continuing Medical Education (CME) credits. This training includes attending medical conferences as well as other lectures and courses, where health professionals learn about the latest medical discoveries and treatments.

The Selection Process

Deciding which pediatrician you will trust with the care of your new baby is a big decision, and one that is made differently by different parents. Although there might not be one best way to choose a good pediatrician that you will be happy with, there are some things that you should *not* do.

- Don't just pick a doctor from the phone book or from a list provided by your insurance company.
- Don't pick whoever is "on-call" when your baby is born.
- Don't go to a pediatrician that someone else likes unless you ask what they like about the doctor.
- Don't go to a doctor just because the office is in a convenient location.

It is important to choose a pediatrician before your baby is born so that if anything goes wrong, you will know who is taking care of your baby and advising you on medical decisions that you must make. Choosing the right doctor may mean avoiding unnecessary tests or treatments from a provider who is overly aggressive or, on the other hand, avoiding a doctor who misses something important because of an inappropriate "wait-and-see" attitude.

Getting Recommendations

Your choice is fairly easy if you already have a pediatrician who has been caring for your other children or if your own pediatrician is still practicing. If not, the best way to find a pediatrician is to get recommendations from friends or family members who have a pediatrician that they like. But it is important to find out *why* they like their doctor. Is it simply because the office is efficient and they can get in and out quickly? Or is it because they always get an antibiotic when they want one?

When accepting someone's recommendation, make sure that you are comfortable with the reason why they like the pediatrician, and that this reason has something to do with being an educated and competent doctor (not a personal preference for the way the waiting room is decorated, for instance). The same applies when a person recommends against a doctor, because the reason for being unhappy with that particular pediatrician may be something that wouldn't bother you. Your partner's own OB/GYN doctor might also be a good source of a recommendation, but again, ask why she is recommending the pediatrician.

FACT

The American Board of Pediatrics reports that there are 77,328 Board-certified pediatricians in the United States, and an additional 2,500 new pediatricians graduate from residency training programs each year. Only 9 percent of them practice in rural areas, though, so whether it will be easy for you to see a pediatrician is likely to depend on where you live.

Practicing Styles

Although parents often focus on office hours, hospital affiliations, and length of wait times, one of the most important things to focus on is the pediatrician's style of practicing medicine. Does he wear a white coat and tie and seem very formal, or does he dress casually and have a playful, informal style? Does he spend a long time explaining things, or does he provide you with reference material that you can take home and read?

Recognizing the pediatrician's style is important, because just as we each become friends with different types of people, there will likely be a particular pediatrician's style with which you and your baby's mother will be most comfortable.

Your Expectations

It is also important to consider your own expectations when you choose a pediatrician. Do you want to always be able to talk to the doctor when you call for advice, and not have to speak with a nurse? Do you expect these calls to be able to last fifteen or thirty minutes?

If you have moved or your previous pediatrician is no longer practicing, you can't always expect to have the same relationship with your new doctor. Just because your previous pediatrician gave you her home phone number to use at any time does not mean that your new pediatrician will do the same thing. The one thing you should expect is that building a relationship takes time on both ends, although with time you may get those same privileges from another doctor.

FACT

The most common reasons for a child to go to the doctor, besides well visits, include having an ear infection, an upper respiratory tract infection, and gastroenteritis, with diarrhea and vomiting.

Solo Versus Group Practice

As you look for a pediatrician, you will notice that some doctors practice all by themselves in a solo practice, while others work with a large group of other doctors. While it shouldn't be the most important factor when you choose a pediatrician, you should understand some of the differences between solo and group practice pediatricians, as well as the major pros and cons of each.

Solo Practice Pediatricians

One of the main benefits of going to a pediatrician in practice by himself is that when you have a visit, you will always see your pediatrician. You don't have to worry about explaining your child's whole medical history to another doctor or seeing someone you don't necessarily like or trust. Even when you call after-hours, you will get to talk to your own doctor.

Another benefit is that a small office will have a small staff. That means that the receptionist, nurses, and office manager are likely to recognize you when you come in and better understand your family's specific needs. You will probably also be able to get common tasks, such as getting a copy of your child's immunization records, done quickly.

Of course, such a small office can be a problem if you don't like or get along with even one of the office's staff members. Another downside is that without any other doctors covering for your pediatrician, you may not always get an appointment when you want one. A small office also may not have the latest medical technology available, so you might have to go elsewhere for simple lab tests and other procedures.

Group Practice Pediatricians

A pediatrician in a group practice shares an office with one or more other pediatricians. With more doctors being available, you probably will be able to get an appointment whenever you want one. You may not be able to see your own doctor or talk to your own doctor after-hours, though.

Another downside is that with a larger office, there will be more office staff and you may not get to know everyone in the office. However, a larger office will have more resources, and will likely be able to provide more services than a solo practitioner will.

Making Your Choice

Before making your final choice for a pediatrician, you should consider some practical matters:

- Is the pediatrician on your insurance plan?
- Is he or she in a convenient location so that you don't have to drive for an hour with a sick child?
- Are the office hours convenient for you?
- How long do you have to wait for an appointment?
- Will you always see your own pediatrician?
- How long will you be kept waiting in the office?
- Is someone available when the office is closed if you need help?
- Is the office affiliated with a children's hospital?

Although you could wait until your prenatal visit to consider these questions, you could also do a little homework on your own and call the offices to save some time. One "wrong" answer may not be enough to disqualify a potential doctor, but if you get several unsatisfactory answers, especially for the questions that are most important to you, then scratch that doctor's name off of your list of candidates.

Once you find a pediatrician that you like, be sure to take some steps to keep the relationship healthy, such as by showing up for your appointments on time, not showing up without an appointment, and not waiting until after-hours to call with nonurgent problems.

Next, find out if the pediatricians that you are considering agree with your positions on important matters, like breastfeeding, antibiotic overuse, circumcision, and so on. If not, are they at least flexible and willing to help you do things the way you want to, even if they disagree with your methods?

The New Dad Consult

Although the first visit with a pediatrician is often called a "new mom consult," it is usually best if both mom and dad go to any prenatal visits to meet the doctors that you are considering. After you make a list of candidates from recommendations and the questions found in this chapter, try to schedule a prenatal visit to meet each doctor. While some doctors charge for these "interviews," most provide them as a free service.

You will want to ask several questions about issues that are important to you, but the main point of these visits is simply to find out if you feel comfortable with the pediatrician and to see how his office works. For example, if you see a waiting room that is overflowing with frustrated parents who seem to be waiting for long periods of time, you might end up waiting for your visits, too, unless there was an emergency that put the office behind schedule. If you show up early for your prenatal visit and see a regular stream of kids come in and quickly go back to see the doctor, then you have likely found an office that is run very efficiently and which you might want to go to yourself.

You Can Change Your Mind

Even with a lot of recommendations and a good prenatal visit, it will still take a few "real-world" visits to find out if you have found the right pediatrician for you. It could be that there is a policy you didn't know about, or maybe the doctor was simply on her best behavior for the "interview." If you later encounter problems with your pediatrician or her office and you can't resolve them, start the process over and look for another pediatrician.

Pediatric Specialists

Your pediatrician will be able to handle almost all of your new baby's health-care needs. The average pediatrician is well trained to help with all of the problems new parents face, from advice about day-to-day basics, such as feeding and sleep issues, to caring for your baby when he is sick. (See Chapter 15 for more information on what to expect during visits to your pediatrician's office.)

FACT

Some pediatric specialists train for more than fourteen years to learn to provide their specialty care. A pediatric plastic surgeon, for example, in addition to four years of college and medical school, three years of a surgery residency, and three years of plastic surgery training, undergoes additional training in pediatric plastic surgery.

There may, however, be times when your baby needs more care than your pediatrician can provide. Maybe he is not gaining weight well, is having seizures, or is not meeting his developmental milestones, and you and your pediatrician need some help figuring out what is going on. Or your baby may have a common illness, like reflux, allergies, or asthma, but isn't responding to traditional treatments. Any of these situations might lead a new parent to seek an evaluation by a specialist.

Types of Specialists

There are many different specialists who care for kids. Especially for older children, you might end up seeing a specialist who cares for both kids and adults, or you could see a pediatric specialist who only cares for children.

Many pediatric specialists are also pediatricians. After completing their general pediatric training, they then go on to do a three-year fellowship and get their specialist training. These types of specialists include, among others, pediatric cardiologists, endocrinologists, gastroenterologists, hematologists, and pulmonologists. There also are pediatric specialists in genetics, nephrology, neurology, emergency medicine, and infectious disease.

Other types of pediatric specialists, including most of the ones who do surgery, are not usually pediatricians. They do complete additional pediatric specialist training, though. These include pediatric surgeons, neurosurgeons, ophthalmologists, and pediatric orthopedic surgeons.

You should usually ask your pediatrician before going to a specialist, even if you don't need a referral. That way, you can be sure to see a doctor that your pediatrician knows and trusts.

And then there are specialists who see and care for kids, but don't necessarily have any advanced pediatric training and are not board certified in a pediatric specialty. However, that doesn't mean that they shouldn't see your child, because they usually have some training in managing pediatric problems. Specialists who see both kids and adults might include general surgeons, allergists, and dermatologists. Your pediatrician can help you choose the specialist who would be best to see your child when and if it becomes necessary.

There are many other health-care professionals who are not doctors but still can help take care of your child's health-care needs. These include speech, occupational, and physical therapists to manage and treat developmental delays, and lactation consultants to help with breast-feeding problems.

Second Opinions

One of the most common reasons to see a specialist is because your pediatrician thinks that it is necessary. Another reason, though, is simply because you want a second opinion. You might disagree with your pediatrician, either because she is being too aggressive or not aggressive enough, or you may just feel more comfortable and better reassured with a specialist's opinion. Don't be afraid to ask for a second opinion if you want one.

Although getting a second opinion from a specialist should be an easy process, there are a few potential roadblocks that you might encounter. One common problem is that there may not be a specialist available in your area or there might be a long waiting list to see the doctors who are around. In either situation, you might ask your pediatrician to call a specialist to get further advice about what to do for your child.

Another problem might be that your pediatrician simply refuses to refer you to a specialist. You shouldn't have to beg for a referral, and if your pediatrician can't convince you that it isn't necessary, then you might want to go to a different pediatrician.

Last, your insurance company might refuse to authorize the referral. A letter of medical necessity from your pediatrician should be enough to override this refusal, though you may have to ask about an appeal process to get the referral approved.

Chapter 15

Going to the Pediatrician

Your infant will make lots of visits to your pediatrician's office during his first year of life. While most of these visits ideally will be for well-child checkups and immunizations, you may also have to go in for a few sick visits when your child is not feeling well. Knowing what to expect can help you make the most of these visits.

Preparing for Your Visits

You don't often hear parents complain about spending too much time with their pediatrician, so it is important not to waste what time you have in the office. Taking care of your sick child and supervising his siblings running around the room are just a few of the things that can distract you during your visits. Preparing a list of questions can help you to not forget anything important. (You'll learn more about what to put on this list later in this chapter.)

The first step in preparing for your visits to the doctor is deciding who actually is going to take your baby to the office. Will it be mom, dad, a grandparent, or another caregiver?

Although you often don't have much choice because of work schedules and other constraints, ideally both mom and dad would come to each visit. That way each parent can ask his or her own questions and get a better understanding of how the baby is growing and developing.

If it isn't possible for both parents to come to the visits, then at least one parent should come. Having only a grandparent or other caregiver bring the child to the visit can make the visit more difficult, unless this person spends a great deal of time with the child and has a good understanding of what is going on.

Well-Child Visits

There will be a lot of visits to your pediatrician for checkups during your baby's first year. These checkups, or well-child visits, include an evaluation of your baby's growth, development, and feeding habits; a complete physical examination; a discussion of what you should be doing to take care of your baby's needs; and usually some vaccines. Because appointments for well-child visits are planned far in advance, both parents should make every effort to attend. This is especially important in your baby's first months, when it's likely that both mom and dad have a lot of questions.

Recommended Checkup Schedule

Most pediatricians stick to a standard timing schedule for well-child visits as recommended by the American Academy of Pediatrics. This schedule calls for visits at these ages:

- Two weeks
- Two months
- Four months
- Six months
- Nine months
- Twelve months

If your baby was discharged home early from the hospital (less than forty-eight hours after being born), then your first visit to your pediatrician should be within another twenty-four to forty-eight hours. This is especially important if your baby is breastfeeding.

What to Expect

At each well-child visit, in addition to a standard history and physical, your pediatrician should have your baby's height, weight, and head circumference recorded and plotted on a growth chart to make sure that he is growing well. It is also important that the exam include a testing of your baby's red reflex, which is part of an eye exam, and a hip check to evaluate for developmental dislocation.

ALERT!

If your pediatrician is leaving out major parts of a traditional well-child visit, such as not measuring his height, weight, or head circumference, or not checking your child's hips or eyes during the physical exam, you might want to change to another doctor.

Other tests will include getting a hematocrit or hemoglobin level to screen for anemia. This test is done sometime during the first year, often at the nine-month checkup. It's likely that your baby also will be either screened or tested for tuberculosis and lead poisoning sometime during his first year of life.

When attending a well-child visit, be prepared to answer the following questions about your baby:

- How often is he breastfeeding or taking a bottle of formula?
- What new foods have you introduced since the last visit?
- What new milestones has your baby picked up, such as rolling over, sitting up, or standing?
- How well is he sleeping at night and for his naps?
- In what position is he sleeping?
- Where is he sitting in the car, and in what kind of car seat?
- Has he had any reactions to his immunizations?
- Are you giving him a vitamin or any other medications?
- What concerns do you have about his development?

If your child has a chronic condition, such as asthma or eczema, don't wait until your well visits to talk about them. If you do, it will take away much-needed time for your pediatrician to talk about your child's nutrition, growth, development, and safety. A separate visit to talk about your child's illnesses is usually a better idea.

Be prepared so that your baby's doctor can more easily determine how well your child is doing. Questions you might ask your doctor include which foods to start next, what milestones to watch for, and what things you should avoid doing. (Also see Appendix B for a Well-Child Visit Worksheet that you can take with you to the doctor's office.)

Sick-Child Visits

Hopefully most of the visits to your pediatrician during your baby's first year will just be for well-child visits, but there may be times when your baby is sick and needs to see the doctor. Keep in mind that just because your child doesn't have a runny nose, cough, or fever, it doesn't mean that he isn't sick. Other symptoms or illnesses that might prompt a sick visit, especially during the first year, include:

- Eczema
- Allergies
- Colic
- Poor weight gain
- Diarrhea
- Constipation
- Thrush
- Blocked tear ducts
- Developmental delays

Behavioral problems might also be a good reason to schedule an appointment with your pediatrician, instead of just trying to get advice over the phone. Such problems might include the child not sleeping well, being very fussy most of the time, not feeding well, or refusing solid foods.

FACT

When your child is sick, don't wait until the last minute to make an appointment. The earlier you call once your pediatrician's office opens in the morning, the sooner you will get an appointment. If you wait until late in the day you might be asked to wait until the next day for an appointment, even for a problem that has been going on for several days.

You should usually expect a same-day appointment when your child is sick, unless your child's condition is a long-term or nonurgent problem, such as acne or bowlegs. It is unreasonable to expect a parent or child to wait even one or two days when the infant has an ear infection, fever, or difficulty breathing. You probably should look for another doctor if you are regularly made to wait several days for appointments when your baby is sick.

What to Expect

During sick visits your child should be weighed and have his temperature taken. Next, after talking about your child's problems and symptoms, your pediatrician should perform a complete physical exam. Warning signs to look for include doctors that quickly prescribe an antibiotic each time you walk in the door or regularly leave out parts of the exam, like not looking in your baby's ears or mouth. If your child has a fever and was up all night crying, your doctor should look at her ears before concluding that she has an ear infection.

Questions the Doctor May Ask

Parents often assume that a doctor can tell what is wrong with a sick child just by the physical exam. In reality, the history (or story of the child's illness) is often even more important. For example, suppose a child has a cough and runny nose. If he is eating and drinking well, isn't too fussy, isn't having trouble breathing, and the symptoms just started yesterday, then he likely just has a cold and doesn't need any antibiotics. If, however, he has had two weeks of symptoms that are now worsening, and has begun to have a fever, he might have a sinus infection and may need antibiotics. Both cases would likely have the same physical exam; it is the description of the illness that would get him the right treatment.

Some questions that you should be prepared to answer during each visit can include:

- How long has your child been sick?
- What are all of his symptoms?
- When are the symptoms worse?
- How have the symptoms been changing?
- What makes the symptoms better?
- How has being sick affected his eating and sleeping?
- Has he been around anyone else who's been sick?
- What medications have you been giving him?
- Why do you think he hasn't been getting better?
- What are you most worried about with this illness?

Questions to Ask Your Doctor

Parents seem to have a million questions that they want to ask their pediatrician, but they often forget them during the visit. Preparing a list of questions and bringing them to your visits can help to make sure that you get all of your questions answered. Some good questions to start with at a sick visit include:

- What is my child's diagnosis?
- What causes this?
- What treatments are you prescribing, if any?
- What are the side effects of those treatments?
- Are there any alternatives to those treatments?
- When should he start getting better?
- What are some signs to watch for that might mean he is getting worse?
- When can he return to day care?
- Do I have to limit his diet or activity?
- Should I bring him back for a recheck?

Getting answers to these questions (and making note of the answers) is especially helpful if only one parent can make it to the visit and needs to explain everything to the other. (See the Sick-Child Visit Worksheet in Appendix B to help you prepare for these visits.)

ALERT!

Don't leave your pediatrician's office if you are not sure that you understand everything that you have been told about your child's illness, prescribed treatments, or what to watch for if he gets worse.

Rechecks

Parents often tend to overlook visits to the doctor that are mainly to recheck a previously diagnosed condition, such as reflux, asthma, or an ear infection. After all, what is the point in going to the doctor when your baby is better?

These visits are very important, though. They can help your doctor recognize when a condition such as poor weight gain or failure to thrive is worsening, and help him decide when to start or stop a daily medication for conditions such as allergies or asthma. If your pediatrician recommends that you return for a recheck, be sure to schedule and keep the appointment.

When to Call Your Pediatrician

Ideally, you have a doctor who is available when you need her. That means you are able to call the office during the day and talk either to an advice nurse or the doctor herself, and also that you are able to call after-hours, when the office is closed. Having a doctor you can call after-hours is especially important, because that can help you avoid needless worrying and unnecessary trips to the emergency room.

Review your pediatrician's procedures for handling after-hours and emergency situations *before* you need them so that you know what to do in an emergency. Can you call the office or an answering service that will page your doctor, or are you expected to just go to the emergency room?

Still, if you call your pediatrician each and every time that you have a question, you might be making several calls a day. And although a patient doctor's office will understand that you are a new parent and will be helpful, you will quickly feel like a nuisance and might stop calling, even when you really need to.

So when is it necessary for you to call? While it really isn't possible to warn you about every situation that merits calling your pediatrician, it is especially important to call if your baby has any of the following symptoms:

- A rectal temperature of 100.4° Fahrenheit or above (when the baby is less than three months old)
- A temperature above 101° Fahrenheit (from three to six months)

- A temperature above 103° Fahrenheit (after six months)
- Trouble breathing
- Fussiness that doesn't improve when you hold her, especially if she also has a fever, poor appetite, or other symptoms
- Projectile vomiting or vomiting up a dark green substance
- Vomiting and/or diarrhea that is causing dehydration
- Bloody diarrhea
- Poor appetite, not eating well
- Excessive sleeping or difficulty waking her up
- Problems breastfeeding to the point at which you need to supplement more than you want to

It is hard to have specific guidelines about when to call if your older infant has a fever, so even if your seven-month-old has just a low-grade fever of 101° and you are concerned, be sure to call your pediatrician. You should also trust your instincts and call any other time that you think your baby is ill and you need help.

Parenting or general questions about feeding or sleeping are usually less urgent. If possible, you might save these questions for your well-child visits or group them together so you aren't calling your pediatrician every day. If you have a lot of questions, you may even want to schedule an extra visit with your pediatrician in order to go over them.

Kids in the ER

Unless you go to a children's hospital or a hospital with a pediatric emergency room, you will likely feel out of place in the ER with your child. Adult-size beds, no kid-friendly decorations, and personnel who might not feel comfortable caring for kids can make a trip to the emergency room difficult and stressful for parents of young children.

Although parents may think that the doctors, nurses, and other people working in the ER have specific training in taking care of pediatric patients, that is unfortunately not always true. That can lead to your child being misdiagnosed, overtreated, or having too many unnecessary tests done.

To help avoid these types of problems, try to call your pediatrician before you head to the ER, unless it is a true emergency. Once you arrive you might also ask what type of pediatric training and experience the ER staff has, ask them to call your pediatrician to review the diagnosis and treatment plan, or ask for a transfer to a facility that has board-certified emergency medicine physicians or pediatric specialists.

QUESTION?

How do you know if the hospital staff seeing your child has pediatric experience?
The easiest way is to just ask questions about their training or how often they have seen a child with the same symptoms or diagnosis as your child. If a procedure is going to be done on your child, you might also ask about the experience level of the person doing it.

For nonemergency situations, remember that you are almost always better off going to see your own pediatrician than going to an emergency room.

The Pros and Cons of Antibiotics

Are antibiotics one of the greatest advances in medicine or a threat to the health of your children? Although the word "threat" might be a little strong, the basic answer is that they are both. That antibiotics have been helpful goes without saying. Thanks to the use of antibiotics, today's pediatricians rarely see kids with problems like rheumatic fever or mastoiditis (a complication of untreated ear infections) and kids are able to survive serious infections such as meningitis, pneumonia, and infections of the blood and bones.

Antibiotics don't help every kind of infection, though. They won't help when your child has a simple cold—even if he has a green runny nose—or any other infection caused by a virus. Overusing antibiotics, or using them when they aren't needed, also carries the risk of creating bacteria that become resistant to the antibiotics. This means the antibiotics don't work when they really are needed.

Resistant bacteria are one of the main reasons that your child might need two or three different antibiotics to treat a chronic ear or sinus infection, and why some bacteria, like MRSA, that cause skin infections can't be treated with standard medications. To help prevent the overuse of antibiotics, don't ask for an antibiotic every time that your baby has a fever, green runny nose, or a cough, or when your pediatrician says that it isn't necessary. Just because you see your pediatrician doesn't mean that you have to walk out with a prescription for an antibiotic.

Recommended Vaccinations

Just like antibiotics, vaccines also can be seen as both an extraordinary medical advance and a threat to your child's health. Even though vaccine experts generally agree that no vaccine is 100 percent safe or effective, it is clear that they are helpful for the majority of children. If you are uncertain whether you want to immunize your child, be sure to talk to your pediatrician about your concerns so that you can make an informed decision. Most of the common problems from vaccines are limited to local reactions at the location where your child got the shot, such as redness, swelling, and soreness. Many vaccines can also cause rashes and fever, but severe reactions, like a serious allergic reaction, seizures, or high fever, are very rare.

FACT

A recent controversy has been the worry that vaccines containing thimerosal, a form of mercury used as a preservative, can put children at risk of developing autism. Although this has not been proven, thimerosal has been removed from most of the vaccines that your child will get.

Routine Vaccinations

There are several vaccines that are commonly given to children at their routine checkups. These include all of the following, which are included in the Recommended Childhood and Adolescent Immunization Schedule that is published by the American Academy of Pediatrics each year.

Hepatitis B

This vaccine, which protects against the hepatitis B virus, a common cause of liver disease, is given as a three-dose series to infants. The first dose is often given at birth or before hospital discharge. The second dose is usually given when an infant is one to four months old, and the last dose when they are between six and eighteen months old.

DTaP

The diphtheria, tetanus, and acellular pertussis vaccine has fewer side effects than the older DTP vaccine. The first three doses are given at two, four, and six months.

IPV

Although kids used to get the oral polio vaccine (OPV), because of the risk of it causing vaccine-associated paralytic polio, this vaccine is now given as an inactivated shot. Your infant will get doses of this vaccine at two and four months, and a third sometime between six and eighteen months.

Hib

This vaccine protects against the *Haemophilus influenzae* type b bacteria, which can cause meningitis, epiglotitis, pneumonia, and skin, bone, and blood infections. It is given at two, four, and six months, with a booster dose at twelve to fifteen months.

Prevnar

Although often thought of as the "ear infection vaccine," this vaccine also protects against meningitis, pneumonia, and blood infections caused by the *Streptococcus pneumonia* bacteria. Like Hib, it is given at two, four, and six months, with a booster dose at twelve to fifteen months.

Twelve-Month Shots

In addition to the booster doses of the Hib and Prevnar vaccines, infants get the MMR (measles, mumps, rubella) and the chickenpox vaccine when they are twelve to fifteen months old.

Flu Shots

Parents are often surprised at the idea of giving a flu shot to their baby, but it is approved for infants six months and older. Why would you want to give your baby a flu shot? One of the main reasons is that younger children are thought to be at big risk for flu complications, just as elderly people are. So even if your baby is healthy, a flu shot might be a good idea to help her avoid getting sick. In fact, it is now recommended for all children between the ages of six and twenty-three months.

Combination Shots

Nobody likes the fact that infants have to get so many shots, especially if they have to get four or five separate shots during a single visit. Your baby might get fifteen separate shots before his first birthday, including three doses of several vaccines. However, that number can be greatly reduced with the use of combination vaccines.

One of these, Pediarix, combines the DTaP, IPV, and hepatitis B vaccines into a single shot, which can cut the number of shots from fifteen to only nine (or ten if your baby also got the birth dose of the hepatitis B vaccine). Comvax, a combination of the Hib and hepatitis B vaccines, is another commonly used combination shot. If you are concerned about your baby's reaction to all those needles, speak with your pediatrician about the possibility of receiving these combination shots.

Disagreeing with Your Pediatrician

No matter how good your relationship with your pediatrician is, there may come a time when you don't see 100 percent eye-to-eye. Because there are few parenting or medical issues that have only one right solution, disagreeing doesn't mean that one of you is wrong.

In situations like this, instead of simply switching to another doctor, which many parents do, it can help to talk about your concerns. Do you think that your doctor hasn't done enough tests or that he is being too aggressive? If your pediatrician knows what you are worried about, it can make it much easier for him to either reassure you about why he believes he is right or to consider coming up with an alternate treatment plan.

Another option that should be available for you is to get a second opinion from another pediatrician. Be careful, though, because if the opinions differ, it can be difficult to know which one to believe. Do you believe the second one just because her opinion is more in line with your own thoughts? Or do you then get a third opinion? Don't let yourself become trapped in this vicious cycle. Eventually you are going to need to take all the information that has been presented to you and make an informed decision about your baby's treatment.

A second opinion should always be an option, whether your pediatrician wants one or simply because you want one. You might look for another doctor if your pediatrician refuses to allow you to get a second opinion.

Instead of seeing another pediatrician, you may decide to get a second opinion from a pediatric specialist. For example, if your child has had a lot of ear infections, but your doctor doesn't believe in ear tubes, you may decide to see a pediatric ear, nose, and throat specialist for a more thorough evaluation and explanation of the situation and possible treatments.

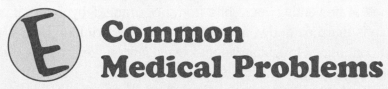

Chapter 16

Common Medical Problems

Your baby's first year will bring a lot of fun and exciting firsts, including her first smile and first steps. The first day that she's sick, whether she has a runny nose, vomiting, or a sore throat, won't be one of the firsts that you are looking forward to, though. Being prepared will make it easier for both of you.

Diarrhea and Vomiting

It may just be because they know they are going to have to clean it up, but for dads, diarrhea and vomiting are among the more distressing symptoms of illness in a child. However, both of these symptoms are generally easy to treat. When caused by a virus, as they typically are, the basic treatments are aimed at preventing your child from becoming dehydrated. If the only symptom is diarrhea and your child is eating and drinking well, you often can just continue her regular diet and give a few ounces of an oral rehydration solution each time she has diarrhea.

Treatment becomes more complicated if your child also is vomiting a lot and is unable to keep down fluids that treat and prevent dehydration. If she continues to vomit, is becoming more dehydrated, or if you are not sure what to do, call your doctor.

Fruit juices, fruit drinks, soda, and sports drinks all have too much sugar and are not a good idea for infants with diarrhea and vomiting. An oral rehydration solution with the right mix of sugar and electrolytes, like Pedialyte, is usually a much better choice when treating a child with a stomach virus.

Parents often unnecessarily restrict what their kids eat when they have diarrhea and vomiting. This usually isn't necessary, but if your child doesn't want to eat, then in addition to fluids, you might try the typical BRAT diet, which stands for bananas, rice, applesauce, and toast. Yogurt, with acidophilus, is also thought to help treat diarrhea, and might be helpful for your older infant.

Acute Diarrhea

Diarrhea that starts all of a sudden, called acute diarrhea, is usually caused by a virus, such as the rotavirus. Symptoms usually include large amounts of watery diarrhea, vomiting, and a low-grade fever. It is estimated that the average child gets two or three episodes of diarrhea caused by a virus each year, so your child will likely catch one of these infections at some point, especially if she is in day care.

There are also several bacteria that can cause acute diarrhea, including *Salmonella*, *Shigella*, and *E. coli*. Unlike viral infections, diarrhea caused by bacteria often has blood and mucus in it, and the child may have a higher fever.

A food intolerance, especially if you have recently introduced a new food or drink, might also cause diarrhea, so review your child's recent diet history to see if you have made any big changes.

Chronic Diarrhea

Once diarrhea lasts more than a few weeks, it is known as chronic diarrhea. This type is less likely to be caused by a simple viral infection. Common causes of chronic diarrhea can include food and lactose intolerances, parasite infections, and malabsorption, which means food isn't being digested properly. Babies with malabsorption often have very foul-smelling and greasy stools. If you suspect this condition it is worth a call to your doctor, as causes can include cystic fibrosis, celiac disease, and many other chronic conditions.

Other Causes of Vomiting

Vomiting accompanied by diarrhea and a low-grade fever, particularly when other people are sick with the same symptoms, is often caused by a simple stomach virus. Vomiting can be a symptom of more serious conditions though, some of which are medical emergencies.

Pyloric stenosis is one common cause of vomiting without other symptoms. Pyloric stenosis is most common in younger infants, and peaks at about the age of three weeks. A common symptom is projectile vomiting after eating.

In older infants, intussusception may be another cause of vomiting. The most common cause of intestinal obstruction in younger children, intussusception also can cause a distended abdomen, irritability that may come and go, and bloody stools that are mixed with mucus.

Other serious causes of vomiting can include conditions that range from intestinal obstructions to brain tumors. These conditions are much less common than the more usual stomach viruses and food intolerances that cause vomiting, but to be safe, see your doctor if your baby has persistent vomiting for more than twenty-four hours or if she has other serious symptoms that you are worried about.

ALERT!

If your child has bilious vomiting, which appears dark green, it can be a sign of an intestinal blockage, such as a malrotation and volvulus. This is always considered to be a medical emergency and requires quick medical attention.

Recognizing Dehydration

Although the average infant with diarrhea can drink enough to stay hydrated, if she has large amounts of very watery diarrhea it is possible for her to quickly get dehydrated, especially if she is also vomiting. Being able to recognize dehydration is important and can help to make sure your baby gets the medical attention she needs. Early treatment can also help you avoid unnecessary trips to the doctor or emergency room.

One of the first signs of dehydration to watch for is whether or not your child is still urinating. If she is having a soaking-wet diaper every six to eight hours, then she likely isn't dehydrated. If she is still having wet diapers, but they are not as wet as they usually are, then she is mildly dehydrated and might get worse without treatment.

The next sign that an infant is dehydrated is a dry and sticky mouth. It is a good sign if your infant's lips and tongue still seem moist or if you can see saliva in her mouth. Late signs of dehydration, which can indicate a medical emergency, can include not making tears, having sunken eyes, a sunken fontanel or soft spot, and a lot of weight loss. At this point, a dehydrated infant might also be lethargic and hard to wake up and may have doughy skin. If you think your infant is dehydrated or if you can't tell, be sure to seek immediate medical attention.

Constipation

This is one of the less serious conditions that worries parents. It is important to remember that it is often normal for infants to strain, groan, and sometimes even cry when having a bowel movement. As long as the bowel movement is soft and watery and not big and firm nor small, hard, little balls, than your child likely isn't constipated.

Although exclusively breastfed babies rarely get constipated, they can normally have infrequent bowel movements beginning at around two to three months of age and until you start baby foods. Again, as long as the bowel movements are soft, this slowdown in having stools is likely normal, even if your child has only one dirty diaper a week. Infrequent bowel movements can be more concerning in the baby's first few weeks of life, though, when it can be a sign that she isn't getting enough breastmilk to drink.

Your infant also may get constipated when you introduce solid foods, like cereal. Once she gets used to her new diet, the constipation often goes away without treatment.

FACT

Although constipation is usually caused by a diet low in fluids and fiber, severe and persistent constipation can be caused by Hirschsprung's disease. A barium enema or biopsy are among the tests your doctors might call for if they are worried about Hirschsprung's disease.

For an infant with persistent constipation, it can help to give him extra water, juice, and baby foods with fiber. If your baby drinks formula and has a great difficulty with constipation, you might have to change to a soy or elemental formula to soften his stools. Rarely, a stool softener might be needed. Things to avoid are regularly giving your child suppositories to help him go, or using enemas. You might ask your doctor about Hirschsprung's disease if your child has never had a normal bowel movement on his own.

Colds and Coughs

It often seems that runny noses and coughs are as much a part of early childhood as diaper changes and baby food are. Especially if your infant is in day care, it might seem that he always has a runny or crusty nose. Do you know how to determine whether that runny nose is a sign that you should see a doctor?

The Common Cold and Sinus Infections

The most frequent cause of a runny nose in younger kids is the common cold. Like most other viral infections, there is no treatment for the common cold, and you often just have to treat your child's symptoms until he gets over them on his own.

These symptoms typically begin with a clear runny nose, low-grade fever, and a cough. Over the next few days the symptoms may worsen, with a higher fever and worsening cough. The runny nose might become yellow or green before going away over the next one to two weeks. It is important to understand that this is the normal pattern for a cold and does not mean that your child has a sinus infection or needs antibiotics. The belief that any runny nose that turns yellow or green is a sinus infection has led to the great overuse of antibiotics and the creation of resistant bacteria that are difficult to treat. Of course, if your child is very fussy, is not eating or drinking, or has trouble breathing, then a trip to your doctor is a good idea.

To help your infant feel better during his cold, you might use saline nasal drops and frequent suctioning with a nasal aspirator to clear your infant's nose, a cool-mist humidifier or vaporizer, and an age-appropriate dose of a pain and fever reducer and/or a cold and cough medicine. When considering using a pain and fever reducer, remember that children and infants should not take aspirin because of the risk of Reye syndrome, a life threatening liver disorder.

While a yellow or green runny nose is typically caused by a common cold, if the infection lingers for more than ten to fourteen days and is worsening, or if the child has a high fever for more than three or four days and appears ill, then he may really have a sinus infection that requires antibiotics.

Bronchiolitis

Often starting out with typical cold symptoms of a runny nose and mild cough, infants with bronchiolitis will develop wheezing, a worsening cough, and trouble breathing as the infection gets in their lungs.

Usually caused by the respiratory syncytial virus (RSV), bronchiolitis can quickly turn into a serious infection requiring treatment with nebulized or aerosolized medications, such as albuterol, and it sometimes requires that children be hospitalized to get intravenous fluids, oxygen, and further care. Younger infants, especially those born premature, are especially prone to serious infections and complications from bronchiolitis.

Synagis is a shot that can be given to children who are at high risk for complications from respiratory syncytial virus (RSV) infections. The shot is given each month when RSV infections are most common, and is especially important for premature babies who will be less than six months old at the start of RSV season in early October.

Bronchitis

The same viruses that cause the common cold can also cause bronchitis, an infection of the bronchial tubes that lead to the lungs. Symptoms are also similar, with a cough, but the cough might be more productive than it is with a cold, and your child may not have much of a runny nose. Although the cough from bronchitis might last several weeks or longer, it doesn't usually need treatment with antibiotics, and can be treated with over-the-counter cold and cough medicines until it goes away on its own.

Croup

Croup is one of the scarier respiratory infections that your infant can get. Unlike most other viral infections, which start with mild symptoms that gradually worsen, an infant with croup usually wakes up in the middle of the night with a loud cough that sounds like a barking seal, and she may have trouble breathing.

Initial treatments might include going into the bathroom, closing the doors, and turning on all of the hot water. Holding your child in this "steam-room" will usually help her to breathe. Just be sure to keep her away from the hot water. Other treatments might include using a cool-mist humidifier or simply walking outside if it is a cool or cold night.

More serious cases of croup are usually treated with steroids or a nebulized medicine called racemic epinephrine. Call your doctor or go to the emergency room if your child with croup is very irritable or is having a hard time breathing.

FACT

Although most people are familiar with the typical symptoms of the flu, including a high fever, runny nose, dry cough, decreased activity, nausea, vomiting, and diarrhea, they can be hard to recognize in your baby, because you can't tell whether she's just fussy or complaining about muscle aches. If you want to prevent your infant from getting the flu, make sure she gets the flu vaccine during flu season, beginning when she is six months old.

Whooping Cough

You should also be aware of the symptoms of whooping cough, or pertussis, which has made a resurgence in recent years because the vaccine wears off after several years. When younger children get pertussis, after a few days or weeks of cold symptoms, they often get coughing spasms or fits, which can be followed by the typical "whoop" as the child gasps for air. Many children also vomit after these coughing fits, which is known as post-tussive vomiting.

Routine immunization with the DTaP vaccine protects most infants from the bacteria that causes whooping cough. Unfortunately, the protection wears off in teens and adults, and it takes at least three doses to get protected. This leaves many infants unprotected until at least their six-month well-child checkup, at which time they get their third dose of DTaP.

To protect your younger children from whooping cough, you should keep them away from any older child or adult with a chronic cough or bronchitis, which is often the only symptom at that age. Because this condition is often overlooked, be sure to tell your doctor if you are worried that your child might have whooping cough. In addition to treatment with the antibiotic erythromycin, younger infants who have whooping cough are often hospitalized because of the risk of apnea, a condition that may cause a child to stop breathing.

Chronic Coughs

An infant with a chronic cough that lasts more than a few weeks can be frustrating to care for and treat. Is it a cold, sinus isnfection, bronchitis, or pneumonia? Or is it being triggered by allergies, asthma, or reflux? A chest x-ray, physical exam, and detailed review of all of your child's symptoms can help you figure out the cause of the cough. Persistent coughs might also need further evaluation by a pediatric pulmonologist.

Allergies and Asthma

It is a common misunderstanding that younger children don't get allergies and asthma, which often leads to them being undiagnosed or undertreated. Complicating matters even further is the fact that most viral illnesses, which are very common at this age, can also cause runny noses, coughs, and wheezing, just like allergies and asthma. However, if your child always gets sick with a cough or runny nose, you should suspect allergies, asthma, or both, especially if these conditions run in the family.

Allergies

Infants with allergies are often misdiagnosed as having colds and sinus infections. Because the average child has six to eight upper respiratory tract infections each year, it is possible that kids who almost always have a runny nose do indeed continually get sick. However, a more likely reason for a chronic runny nose is allergies, especially if your child typically has a clear runny nose and no fever.

In addition to being difficult to diagnose, allergies can be difficult to treat at this age, because few medicines are approved for use in children so young. One good choice is the antihistamine Zyrtec, which is approved for use in infants over six months of age.

Although it was long thought that having pets was bad for kids at risk for allergies or asthma, several recent studies have shown that children who grew up around allergens might have a decreased chance of developing allergies and asthma later in life. Some experts believe that the recent increased incidence of allergies and asthma is because we live in too "sterile" an environment, and pets may help to make it less so.

Asthma

Asthma can also be difficult to diagnose at this age, when kids may just have a chronic cough and not the typical wheezing that other children have. Some features that might indicate asthma as the cause of a chronic cough include worsening of the cough at night or with any kind of activity, especially once your child starts walking and running around.

The importance of daily preventive medications to manage asthma is now well known. Medicine such as inhaled or nebulized steriods can prevent further asthma attacks and allow your child's lungs to heal, so early diagnosis is important.

Avoiding Triggers

In addition to preventive medicines for allergies and asthma, it can be even more helpful to learn what is triggering your child's symptoms and then avoid those things. Common triggers can include:

- Secondhand smoke
- Pet dander
- Dust mites
- Mold
- Pollens
- Foods and food additives

- Strong odors
- Air pollution
- Cockroaches, rodents, and other pests

Things such as changes in the weather, gastroesophageal reflux, and viral infections also have been known to cause allergic reactions, although these things obviously are harder to avoid than are the triggers listed here.

Common Rashes

After colds and ear infections, a rash is one of the more common reasons for a visit to the pediatrician. Rashes can range from small red bumps and itchy, crusted plaques to welts from head to toe.

FACT

Advice to avoid daily baths is now considered "old school." Most experts now recommend that a daily bath is good for the skin, as long as you use lukewarm water and a mild soap, and then gently dry the skin and apply a moisturizer within a few minutes after the bath.

Eczema

Eczema is one of the more frustrating rashes, both because it is so itchy and because it usually keeps coming back. It often affects children with other allergic-type diseases such as allergies and asthma. Usually beginning at about age six to eight weeks, infants with eczema develop itchy, red patches on their cheeks, elbows, knees, and eventually the rest of the body if it gets very bad.

Treatments for eczema usually include a topical steroid cream, either over-the-counter for mild cases or prescription strength for persistent cases, when the rash flares up and regular use of moisturizers as a preventive measure. Flares can sometimes also be prevented if you can find and avoid common triggers, such as harsh soaps, wool clothing, overheating, and frequent baths without using a moisturizer.

Hives

Hives are large, red, raised areas that come and go quickly and are very itchy. Unlike most other rashes that affect children, each hive usually only lasts a few hours before it disappears and another pops up somewhere else. Hives are a common allergic reaction in children, often triggered by foods, such as peanut butter, egg whites, milk, and soy. They also can be triggered by medicines or even by infections. If possible, try to find and then avoid known triggers. You usually can treat hives with an oral antihistamine, like Children's Benadryl.

Ringworm

Ringworm is a fungal infection that can occur on a child's skin or scalp. On the body, the rash looks like a ringlike red area with scales, and it's usually easily treated with a topical over-the-counter antifungal medication. Scalp fungal infections can cause areas of baldness and scaling and are much more difficult to treat, requiring a prescription for an oral antifungal medication.

Diaper Rashes

A diaper rash is one of the more common rashes that your baby might have during his first year. It is often caused by irritation and can be prevented with frequent diaper changes and use of a barrier-type diaper rash medication, such as A+D, Balmex, or Desitin. Various diaper rash creams and ointments also can be used to treat most diaper rashes. If the rash doesn't go away, especially if it is bright red and surrounded by small red bumps, then it may be caused by a yeast infection. You should use an over-the-counter or prescription strength antifungal cream in addition to a diaper rash medication to clear up this type of secondary infection.

Sore Throats

Although sore throats in older children and adults are commonly a sign of strep throat, most sore throats in infants are caused by viruses, and therefore don't require treatment with antibiotics.

Hand, Foot, and Mouth Disease

This is a common viral infection that is often overlooked because most parents aren't able to get a good look in their infant's mouth when he is sick. A child with hand, foot, and mouth disease (HFMD) usually has a fever, irritability, and ulcers in the back of the mouth. This infection is easier to recognize if the child also has the typical blisters on the palms of the hands and soles of the feet.

Unfortunately, there is no treatment for this common illness. The symptoms can last for seven to ten days, during which time your child will be contagious to others. Symptomatic treatments with pain and fever reducers and making sure your child drinks enough so that he doesn't get dehydrated can be helpful until he recovers. Appropriate pain and fever reducers might include ibuprofen if your infant is over six months old, or acetaminophen. Remember to not give your child aspirin because of the risk of Reye syndrome.

Gingivostomatitis

This is another viral infection (this one is caused by the herpes virus) that can cause blisters in a child's mouth. Unlike HFMD, this infection typically causes ulcers on the tongue, gums, and lips and not on the hands and feet.

In addition to a fever, the painful ulcers can make your child irritable and cause decreased appetite. Antibiotics don't help this infection, and the main treatments are aimed at helping to control your child's symptoms.

Tonsillitis and Strep Throat

Parents often confuse the term "tonsillitis" with strep throat. It can help to remember that tonsillitis is a generic term for an infection or inflammation of the tonsils, but it doesn't refer to whether the problem is caused by a virus or bacteria. So even if your child has enlarged tonsils that are red and covered with pus, it doesn't necessarily mean that he has strep. Tonsillitis also can be caused by a viral infection, which, unlike strep throat, doesn't require treatment with antibiotics. Younger children are much less likely to get strep than are older children, but you might have your child tested if he has direct contact with someone who does have strep.

Infections and Other Problems

Other common childhood problems that you may get some experience with include ear infections, chickenpox, and other infections.

Ear Infections

Parents often suspect that their child has an ear infection when he starts pulling on his ears, but unless there are other symptoms, like a fever or irritability, the ears are usually normal.

ALERT!

Some of the risk factors that increase your child's chances of getting frequent ear infections are having a parent who smokes, not breast-feeding, drinking a bottle while lying down, using a pacifier, having uncontrolled allergies or gastroesophageal reflux, and attending a large day care.

More typically, an ear infection will develop a few days or weeks after having a cold. A child will experience ear pain, irritability, fever, and a decreased appetite when he gets an ear infection. Although symptoms sometimes go away without treatment, doctors still commonly prescribe antibiotics, especially for children under the age of twelve to twenty-four months.

An ear infection shouldn't be confused with simply having fluid in the middle ear, which commonly occurs after an ear infection. This fluid doesn't usually require treatment and will often go away in two to three months. If it isn't going away, a child may need treatment with ear tubes, especially if it is causing a hearing loss. Frequent or persistent infections can also be a sign that your child needs ear tubes.

Chickenpox

Chickenpox is much less common since children began getting routine immunizations that protect against it. However, because children don't get this immunization until their first birthday, your child can be at risk if he is exposed to someone with chickenpox during his first year.

Symptoms usually begin ten to twenty-one days after exposure to a person who has chickenpox, and include fever and a rash. The rash begins as small, itchy, red bumps that quickly become blisters. These blisters will crust over before fully healing in about seven to ten days. They can be treated with an anti-itch medication, like calamine lotion, or an Aveeno oatmeal bath.

Thrush

In addition to causing diaper rashes, yeast can also cause an infection in your child's mouth. Once infected, an infant develops white patches inside the mouth, typically on the tongue, the inside of the cheeks, and on the lips, gums, and the roof of the mouth. This common infection is typically treated with the oral anti-fungal medication Nystatin, although persistent infections are often treated with fluconazole, a stronger medication. Be sure to clean your baby's pacifiers and the nipples for bottles, which can sometimes be the source of the yeast that causes thrush. Breastfeeding mothers should also be sure that they don't have a yeast infection of their nipples, which would also require treatment.

Roseola

A common infection of younger children, roseola begins with a high fever and mild upper respiratory infection symptoms, like a runny nose. After a few days, the fever breaks, and the child develops a pink or red rash all over his body.

It is the characteristic pattern of the rash developing once the fever breaks that makes this infection easy to recognize. Unfortunately, that means that you usually can't make the diagnosis until the end of the illness, and so your child might have to go through testing to look for other more serious causes of fever, like blood and urine infections, while he has the high fever.

Fifth Disease

Although not very common in younger children, Fifth disease has such a characteristic presentation that it is important to be familiar with it.

Like most other viral infections that cause rashes, children with Fifth disease typically have mild cold symptoms, but in this case these are followed by their cheeks getting red. This redness gives rise to the other name for this illness, "slapped-cheeks" disease. After a few days, the redness is replaced by a pink, lacelike rash on the child's arms and legs. And although the rash may come and go for several weeks, it requires no treatment and will go away without problems.

Adults who are exposed to someone with Fifth disease and who aren't immune can get a more serious infection that is accompanied by arthritis. Pregnant women are also at big risk if they get Fifth disease. If a pregnant woman is exposed to a child who is infected with this disease, she should call her obstetrician.

FACT

In addition to the better-known viral infections that cause rashes, such as chickenpox, roseola, and Fifth disease, it is important to understand that most other viral infections can also cause rashes. These types of rashes typically occur as small red bumps that blanch, or disappear briefly, when you press on them. They usually fade as the infection goes away.

Fever

Fever is a common symptom of most childhood infections. It is more worrisome when a child has a high fever and no other symptoms, because instead of having a simple cold or ear infection, she might have something more serious, like meningitis or a urinary tract infection.

Fever that lasts longer than the typical three to five days also can be a sign of a problem, including noninfectious causes of fever, like juvenile arthritis and Kawasaki's disease. Be sure to keep in close contact with your doctor if your child has an unexplained or persistent fever.

Frequent Illnesses

Although parents worry when their kids get sick a lot, it is important to remember that the average child gets six to eight upper respiratory tract infections, such as colds and sore throats, and two to three episodes of diarrhea each year, especially if he is in day care.

Frequent infections can be a sign of a serious immune system problem though, especially if your child has had poor growth and several serious, life-threatening infections that required hospitalization, such as:

- Meningitis
- Pneumonia
- Blood infections
- Bone infections
- Chronic diarrhea

Chronic skin and sinus infections, although not usually life-threatening, also can be a sign of an immune system problem. Your pediatrician or a pediatric immunologist can test your child for the more common immune system disorders, including cystic fibrosis, severe combined immunodeficiency (SCID), common variable immunodeficiency (CVID), and X-linked agammaglobulinemia.

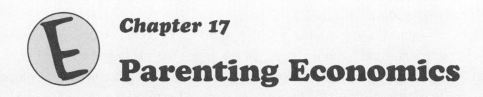

Chapter 17

Parenting Economics

The economics of raising a new baby is going to mean different things for each family. A father with a lot of credit card debt who is living paycheck to paycheck is going to have different needs and priorities than a father who is more well-off and is already planning his baby's college fund. Although it can be a stressful topic, thinking about your family's finances is important, no matter what your situation.

First-Year Expenses

According to the USDA Expenditures on Children by Families, 2002 Annual Report, the average cost of raising an only child in a two-parent family is about $215,000. That considers most expenses that you will have for your child from birth to age eighteen, including housing, food, clothing, health care, and transportation.

In addition to housing, which at about $4,000 is likely to be the largest single annual expense, some of the other big expenses will be for formula, baby food, diapers, clothing, and child care. A family with before-tax income of $39,700 to $66,900 can expect to spend a total of about $11,500 during this first year. Although each family has its own standard of living, generally families with smaller incomes will have lower expenses the first year, at about $8,200, and higher-income families will have higher expenses.

Infant Formula

Formula can be a big expense during your baby's first year. If you figure that the average baby drinks about 28 ounces of formula each day, then you will be paying about $1,400 for a year's supply of a popular infant formula, such as powdered Enfamil LIPIL with Iron. You will pay even more if you go with a concentrated liquid or ready-to-feed formula, or if your baby needs an elemental formula, such as Nutramigen.

On the other hand, you might be able to save some money by going with a store-brand formula. And of course, you can eliminate this expense altogether by having your baby breastfeed exclusively until at least his first birthday. (See Chapters 5 and 11 for more information to help you make the decision between breastfeeding or formula.)

When comparing the price of formula, consider how many ounces of formula each package makes. Although different brands all seem to be the same size, some make fewer ounces and so you are not saving as much money as you are made to think.

Diapers

In your baby's first few months, he may need up to ten or twelve diaper changes a day. You may not be too happy about changing those diapers when you realize that each name-brand disposable diaper is costing you about twenty-five cents. And they just get more expensive as your infant gets older, although you will likely be changing your baby less often. By the end of the first year, you can expect to have spent about $750 to $1,000 on diapers and diaper pail refills.

You can save money by using cloth diapers, but only if you launder them yourself. Using cloth diapers and a diaper service that launders them for you probably will cost you just as much as disposable diapers. And remember, laundering cloth diapers yourself will increase your monthly water and detergent use significantly.

One Income or Two?

The decision about whether or not both parents should work after they begin having kids is a lot more complicated than most people realize. There isn't just the extra income to consider. You also have to consider many other pros and cons, including commuting expenses; benefits received in addition to income, such as insurance or a 401(k) plan; the cost of day care; and the amount of taxes you pay on that income.

For people who have free, familiar day care, such as a grandparent or other family member who can watch the baby during the day, or for parents who are both very committed to their careers, choosing to continue in a two-income lifestyle may be a very easy decision to make.

Likewise, if a family plans to have one parent stay home, and one parent makes much more money than the other and has better benefits or a stronger future at the job, they also will have an easy decision to make. But it becomes harder to make this decision when you're not sure how to downsize your spending to fit one income, or when one parent makes much less money but is the only source of health insurance or a company retirement plan. Consider using a day-care cost calculator on the Internet or talking to a financial advisor if you are having a hard time deciding whether it makes more economic sense for both parents to work or for one to stay home.

ALERT!

When considering the expenses of putting a child in day care versus keeping her home, you should consider that your child is much more likely to get sick when in day care. Be sure to factor in the cost of doctor visits, medications, and your own time off work because of the increased number of sick days.

Child-Care Options

Along with deciding whether you will finance your family's expenses on one income or two, you need to decide who will care for your baby during the day. If one of you is going to stay home, who is it going to be? Even if you both want to continue working, there are still options that allow you or your partner to care for your child, or you can choose from some other types of child-care providers.

Who Will Stay Home?

When one parent stays home, it is often the mom. It does seem that more and more mothers work outside the home, either because of economic necessity or because they enjoy working and want a career, but there are still many stay-at-home mothers. Recent statistics show that about 30 percent of children in two-parent families have a mother who stays home to care for them.

Although often viewed as a "dream job," staying at home can be hard for many new mothers. In addition to the sometimes unappreciated work of caring for their kids and their home, the lack of contact and communication with other adults can be too much for some mothers. A helpful dad and a good support system can make it easier for a stay-at-home mom who is struggling.

The traditional roles of a career dad and stay-at-home mom also are sometimes reversed. More and more dads are staying home and caring for their kids while mom goes to work. Sometimes this continues until the children are grown, while other times mom and dad take turns staying home for a few years at a time.

There are many reasons why dads will stay home. Sometimes it is out of necessity, when dad loses a job and can't find work. Or maybe mom has a much higher paying job and it makes more sense for her to be the "breadwinner." But often, the reason is simply that dad wants to stay home, care for his kids, and have more time to spend with them. As more and more dads stay home with their kids, this should be viewed as a good option for families who don't want to put their kids in day care or hire a nanny.

Paternity Leave

Depending on how large a company you work for, you may be entitled to up to twelve weeks of leave when you have or adopt a new baby. This paternity leave is mandated by the Family and Medical Leave Act (FMLA), but it has many restrictions and mainly applies to people who work in government jobs or for larger employers. If you work for a company that has fewer than fifty employees, you may not be entitled to paternity leave at all.

FACT

In addition to the federal Family and Medical Leave Act, dads living in California have another option to help them stay home when their baby is born. The California Paid Family Leave program allows workers to take up to six weeks of partial paid leave to care for a new baby.

Unfortunately, even when you do qualify for paternity leave, that time off will likely be unpaid. Can you afford to take three months off of work? If not, consider taking just one or two weeks of leave or use some paid vacation time instead. If you plan for it in advance, you may be able to take more time off when your baby is born. This might mean saving up sick days and vacation time, or working extra before the baby is born and saving up some money to get you through your paternity leave.

Working at Home

Staying home and caring for a baby is a full-time job in itself for most parents. That makes it hard to understand how anyone could stay home, care for the baby, plus have another job on the side. Especially in the first few months and years, when your baby is going to demand a lot of your time, working at home can be difficult. However, some people have been known to make this work for them. For example, working at home may be an option if you have a very flexible, part-time work-at-home job and you have extra help around the house. Be sure to carefully consider the demands of this option before deciding whether you or your partner can make this kind of commitment to an employer. Be realistic with yourself about what the job requires, and whether it will be possible to meet those demands as well as the needs of your infant.

Opposite Shifts

Another way to avoid day care or a nanny, even when both parents are working, is for parents to have opposite work shifts. With this type of arrangement, one parent may work at night, while the other works during the day. Or one parent may just work a few shifts on the weekend, when the other parent has time off.

Having different work schedules does allow one parent to always be home with the child, but it can put a big strain on the rest of family life. Because one parent will likely be coming home as the other is leaving for work, it doesn't give the couple much quality time together.

That big drawback makes this type of arrangement most useful for families in which the parents already were working in opposite shifts when they had their baby. Maybe one parent has a traditional daytime office job, while the other works the night shift as a nurse, police officer, or in tech support. These new parents are probably already used to their arrangement. It may not be as good an idea for parents who look to move to opposite shifts after they have their baby.

Day Care or a Nanny?

If you decide that both parents are going to go to work each day, next you will have to decide who is going to take care of your baby. This decision will be easy if you have a trusted family member who is willing to baby-sit each day. If this isn't an option for you, the usual choices are enrolling your baby in a group or home day care or hiring a nanny to watch your baby in your house.

Each option has it own pros and cons, so be prepared to do some research. For example, a nanny is the most expensive option and it means trusting one person to be alone with your child, but your child will be around fewer kids and will be less likely to get sick often. A group day care will expose your child to a lot of other kids (and their germs). While he might get sick a little more often in a group day care, these facilities are also often thought of as being the most well supervised, as there are many other people around and your child isn't usually alone with just one caregiver. Check out the options in your area carefully, and don't hesitate to ask plenty of questions before signing up anyone's services.

Health Insurance

The need to have health insurance is one of the easier financial topics for most parents to understand. Even regular visits to your pediatrician can be expensive, but if your child develops medical problems or ends up being hospitalized, the expenses can quickly add up and cripple a family financially.

If you don't have health insurance or if you don't have coverage for immunizations, look for a doctor who participates in the federal Vaccines for Children (VFC) Program. In this program, eligible children can get free or low-cost vaccines (although you may have to still pay for an office visit or vaccine administration fee depending on where you go).

Having health insurance is an important way to protect your child, both financially and healthwise. Without health insurance, your children:

- May not get all of their vaccines on time
- May have to go to the emergency room instead of visiting their regular pediatrician
- May miss out on treatments to prevent chronic illnesses (such as allergies and asthma) from getting worse
- May not get medications they need because you can't afford them

Health Insurance Choices

In general, the more benefits you get, the more expensive your insurance package will be. Less expensive health insurance isn't going to be very helpful, though, if it doesn't meet your needs, so put some thought into which plan you choose.

Your options for insurance plans may be limited, especially if you're getting coverage through an employer. But there are still some things to keep in mind. In general, indemnity plans, which allow you to see whichever doctor you want and send the bill to your insurance company, will provide many more choices. However, they are likely to be much more expensive than managed care plans, such as Preferred Provider Organizations (PPOs) and Health Maintenance Organizations (HMOs). Here are some other things to consider when choosing insurance that will cover your new child:

- If possible, choose a PPO or POS (Point of Service) plan. These plans usually offer more choices and more independence, such as seeing specialists without a referral. If you choose an HMO, make sure that there are pediatric specialists on the plan.
- Make sure that vaccines are a covered expense, especially during your baby's first year, because he will be getting shots at most visits.
- Consider getting prescription drug coverage. Most antibiotics and other medications can easily cost $40 to $100 each and may be more than the doctor's visit costs.
- If there is a children's hospital in your area, make sure that it is on the health insurance plan that you choose.
- Try to get insurance through a group health plan if your baby or any other family members have a chronic illness that might count as a pre-existing condition. With an individual plan, that condition likely won't be covered for at least a year.

You should also consider what your copays and deductibles are. Choosing a health insurance plan that costs $100 less per month doesn't make sense if you are going to be paying $1,500 or $2,000 extra each year in copays and deductibles.

In the end, you will have to balance the cost of the insurance plan with your own needs. Would you rather have a less expensive plan and have to deal with fewer choices and some inconveniences? Or is it more important that you have better coverage, even if you have to pay more?

FACT

In the United States, almost 8 million children don't have any health insurance coverage. Many of them qualify for free or low-cost insurance coverage, though, either through Medicaid or a state children's health insurance program.

Medicaid

For families who can't afford insurance, their state's Medicaid program may be a way for them to get health coverage for their children. Whether or not you qualify will depend on your eligibility group, how much money you make, and which state you live in. You can look for more specific eligibility criteria or apply at your local Medicaid office, which you can find in the government listings (the "blue pages") of your phone book under "medical assistance."

State Health Insurance Programs

If you can't afford private health insurance and you don't qualify for Medicaid, you may have another option. Each state now offers free or low-cost health insurance for children who qualify. In most states, your child must be under the age of eighteen and your family of four must earn less than about $34,100 a year in order to qualify.

These children's health insurance programs (CHIPs) are a good way for low-income working families to get their children covered by insurance. In addition to doctor visits, these plans pay for vaccines, prescription medications, and hospital stays. To find out whether you qualify or to learn more, visit *www.insurekidsnow.gov* or call 1-877 KIDS NOW (1-877-543-7669) to contact your state's specfic program.

More Insurance

How much insurance do you need? Another way of asking that is how much insurance do you have to pay for? Health insurance. Auto insurance. Homeowners insurance. It seems like a never-ending list of protection that you need to pay for and hope that you will never need to use.

Once you have a family, there are a few other kinds of insurance that are equally as important as health insurance. If you are the primary provider and something happens to you, will your family be able to make it financially? Making sure that your family has some protection in case you die or become disabled is something you should be sure to take care of now. If the worst happens, having insurance will make difficult times a little easier for your family.

Life Insurance

Once you become a father, life insurance is essential. If you are an important source of financial support for your family—whether or not you are married, and whether or not your baby's mother also works—you need to make sure that support continues, even if you aren't around anymore.

How much life insurance do you need? That depends on what other source of income your family will have if you die, and what other assets you have. If your life insurance policy is going to be the primary source of money for your family over a long period of time, then you should get as much life insurance as you can afford. And the best time to buy it is when you are just starting to think about having a baby.

Don't overlook the need for life insurance for a stay-at-home parent. Although not technically a "breadwinner," if this parent dies, will you be able to afford day care or a nanny for your baby? If not, make sure that both you and your partner have life insurance.

Fortunately, life insurance doesn't have to be that expensive to buy. Especially if you are young, healthy, and don't smoke, you should be able to obtain term life insurance at a very reasonable rate. For example, if you are in your twenties or thirties, you can get $500,000 of coverage in a 20-year policy for only about $300 a year. That means that if you die within 20 years, then your beneficiary will get $500,000 tax-free to care for your family. You can increase your coverage to $1 million and still just pay about $500 a year.

What happens after 20 years? Ideally, by that time you will have amassed other assets that can provide for your family, or your children will be grown and able to support themselves. Or, for a few hundred dollars more each year, you may be able start off with a 30-year policy instead.

Disability Insurance

Less well known than life insurance, disability insurance can help provide you and your family with financial support if you are injured and are no longer able to work. Because a younger father is much more likely to become disabled than to die, long-term disability insurance can be important to have. It will help to supplement any Social Security benefits that you will get, help pay your bills, and help your family to maintain their current lifestyle if you can't work anymore.

Because your family will be more likely to need and benefit from disability insurance, many experts consider it even more important to have than life insurance. Of course, having both types of insurance is best. Talk to a financial advisor if you can only afford one and aren't sure which to choose.

Starting a College Fund

With all of the other things you have to worry about, thinking about how you will pay for your child's college education may be at the bottom of the list. However, if you consider that using current estimates, the cost of college will likely be more than $30,000 a year for a public college and more than $70,000 a year for a private college by the time that your new baby is ready to start school, you may already be behind if you haven't started saving yet.

Of course there are alternatives if you are unable to pay for your child's college expenses, such as loans, grants, scholarships, and other types of financial aid. Or your child may be able to work part-time as he goes to school, or attend a community college. But if you want to be able to financially support your child as he attends the college of his choice, the earlier you start saving, the easier it will be.

When should I start saving money for my child's college education?
The simple answer is as early as possible. That may mean even starting before your baby is born. The more money you save and the sooner you start saving it, the more likely that you will have enough to fund your child's college education.

Prepaid Tuition Programs

Prepaid tuition is a popular option for many parents. This type of plan, often called a 529, is an education savings plan with special tax benefits. It allows you to fund one or more years of tuition now, to be used when your child is ready to start college. Unlike many other types of plans, these state prepaid tuition programs are guaranteed to pay for college in the future, even as tuition prices go up. Besides the many tax advantages, another benefit is that other family members, such as helpful grandparents, can contribute to the plan.

There are two downsides of prepaid tuition programs: they only pay for tuition (you will still have to save for room and board), and not all states offer them. Also, for states that do offer them, the cost is likely to continue to increase each year, so paying for the plan as early as possible is a good idea. Keep in mind that prepaying your child's tuition at one school doesn't necessarily mean that he has to go to school there. Many plans allow you to transfer your money to another school.

College Savings Programs

College savings programs are another type of state 529 plan, into which you can contribute money to pay for college later. Unlike the prepaid tuition programs, there is no guarantee that the invested money will be enough to pay for all of your child's expenses. On the other hand, you can use the money for tuition, room and board, and any other college-related expenses. They also have low minimum contribution limits, which can make it easier for you to start saving for your child's college education.

More Alternatives

Alternatives to Section 529 college savings plans and prepaid tuition plans can include starting a Coverdell Education Savings Account (formerly known as an Education IRA) or a Uniform Transfers to Minors Act (UTMA) account, or purchasing U.S. Savings Bonds to pay for your children's college expenses. Other traditional investments, including stocks, mutual funds, and real estate, are more options. They don't usually offer the tax advantages of the other programs, though. In general, a 529 plan is going to be the easiest to set up and maintain. Talk to a financial advisor if you aren't sure which option is best for you.

Planning Your Retirement

Just as it is never too early to begin saving for your child's college education, it is never too early to begin planning for your retirement. Most experts would say that saving for your retirement is even more important than saving for college. After all, there will be other options if you don't have enough money for your child's college expenses, but you will have fewer options when you are ready to retire.

If you aren't funding your retirement plan at work, consider cutting back on other expenses so that you can. Since you can put this money away tax-free, you are throwing away money if you don't, especially if your employer provides a matching contribution.

The easiest way to set aside money for retirement is to contribute to a retirement plan at work. That is especially a good idea if your employer offers any kind of matching funds. The first step in planning for retirement is often making sure that you are contributing the maximum amount that you can to your job's retirement plan.

If you don't have a retirement plan at work, you may have to save on your own. An Individual Retirement Account or Roth IRA is a good way to do that. In addition, you can plan on your own savings and investments to help finance your retirement. If you aren't sure how to get started or are afraid to start, a financial planner can help you.

More Future Expenses

Your own retirement and your child's college education are the major investments you should begin funding as soon as possible. But they're not the only things to prepare for. Unless you're willing to live paycheck to paycheck, unprepared for any financial emergencies, there are other things that you should start saving money for. Are you going to need a new home as your family gets bigger, or a new car? Do you want to have some money saved in case your kids need braces?

Financial Emergencies

Ironically, emergencies are one of the most important things to plan for. Besides your long-term disability insurance, do you have enough of a reserve to get by on if one or both parents can't work for a while and you miss a few paychecks? Will you be able to pay your rent or mortgage or even be able to buy groceries? If a stay-at-home parent gets sick and can't care for the kids, do you have enough money to pay for day care until the parent is better?

Saving a good three to six months' worth of your regular monthly expenses in a savings or money market account can help you be financially prepared for an emergency. Until you have that reserve or buffer built up, you should put off other unnecessary expenses, such as going on vacation or buying a new TV. Of course, you have to actually know what your monthly expenses are first, so figure out your total monthly expenditures and a regular budget and then start saving.

More Kids

Having more kids does introduce a lot of new expenses, including diapers, food, and perhaps increased child-care expenses. One of the highest expenses may be simply the medical cost of having another child. And of course, you will have to think about planning for more than one child to go to college. Fortunately, many other expenses are fixed and so your total monthly expenses might not go up as much as you think as you have more kids. For example, unless another child causes you to outgrow your home or car, your housing and transportation expenses won't increase. And you should be able to use a lot of hand-me-down clothing and baby products from your first child, so you probably won't need to buy another crib, changing table, highchair, or other baby accessories.

Financial Goals

Once you have your emergency fund saved up and you have a plan to fund retirement and college expenses, you can begin to think about other short-term and long-term financial goals.

Your biggest goal should be to avoid any "bad" debt, such as large credit card bills with high interest rates. Paying off this type of debt, and avoiding building up more of it, is even more important than saving for college or building up an emergency fund right now.

Your goals might include buying your first house, remodeling the house you live in now, or moving into a bigger one. Other financial goals might include taking a family vacation, buying a boat, starting a business, buying a vacation home, or buying a new car. By planning in advance for some of these expenses you can avoid building up a lot of "bad" debt and having large credit card bills that you can't pay.

Chapter 18

The High-Tech New Dad

If you are into high-tech gadgets, having a baby offers a lot of excuses to get some new toys to play with. From a digital camera and video camcorder to record all of your baby's "firsts" to computer equipment to create movies, there are all sorts of things you may want to buy. These gadgets can be pricey, though, so don't rush out and buy anything until you do a little research. (And make sure that you've covered all of the economics essentials in Chapter 17 before you spend too much money on these toys.)

Digital Cameras

You could use a traditional camera to take pictures of your baby, but these days, a digital camera is an almost essential item for a new dad. Babies don't pose very well, so with a traditional camera you are going to be stuck with a lot of bad pictures and might even miss out on getting a good picture of certain events. Did you really catch one of her first smiles, or did she turn away too quickly? With a film camera, you won't know until you get the pictures developed, but you will be able to preview your digital pictures almost instantly.

Taking Pictures

One of the biggest advantages of having a digital camera is that you can take an almost unlimited number of pictures with them. After the initial cost of the camera, you don't have to worry about spending money buying film or having it developed. You simply take your pictures, transfer them to your computer, and then start all over again.

QUESTION?

How can I share my digital photos with other people?
In addition to making prints, you can share your digital photos with friends and family members by sending them by e-mail, posting them on a Web site, creating an online photo album, or making a CD or DVD slideshow or sending them to a digital frame.

Because you don't have to pay for each picture you take and you don't even have to keep them if they don't turn out well, it makes it easier to get at least a few good pictures of your baby. Are you hoping to get a picture of her first steps that shows the big smile on her face? Then take five or ten pictures and use your camera's preview function to see if you captured the moment. If you didn't, keep trying. Once you get the picture you want, transfer it to your computer and save it or send it to your friends and family.

Viewing Your Pictures

One of the downsides of having a digital camera is that you don't always have a physical picture that you can hold and carry around with you. While you could always print your pictures from your computer using a color printer, that can use up a lot of ink and get expensive. New services make it easy and inexpensive to make real prints of your digital pictures.

One of the easiest ways to inexpensively create high-quality prints of your digital pictures is to use an online photo service to do everything for you. These companies, such as Ofoto and Shutterfly, allow you to upload or transfer your photos to them over the Internet and then view, edit, and order prints. For only twenty-five to twenty-nine cents each (plus shipping), you can get high-quality pictures sent right to your home. You also can create your own greeting cards, calendars, and online photo albums with your pictures.

If you don't want to make real prints of your digital pictures, you can also just view them online. Using your computer, you can set up digital photo albums or slide shows to look at and organize all of your pictures. There is even software that will let you create a photo slideshow and burn it on a CD or DVD so that you can simply watch it on TV, just as you would a movie. Or you can use a digital photo frame, which is an electronic frame that can store and display your digital photos, to carry your pictures around.

Choosing a Camera

Deciding which digital camera to buy can be a little overwhelming. Although they all basically function the same way, you have a lot of choices among different brands and features. Among the features to look at are the camera's storage capacity, whether or not it has an optical zoom, the camera's size, its compatibility with your home computer, and the number of megapixels it has. Of course you also have to consider how much money you want to spend.

Most of these choices will be based on your personal preferences. If you plan on taking a lot of pictures, especially when following your infant around, you should try to choose a small or compact size camera. These can easily fit in your pocket and so can be readily available when you need to capture a special moment. Other features to look for include an optical zoom, so that you can get close up for some pictures, and the ability to record short movie clips. A preview LCD screen is an essential feature, so that you can view the pictures you have just taken. That way you will know if you got a good picture or if you need to delete it and try again.

But what about the issue of megapixels? Do you want two, three, or four? Or do you want a newer, more high-end digital camera with eight or ten megapixels? For the average user, a two- or three-megapixel camera is going to be more than enough. You can take pictures with more detail using a camera that has more megapixels, but unless you plan to routinely print 8" x 10" or larger prints, that probably isn't necessary. Even the file sizes of pictures from a two- or three-megapixel camera are rather large and have to be reduced to send through e-mail or post on a Web site.

To create a 4" x 6" printed photo that is similar in quality to a 35mm film camera, you must have a digital camera with at least two megapixels. To print good quality 8" x 10" inch prints you will need a camera with three or four megapixels.

Keeping all of these features in mind, you should be able to get a good digital camera for $100 to $300. It may also be a good idea to spend a little extra and get a larger memory card so that you can store more pictures.

Camera Phones

Although it is easy to take pictures with a digital camera, transferring those pictures to your computer and then posting them on a Web site or e-mailing them can take time. A much easier way to take and send simple pictures is to use a mobile phone with a built-in camera. If you're considering a camera phone, just imagine using it to take pictures of your baby and then quickly sending them to his mother, or a friend or family member. Could there be a more hassle-free way to show off your pride and joy?

Once you take a picture, you can either send it to other people with compatible mobile phones or send it as e-mail. You also can easily post these pictures on a Web page for even easier viewing. Using a moblog (mobile weblog), you can instantly post the video clips and pictures you take from your camera phone. You can set up your moblog through a mobile phone carrier or an online service, such as ✐*www.textamerica.com.*

Is your baby walking for the first time? Take a picture and send it to your moblog and everyone else can join in the excitement as well. If you are a dad who travels a lot, video clips from a camera phone can be a good way to say goodnight and keep in touch with your baby.

FACT

The line between digital cameras and camcorders is becoming more and more blurred, as digital cameras are able to record short video clips and camcorders can take digital photos.

Video Camcorders

A camcorder is another great way to create a record of your baby as she grows up. Most people start out recording their baby's delivery, and then just keep recording each special moment after that. Your baby's first smiles, the first time she starts rolling over, and her first steps are just a few of the events that you will want to record and watch later.

So which camcorder is best for you? As with a digital camera, you should go with a camcorder that has all of the features you need, but is still afford-able. You will first have to decide if you want a digital or analog camcord-er. What's the difference? An analog camcorder simply records on regular videotape, like those in the 8mm, Hi8, and VHS format. Newer digital cam-corders offer better quality and make it easy to transfer your video to your computer for editing.

Other features to look for include image stabilization, small size, optical zoom, and an LCD display to view your movies. If you want the latest tech-nology, go with either a camcorder that records straight to DVD or a tapeless camcorder that records on a memory card, and is therefore extremely small and slim. Although a tapeless camcorder may be the most compact option, keep in mind that the quality is not as good as other types of camcorders, and unless you upgrade the memory card, you will only be able to record a few minutes of video at a time.

ALERT!

Although it can be nice to have recorded movies of important events, be sure that you don't miss out on actually being a part of those special times because you are too busy behind the camera. Find a good balance between recording things yourself and having other people film events while you participate.

Making Movies

Making movies is easy. Technically, if you have a camcorder, you can make a movie. But what you really end up with is just a collection of videos, both good and bad, that you have recorded one right after the other.

New technology and software let you take this a step further. Instead of just watching the uncut, unedited versions of movies you've recorded, you can now edit your videos. You can rearrange frames and add music, titles, and credits. You also can delete scenes or add other images, such as old family photos, to create a professional-looking movie.

To start making movies, all you need is a digital camcorder, a computer to connect it to, and video editing software. In addition to the very popular iMovie on Apple computers, you can use Microsoft Windows Movie Maker to create movies if you are using Windows XP. You will also need a DVD burner if you want to share and watch your movies on a regular TV.

Baby's First Web Site

Taking pictures and making movies are great ways to record how your baby has been growing and developing his first year. That way you can always look back and have a clear reminder of this rapidly changing time. As you collect all of these photos and videos, you will soon be wondering how you will share them with all of your friends and family members.

Will you send out printed pictures or just e-mail your photos to everyone?

Those are simple options, but they don't offer an easy way to keep those pictures organized. An e-mailed photo also doesn't provide a good way to insert comments about each picture or event.

FACT

A weblog, also called a blog, is a type of Web page that you regularly update, like an online diary or journal. Blogs have become a popular way for families to share what is going on in their lives and it is a great way to post information about your baby. A blog is a good alternative to a more traditional Web site if you plan on making very frequent changes and additions.

A much better option is to create a Web site for your baby. This can be as simple as a single page with a few pictures and a few lines of text that describe the picture, or a larger site with pages for each stage of your baby's development. As you get more advanced, you can add movies, stories, and even a guest book for family members to add their own comments.

But isn't it hard to create a Web site? It can be if you are trying to learn everything on your own and you aren't very Internet savvy. If you don't know what HTML (hypertext markup language) and FTP (file transfer protocol) are, then you might have some learning to do if you want to start a Web site from scratch. Fortunately, there are many easy and free ways to create a Web site, even if you have no experience and don't know where to start. You may be able to set up such a site through your Internet service provider, such as EarthLink or America Online. Or you can use a free online service—for example, ✎*www.babiesonline.com*—to get a site up in just a few minutes.

If you want more control over the look and feel of your baby's site, you might consider learning HTML and creating your own Web site from scratch. For a little extra help, pick up some software that will automate many of the steps for you. Adobe GoLive, Macromedia Dreamweaver, and Microsoft FrontPage all are good choices. You also could read a book or take a class that will teach you how to create your own Web site. Any of these methods will help you get set up in no time at all.

Baby Monitors

Your basic baby monitor might not seem very high-tech. But there are plenty of bells and whistles available beyond a basic baby monitor to make it more of a fun gadget to play with.

Many wireless devices in your home can interfere with each other. If you already have a cordless phone and wireless computer network, you may notice a lot of interference, static, and poor quality when you use a baby monitor. To get the best signal, consider choosing a monitor that has more than one channel and that operates on a different frequency from the other devices in your home.

Audio Monitors

A basic baby monitor simply consists of a transmitter with a microphone that you place in your baby's room and a receiver that you carry with you or just put in the room you're in. Obviously, that's not very high-tech, especially if you get a cheaper model that has a lot of static and a poor range.

Newer models have advanced features such as increased range, dual monitors, and even the ability to put on a projection light show to help soothe your baby. Other advanced features include rechargeable power supplies, lights to indicate the intensity of your baby's cries, and two-way connections, so you can talk to your baby.

Video Monitors

In addition to the basic audio monitors, you now can get a combined audio and video monitor so that you can see what your baby is doing if he is crying in his room during naps or at night. It is also a good way to keep an eye on your older baby if he is playing in another room. An infrared lens allows you to see your baby in the dark as long as the camera is mounted about six feet or less from his crib.

Available in both 900 MHz and 2.4GHz models, video monitors can usually transmit from 100 to 300 feet. Other available features include the ability to receive the signal on your regular TV set, using a monitor that comes with the camera, or receiving the video signal on a handheld color monitor. If you already have a wireless computer network at home and a Palm Pilot or other PDA, you can even set up the monitor so that you can watch your baby on your PDA. Many systems even allow you to have more than one video camera, so that you can keep track of more than one child.

ALERT!

Because a basic baby monitor, whether it is using audio or video signals, is just a transmitter, your neighbors and other people may be able to see and hear your baby too. Keep this lack of privacy in mind and consider other security controls, especially if you are going to watch your baby on the Internet.

Internet Video Monitors

If you want to get really high-tech, you can give yourself the ability to watch your baby when you aren't at home. It may sound like that's impossible, or that it would cost a lot of money to set up, but there are systems that allow you to inexpensively and easily watch your baby on your computer or PDA when you are away from home. If you have a PDA with wireless Internet access, you will be able to see your baby from almost anywhere.

These systems can be a good way for a dad who works outside the home to check in on his baby throughout the day. They can also be a good way for grandparents or other family members to regularly see the baby.

Infant Toys

Your baby's toys might be some of the most high-tech items that you have in the house. These fancy toys can talk, record your baby's voice, and even sing your baby to sleep. Some toys can be controlled by remote control, so you don't even have to go in and reset them if your baby hasn't fallen asleep yet when they stop playing.

Although not all of your toys have to run on batteries, having a few of these types of learning toys can be fun. Balls, blocks, and drums that play music, interactive dolls, and books that talk can hold your infant's attention and encourage her development.

Keep in mind that your older infant is likely to be just as happy playing with toys that don't talk or play music, so don't feel that you have to spend a lot of money and buy every high-tech toy out there.

What Else Do You Need?

There are other devices that high-tech dads might want to have. With all of the time that you are spending in helping to care for your baby, you will likely miss a few of your favorite TV shows. A digital video recorder, like TiVo, can help make sure that you can still watch a few of your programs.

Other high-tech safety devices you can buy might include a wireless video camera for your backyard, or a backup warning device or video camera in your car. Although it won't keep your baby safe, a digital music player, like an iPod, can be a fun gadget to have. Many strollers even include built-in speakers now, so you can hook up your music player and play your baby's favorite songs as you go for a walk. Don't go overboard, though. Remember that there are many things more important to the health and well-being of both your baby and your bank account.

Chapter 19

Grandparenting the First Year

In these days of frequent relocations and small extended families, having grandparents who are an active part of your baby's life can be a godsend. Whether they offer parenting advice and financial support or simply spend time with the new baby, grandparents can be an important part of your baby's life.

Reconnecting with Your Parents

Do you have a good relationship with your parents? Do you talk to them or see them as often as you (and they) would like? Unfortunately, growing apart from your parents is too often a part of growing up. Living far away and dealing with unresolved hard feelings and situations such as divorce can all get in the way of a healthy relationship with your parents as you get older.

Having a baby can give you a wonderful opportunity to reconnect with your parents. You may simply find more time to talk about things, because they are around more now that they're spending time with your new baby. Or you may just have more things to talk about, because just about everything your baby does presents a topic for conversation. Your parents will love to hear about each new milestone as their grandchild meets it, and you also can ask them about your own babyhood, such as whether or not you were a fussy baby and how old you were when you took your first steps.

Unwanted Advice

Grandparents can be a source of invaluable advice and support. In addition to raising their own kids, they had years of experience dealing with all the things that help a family run smoothly. Ideally, that would mean that if you have a problem, you could ask one of your baby's grandparents and get some useful advice.

If your baby's grandparents are having a hard time understanding how parenting, medical, and safety advice have changed, consider inviting them to one of your baby's visits to his pediatrician. That way, they can hear that advice firsthand, ask questions, and learn to better support your methods of raising your baby.

Unfortunately, not every family is in such an ideal situation. Instead of getting helpful advice, you and your partner might be criticized for the way that you are doing things. Or you may get advice that goes against the way that you have chosen to raise your children, leading to hard feelings when you decide not to follow it. Understanding why this happens and trying to avoid miscommunications can help to support a healthy relationship between your own family and all of the grandparents.

Times Have Changed

Parenting advice has changed a lot over the years. There was a time when doctors actively discouraged mothers from breastfeeding and it was recommended that you not hold your baby very much because it might spoil him. Parents also were advised to start solid foods and table foods a lot earlier than we do now. Even childproofing, car seats, and other safety measures weren't widely supported when many of today's new parents were kids.

Because today's grandparents raised their children using different advice, it is not surprising that their recommendations would be a little different from the methods you are now using. Is your two-month-old not sleeping through the night? Then don't be surprised if a grandparent recommends feeding him some cereal to help him sleep. Or maybe you will be told that your baby doesn't need to breastfeed or that she should be put to sleep on her stomach.

Although trying to explain that those things aren't recommended anymore can be helpful, it is hard to do this without making grandparents feel that they did things wrong. After all, those methods likely worked for them and they were following the advice of the time. Instead of dismissing or criticizing a grandparent's advice, you should try to explain why recommendations have changed—for example, that a baby who sleeps on her stomach is at higher risk for SIDS.

Miscommunications

New parents are often at least a little insecure about the way they are doing things with their baby. Are you feeding him enough? Is he as safe and healthy as he should be? Is he growing and developing normally? These are just a few of the things that new parents question about themselves and their baby. With this built-in insecurity, it is not hard to see how any advice or comments from a grandparent could be seen as criticism. And while they really may be criticizing you—that will depend on their personalities and your relationship with them—it's also possible that they are just trying to be helpful. Misunderstandings can cause even further harm to a poor relationship. Often, what a grandparent sees as being helpful might be viewed by a new parent as meddling. Or an idea for new ways to do things might be seen as criticism even when the grandparent is really just trying to help you in this time of need. Talk to them about how their comments are making you and your partner feel. This may help to get them to give advice differently, so that it isn't seen as being critical.

ALERT!

Don't always assume that problems with grandparents are going to come from the in-laws. Your partner may need the most help and support dealing with her own parents if she doesn't have a healthy relationship with them or they don't communicate well.

Supporting Mom

There will be times when any advice from a grandparent, or anyone else, is going to be unwelcome. In the first few days and weeks, many new parents need time to adjust to and bond with their baby. Too much advice at this time, especially when it is not asked for, will likely be unwanted.

When faced with a grandparent who is offering unwanted advice, a father's primary job will be to support his baby's mother. This may mean reassuring her that she is doing a great job or actually telling a grandparent to back off. Particularly when the criticism is coming from your own parents, stepping in early to have a talk about things can help to avoid hard feelings down the road.

Encouraging a Good Relationship

Because grandparents can have such a positive role in the life of your baby, it is important to try to maintain a healthy relationship with them. That can sometimes be hard, though, especially with all of the added stress and anxiety that having a new baby can bring to a family. It can be even harder if you didn't have a good relationship with the grandparents before the baby was born.

How do you balance your need for help with the grandparents' need to be helpful? One way is to clearly define what you think their role should be and try to understand what role they would like to have. Balancing those two things can help to avoid many misunderstandings.

FACT

According to the U.S. Census Bureau, more than 5 million children live with their grandparents. The grandparent is the primary caregiver in the majority of these cases. In about 25 percent of these families, a parent also lives with them.

You also should be specific about what your needs are. Do you need help watching your baby? Or would you rather spend more time with your baby but you need some extra help around the house in order to do this? If you ask for help in very general ways or don't ask at all, then you are less likely to get the help you need.

As a new father, you can help to encourage a good relationship with your baby's grandparents by making sure that everyone gets along, communicating what you and your partner need, and talking to overcome any misunderstandings. Making sure that grandparents have the chance to visit and spend as much time with their grandchild as they would like can also help support a healthy relationship.

A Grandparent's Role

Grandparents can have widely different roles, from being the primary caregivers for their grandchildren or baby-sitting each day to just visiting during holidays and special occasions. Their role also is likely to depend on how healthy they are, what kind of relationship you have with them now, and whether or not they are retired or working full-time. Ideally, your baby's grandparents will be able to have an active role in helping to raise your baby.

Whatever their role, grandparents shouldn't be viewed as a built-in day-care or baby-sitting service, where you just drop off your kids with a list of instructions. By accepting their help, you have some responsibility to also support their need to be a part of your baby's life.

Giving Time and Money

For new parents who are struggling to get things done, having a few extra hands to help care for the baby can be the most helpful thing of all. Grandparents are often more than willing to help out by watching your baby, caring for your other children, or just helping out around the house. With that extra time, you may be able to get a night out or just get a little extra sleep.

If you live with your baby's grandparents, it can be harder to define everyone's roles. You may have to make more compromises about how you would like things to be done. This makes it even more important to talk things over and try to support a relationship that works for everyone.

In addition to time, money is one of the biggest things that is in short supply after having a new baby. You have the costs of getting all of the supplies to prepare for your baby, such as clothes, a crib, a car seat, and so on, plus the hospital expenses for the baby and mother. If you had a premature baby, those hospital expenses can quickly grow to unbelievable amounts. If your baby's grandparents are willing and financially able to help with those expenses, it can make things much easier on you.

Giving Too Much?

Grandparents who are always spoiling their grandchildren aren't appreciated by most parents. It might be okay if the grandparents don't see the kids on a regular basis, and they just lavish them with treats and gifts a few times a year when they are together. But on a regular basis, these constant handouts can interfere with your own parenting and lead to spoiled kids.

Instead of spoiling the children with candy and toys, a better role would be for the grandparents to "spoil" them with affection, love, and time. You might consider asking your parents to set limits on how much they can spend on incidental gifts. If that doesn't work, you could have your children keep the gifts at their grandparents' house and just play with them when they go there.

Family Stories

Your baby's grandparents can be a wonderful source of information about your family. Stories about your own childhood, where your family came from, and what your ancestors did might be lost if you don't hear them from older generations in your family.

Do you know your family's history? If not, now would be a good time to learn more information from your own parents. Some good questions to ask can include:

- Where is our family originally from?
- What did your parents and grandparents do?
- What was it like when you went to school?
- What do you remember about the rest of our family?
- What kind of job did you have?
- What places did you visit?

If you don't record your family's stories, they most likely will be lost, especially once older generations aren't around to continue telling the stories. Are you going to remember everything about your own parents and grandparents when your children grow up and start asking questions? Take steps to record the facts now, while you still have the chance.

In addition to telling family stories, grandparents might write down these stories so that there is a written record that can be passed on from one generation to another. They can use a journal or scrapbook to record all of this information, or you can prepare some questions to ask your parents and write down their answers yourself.

Names for Grandparents

As your baby gets older and begins talking, she will have to call her grandparents something. Will they simply be grandma and grandpa? Or something a little cuter, like the way your child first mispronounces their names? Or will it be an ethnic name or something from your own childhood?

If any of the grandparents have divorced and are remarried, having names for each grandparent can be even more important to avoid confusion. In this situation, your baby may have multiple sets of grandparents and step-grandparents that she will get to know. While an older child may be able to simply say grandma X or grandma Y, for example, that is too complicated for an infant or toddler who is just learning to talk.

Also keep in mind that some younger grandparents may simply not be ready to be called grandma or grandpa. Another name, which doesn't have the same implication for older age, might be a good alternative in this case.

Some common names for grandmothers include:

- Memaw
- Memmie
- MawMaw
- Nanna
- Nanny
- Grammy
- Abuela (Spanish)
- Nonna (Italian)
- Oma (German/Dutch)

Names for grandfathers include:

- Gramps
- Poppie
- Pawpaw

- Pepa
- Poppa
- Grandpapa
- Abuelo (Spanish)
- Nonno (Italian)
- Opa (German/Dutch)

Very often, grandparents get their names by simply waiting to see what their grandchild will call them. Maybe she will just start using a common name, like grandma and grandpa, or maybe she'll come up with a name on her own. It may be a variation on one of these common names or she may mispronounce a grandparent's first name, like LaLa for Laura or SuSu for Susan.

Long-Distance Grandparenting

Even when your baby's grandparents want to have a close relationship with him, it is not always possible. They may live too far away to visit very often. Or maybe they are sick or in a nursing home and are unable to spend much time with him.

Most long-distance grandparents wish that they lived closer to their grandchildren, and many are now taking the big step of actually moving so that they live nearby. Although not always easy or practical, it is sometimes the only way to make sure that they are a big part of their grandchildren's lives.

Whatever the reason for the separation, there are many ways for the grandparents to stay in touch with your baby's life. In addition to the more traditional phone calls and mailing photos, you may be able to use the Internet to keep in close touch. In this day of digital pictures, instant messaging, and e-mail, there is no reason your baby's grandparents can't get to know him, even if it is from a distance.

You also can plan frequent trips, as often as possible, to visit grandparents or have them visit you. If none of those solutions provide enough contact, then you or his grandparents might consider moving so that you can all live closer together. Although not always practical, the many benefits of having a close extended family may make it a worthwhile thing to do.

Adopting a Grandparent

By now you likely have a good understanding of what an important role grandparents can have in your baby's life. But what if your baby's grandparents aren't around? Unfortunately, there are many things that can make it impossible for your baby to get to know her grandparents. They may live too far away to visit very often; they may be deceased; or perhaps you have such a poor relationship with them that you don't want them to be a part of your baby's life.

Can you find a substitute to offer the same unconditional love and support to your baby? Sure you can. More and more families who do not have extended families living nearby are "adopting" a grandparent to fill that role.

People who would be good candidates for an adopted grandparent could be anyone you know who doesn't have grandchildren of his or her own nearby. An older neighbor, coworker, or a member of your church that your family is already close to would all make great adopted grandparents if they are willing.

You might also consider visiting a nearby nursing home to find out whether you could adopt a few residents to be your baby's grandparents. While they might not be able to take your child out or baby-sit, visiting them on a regular basis still would be a good experience for them and for your child as she gets older.

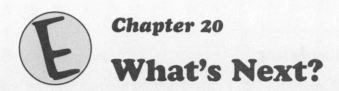

Chapter 20

What's Next?

Congratulations! You got through the first year. It's all smooth sailing from here, right? Well, not necessarily. Each age has its own problems and challenges, so there will still be things that come up that you might be anxious about or have a hard time dealing with. Most parents do consider the first year to be the hardest, though, so you deserve a big pat on the back for making it this far.

The Toddler Years

Your baby's first birthday marks the start of the toddler years. This is the transition period between your baby's total dependency on you in his first year and his increasing independence as a preschool and school-age child. Instead of the small baby that you were bouncing on your knee, you will now have a running toddler that you will be chasing around the house.

Increased Independence

As your child learns to walk, talk, dress, and feed himself, he will also learn to be independent in other ways. He may not want to eat when you want him to or stop playing when it is time for a nap. Or he may begin testing his limits to see what he can do and get away with. These are all normal ways that he will learn to develop and grow during this new developmental period.

Your toddler's growing mobility, independence, and need to explore will make it even more important than ever to keep his safety in mind. In addition to continuing to use a car seat in the back seat, you should inspect your house to make sure that everything is still childproofed. It is especially important that you have taken steps to childproof doors so that he can't get out of the house or into rooms that aren't safe.

Playing with Your Toddler

During your child's toddler years, when he is running around and beginning to talk, playtime becomes more fun for many dads. It was certainly fun to play with your infant too, but now your child can really participate in play. Even when he plays alone, it is fun to watch him manipulate toys, stack blocks on top of each other, and try to figure out how things work.

In addition to simply having fun, your toddler's playtime is an important way that he learns about things. Remember that not every toy has to be computerized or have a lot of lights or sounds, though. Simple toys that he can push, pull, or climb on are just as much fun.

First Words

It's fun when your baby says his first words, especially when that word is "dada." By about thirteen months, most toddlers are able to say dada and mama specifically to ask for or talk to their father and mother. The next word soon follows in the next few months.

FACT

Your baby's first word is often "dada" rather than "mama," just because it is easier to say. It is okay to feel special that his first word is "dada," but because he isn't using it as a label for either you or his mother at first anyway, you probably shouldn't attach too much significance to these first words.

What will your baby's second word be? It could be "cat" or "dog," if you have either as a pet. Or maybe a sibling's name or a favorite toy, like "ball." Hopefully it isn't "no."

Toddler Language Milestones

The rest of your toddler's second year should lead to an explosion in his speech. By the end of the second year, many toddlers know more than fifty words and have started to talk in two-word sentences. You can also expect that he will be able to tell you a few of the things that he wants at this time. For example, he might say "milk" or "juice" when he is thirsty, or "cookie" when he wants a snack.

Even before all of this talking, your child likely will understand things very well. During his second year, he will learn to point to his body parts, like his eyes or mouth. He will also begin to follow some two-step commands, such as "pick up the shoes, then bring them to daddy." At the end of the second year, you can also expect him to begin pointing to things that you name, such as a toy or a cup.

Speech Delays

If your child is a little late in picking up language milestones, it becomes a little easier to spot during the second year. It is harder to know if a younger infant isn't on track, because the differences between the different babbling milestones aren't always easily understood. Once children start to really talk, though, with real words, it is easy to know when they are behind other children of the same age.

It is important to remember that just because your child isn't talking as much as other kids of the same age, it doesn't mean that she is really developmentally delayed. The range of what is considered normal is very broad. For example, one commonly used tool called the Early Language Milestone Scale-2 (ELM Scale-2) says that 25 to 90 percent of children can say four to six words between about eleven and twenty-three months. That can mean more than a full year's difference between the ages when two normal children pick up this milestone.

Not all speech delays are normal, and you shouldn't always take a "wait and see" approach when your child isn't meeting her milestones. A toddler whose speech is delayed may have a hearing loss or other medical problem. If it also seems that your child does not understand or communicate well, she may have a more serious developmental problem that should be evaluated.

The range for when toddlers can say fifty or more single words is almost as broad, with most kids meeting this milestone between about eighteen and twenty-six months. If you do think that your child's speech or language is delayed, you should discuss it with your pediatrician. Getting your child's hearing tested by an audiologist and seeing a speech therapist also can be helpful to evaluate late talkers.

Whole Milk

Knowing what to give your baby to drink is one of the easier decisions that you will have to make this next year. The American Academy of Pediatrics (AAP) is very clear in recommending that kids who aren't breastfeeding should start on milk after they are a year old. If your toddler is still breast-feeding two to three times a day, he won't have to start milk until he weans down to only one feeding or stops breastfeeding altogether.

The AAP recommends that toddlers drink whole cow's milk. Younger children need some fat in their diet and it is not recommended that you limit their fat intake until after they are two to three years old. That means no low-fat or skim milk until later.

Milk Allergies

The decision of what to give your toddler to drink becomes harder if he is allergic to milk. Many infants on soy formulas are able to switch to cow's milk without problems. You should still talk to your pediatrician before start-ing milk if your baby was intolerant of milk-based formulas. If your child only has simple formula insensitivities, and no serious allergy-type symp-toms, your pediatrician might say it is okay to start milk.

If you know your child is allergic to milk and he did well on a soy for-mula, you can simply continue with a soy formula, or you might change to a toddler soy formula. Soy milk is not a very good alternative, because it is low in fat.

If your toddler is resisting milk, you might consider waiting a few weeks and trying again. Going more slowly, for instance switching only one bottle from formula to milk every week, also can be helpful. As a last resort, you might consider mixing the formula and milk together and then slowly putting less and less formula in the bottle to get her slowly accustomed to the taste of milk.

Kids Who Won't Drink Milk

Children who don't have milk allergies, but simply don't like milk, have many options. They can simply continue to drink a toddler formula, whether it is milk or soy-based. Or they can just eat and drink other foods supplemented with calcium. These include cheese, yogurt, orange juice, and many other foods whose labels say that they are a "good" or "excellent" source of calcium. As a last resort, you might also consider flavoring your child's milk.

Toddlers not drinking milk are also likely to need a Vitamin D supplement. In addition, you will have to be sure to make up for the fat and calories that your toddler is missing out on by not drinking milk.

ALERT!

Parents seem to worry more when their children don't drink enough milk, but drinking too much can be almost as bad. In addition to filling up on milk and not eating other foods, toddlers who drink a lot of milk can get constipated and are at risk for iron deficiency. Getting too many calories can be another problem. To avoid these problems, try to limit your toddler's milk intake to 16 to 24 ounces a day.

Getting Rid of the Bottle

About the time that infants switch to milk, most parents consider getting them to also give up their bottles. Making two big changes at the same time can be too stressful for some kids, so you might do one at a time. But which one? Should you switch to milk or to cups first?

It actually may not matter that much. Some parents think that it is harder to get off the bottle later if they first get their toddler used to drinking milk from a bottle. Others find it harder to get their toddler to take formula from a cup, because he has been used to drinking it from a bottle for so long.

Since there is no real "right" way to get your toddler used to milk and cups, you will have to think about what will work best for you. Is your toddler very easygoing and adaptable? Then you may be able to switch to both at once, using a cold-turkey approach and going straight to milk in a cup. If your toddler strongly resists any change, then consider going much more slowly. You might have to change just one bottle to milk every few days or weeks, to allow your toddler to ease into this transition.

QUESTION?

When should you take away your baby's bottle?
You should usually begin to wean your baby from his bottle at around twelve to fifteen months. Taking a bottle for too long may encourage your toddler to drink more milk and juice than he really needs.

If your baby is breastfeeding you can avoid bottles completely by weaning straight to a cup. Especially if your infant is already a year old when he weans, there is no real reason to give him a bottle at all. If he was drinking water or juice from a bottle, then you can switch to a cup at around twelve to fifteen months, whether or not he continues to breastfeed.

Feeding Your Toddler

The biggest transition that comes when you go from feeding an infant to feeding a toddler isn't usually what she is eating. Sure, your toddler will be eating more "real" table food and less baby food. In fact, some kids have given up baby food altogether by the time they are a year old. The big change is usually in their eating habits.

Picky Eaters

Your older infant probably was eating three big meals each day, consisting of cereal, fruits, vegetables, and meats; three or four feedings of breast-milk or formula; and a few snacks. And that is what helped her to triple her weight that first year. All of that food and all of those calories helped fuel your infant's rapid growth.

That growth slows down quite a bit in the toddler years though. Instead of gaining almost a pound a month, your toddler is expected to gain only

5 pounds during her whole second year. This slowdown in growth usually translates into a slowdown in eating, because your toddler needs fewer calories and less food energy now.

Although being a picky eater can be normal, you should make sure that your toddler isn't drinking too much milk and juice. If your picky eater is drinking much more than 16 to 24 ounces of milk or 4 to 6 ounces of juice, then he might be getting so many calories from what he drinks that he is already too full to eat.

So instead of three big meals a day, you may find that she wants to eat only one good meal each day. She may then just pick at other mealtimes. Even if she seems picky and doesn't seem to be eating much, if she is active and growing and developing normally, then she is likely eating enough. To be sure she is eating well, review your toddler's diet with your pediatrician.

Mercury and Fish

Although fish can be a part of a healthy diet, there are a few reasons not to give your toddler a lot of fish to eat. For one thing, kids can be allergic to shellfish and other fish, so those foods should not be introduced to children under the age of three who are at risk for developing food allergies. The other big danger is that many types of fish are contaminated with mercury, which can harm young children, especially if they are breastfeeding and their mother eats fish.

Once you introduce fish into your toddler's diet, you should be careful about the types and amounts of fish that you let him eat. Specifically, younger children should not eat any shark, swordfish, king mackerel, or tilefish. Other types of fish, including shrimp, canned light tuna, salmon, pollock, and catfish, should be eaten in moderation, with no more than two servings of 2 to 3 ounces each per week.

This limit of two servings a week also applies to fish sticks and fast-food fish sandwiches. And only one of these weekly servings should be fish that you catch on your own or albacore or white tuna, which can contain higher levels of mercury. Remember that these limits and warnings also apply to the diet of women who are breastfeeding.

Potty Training

Learning to use the potty is a big milestone for toddlers. You shouldn't expect to be able to stop buying diapers anytime soon, though. The days of trying to potty train at a very early age are mostly over—although you might still be pressured by older family members to begin potty training by nine or fifteen months.

When thinking about potty training, keep in mind that the average child doesn't begin this stage until eighteen months to three years. And most recent studies have shown that starting early, before your child is ready, usually just prolongs the whole process. This means that a child who started early would likely end up being potty trained at about the same time as children who started later.

FACT

The average toddler isn't developmentally, psychologically, or physically ready to begin potty training until eighteen months at the earliest. This, plus the fact that starting very early doesn't lead to finishing any sooner, should discourage you from beginning potty training until your child is ready.

How will you know that your child is ready? Watch for the following signs:

- Staying clean and dry for several hours at a time
- Being bothered by a dirty diaper and wanting to be changed
- Not being overly negative about things in general anymore
- Being eager to please; able to follow simple directions and imitate others
- Having the physical ability to walk to the potty and get on and off of it by herself

It also can help if you are able to determine when your child needs to use the potty. You might already know this because she is consistent in when she goes, or because you can just tell by how she is acting. Remember that if your child isn't ready to start training, you probably should wait. While most children are ready somewhere between eighteen months and two years, some aren't ready until much later.

Discipline Issues

Often, the time of negativism known as the "terrible twos" starts in a toddler's second year. It is at this time that you may start noticing that your child has more temper tantrums and gets angry and frustrated when he doesn't get his way. It is important to understand that this is normal behavior. Can you really expect a toddler to understand why he can't do all of the things he wants to do, when he wants to do them? Of course not. But that *doesn't* mean that you can't work to stop these tantrums and teach him a better way to behave. Instead of giving in to tantrums (which would teach that throwing himself on the floor, banging his head, and screaming is the correct way to get things), you should try to discourage them.

The best ways to discourage tantrums are to stick with regular and predictable routines of when you do things, ignore tantrums when they occur, and try to distract your child if you see a tantrum coming. For behaviors that you can't ignore, such as hitting and biting, stay calm. A strong reaction will only encourage him to do it more.

You can help to prevent temper tantrums by providing a safe environment for your toddler to play and explore in. He can't have a tantrum because you won't let him pull all of the pots and pans out of a kitchen cabinet if you have a latch on the cabinet and he can't get into it in the first place, right?

The most important part of learning to discipline your toddler is that you should be prepared. Don't get in the habit of simply reacting to your child's behaviors, because you will be more likely to just get mad and won't be doing much to encourage better behaviors or reduce bad behaviors. You can avoid becoming the stereotypical authoritarian father by learning how to praise good behaviors, set limits, discipline in a calm and loving manner, and avoid physical punishment, like spanking. Most important, remember that discipline is more about teaching your child how to behave. It is not all about punishment.

Ready for Another?

Early in your baby's first year, you might have been doubting your decision to ever have children in the first place. After all, there were all of the sleepless nights, the hours of listening to crying, and getting spit up on all of the time. You also likely lost some freedom and the ability to be spontaneous in the things you and your partner wanted to do.

FACT

Don't let a few bad experiences with your first child be the only factor that discourages you from having more kids. Just because your first child was a poor sleeper, fussy most of the time, or otherwise "difficult," it doesn't mean that your next one will be too.

Those kinds of thoughts often quickly go away though, and are replaced with feelings of love. That's when you realize how lucky you were to have a baby. And then you start thinking about when you are going to have another one. Should you wait one year? Two? Or more?

Is it better to space kids by several years or have them close together? There are a lot of pros and cons that support both options. What works best will likely depend on your family situation. Here are some factors to consider:

- Having kids close together will mean that you might have more than one infant who needs a lot of care and attention, meaning more diapers to change, more feedings, and more babies to carry around.

- Too much time between babies will mean that you will have to get used to the "baby stuff" all over again.
- An older first child might resent losing out on his "only child" status more if he has longer to get used to being an "only."
- Kids close in age may mean more than one or two kids in day care at the same time.
- Kids spaced far apart will have very different needs, such as an older child needing rides to school and soccer practice while the younger child needs regular naps.
- An older child might be able to entertain and help take care of younger siblings.

As you can see, there are factors that support whatever decision you make. The age at which you and your partner started having kids and how much of a support system you have will be other factors. Talk it over to come up with the situation that's best for everyone in your growing family.

Appendix A

New Dad
Tip Summary

Being a new father can be overwhelming. The checklists in this section can
help you remember what to do and what to
expect during all the phases of your baby's
first year.

Months One Through Three

By the time you get through the first few months, you will likely be a pro at caring for your baby. Changing your baby's diaper and his clothes, feeding him, and keeping him safe will become easier and easier. Reviewing a summary of what you should be doing at this age can still be helpful though. Be sure to do the following things:

- ❐ Put your baby to sleep on his back to prevent SIDS
- ❐ Vary his positioning so that he doesn't develop a flat head
- ❐ Remember that you usually don't need to start solid foods yet
- ❐ Don't confuse a growth spurt and increased breastfeeding as a sign that you have to supplement with formula
- ❐ Talk to your pediatrician if you have concerns about your child's growth or development
- ❐ Continue to use a rear-facing car seat in the back seat
- ❐ Don't leave your baby on places where he can roll off and fall
- ❐ Avoid infections by not exposing your baby to a lot of people
- ❐ Call your pediatrician if your baby has a fever at or above 100.4° Fahrenheit
- ❐ Start using an insect repellent at two months if necessary

Months Four Through Seven

For some dads, taking care of the baby in these months is becoming easier. The baby is doing more things, is bigger and likely seems less "breakable." Other dads find it is more challenging to take care of the baby as he gets older, because older babies are awake more, need to be entertained more, and can place more demands on a dad's time. Both types of dads likely still find that baby care is fun, though. Reviewing these tips can help you make sure that you aren't leaving out anything important:

- ❐ Continue to put your child to sleep on her back to prevent SIDS
- ❐ Continue to vary her positioning and give her tummy time so that she doesn't develop a flat head

❐ Don't start solids foods until your baby is showing signs of readiness

❐ Once you start solid foods, do so slowly, only offering one new food every two to three days

❐ By six months of age, begin giving your baby some water with fluoride

❐ Move your child to a rear-facing convertible car seat if she outgrows her rear-facing infant seat

❐ Avoid sun exposure when possible and use sunscreen

❐ After six months, consider starting to restrict her pacifier use so that she doesn't become overly dependent on it

❐ Use the harness in highchairs and don't leave your baby where she can fall

❐ Begin cleaning her teeth once she starts getting them

❐ Finish childproofing your house before your baby becomes more mobile

Months Eight Through Twelve

As your baby's first year is coming to an end, you are likely feeling like a pro at all of this parenting stuff. Childproofing, diaper changes, feedings, and even baths are second nature to you.

❐ Continue to use a rear-facing car seat until your infant is twelve months old AND weighs 20 pounds

❐ Review how well your home is childproofed, because your child is much more mobile now

❐ Use sunscreen and insect repellent when necessary

❐ Remove crib bumper pads and mobiles if your baby is able to stand up in her crib

❐ Supervise your baby when she eats solid foods in case she chokes

❐ Don't start regular cow's milk before your baby is a year old

❐ Offer juice in a sippie cup (only offer small amounts of diluted 100 percent fruit juice)

❐ Clean your infant's teeth each day

❐ Don't give in to tantrums

Appendix B

Worksheets for Pediatrician Visits

The following worksheets for well-child and sick-child visits can be used to help you get the most out of your visits to your pediatrician.

Well-Child Visit Worksheet

Date:_____

Your Child's Age _____

What is your child's feeding schedule like? What, how much, and how often does he eat? _____

_____

_____

_____

What new milestones has your child picked up since his last visit? Is he . . . (circle all that apply)

smiling | following objects | laughing | grasping things | rolling over

sitting up with support | sitting up alone | cruising | pulling up | walking

Describe any concerns or questions you have about your child's nutrition, growth, development, safety, etc.

_____

_____

_____

_____

Describe any problems your child has had since his last visit, including vaccine reactions, food intolerances, illnesses, etc.

_____

_____

_____

_____

Information to record from your visit:

Height _____ Weight _____ Head Circumference _____

Vaccines given at this visit (circle the ones your child received):
DTaP Hib IPV HepB Prevnar Chickenpox Vaccine MMR

Don't forget to ask about:

- ❑ A Vitamin D supplement for breastfeeding babies (two months)
- ❑ Using an insect repellent (two months)
- ❑ Using sunscreen (six months)
- ❑ A fluoride supplement (six months)
- ❑ When to start solid foods (four to six months)
- ❑ Lead poisoning risk factors (six to nine months)

Your child's next visit will be at _____ months.

Sick-Child Visit Worksheet

Date:_____

What is the main reason that you have brought your child to your pediatrician today?

_____

_____

_____

When did she start getting sick? Has she been around anyone who is sick?

_____

_____

_____

_____

What are her symptoms? Does she have . . . (circle all that apply)

runny nose | cough | fever | vomiting | diarrhea | trouble breathing

irritability | trouble sleeping | poor appetite | rash | ear pain

Other symptoms: _____

_____

_____

_____

When are her symptoms better and worse? How have they changed?

_____

_____

_____

_____

What treatments and medications have you been giving to your child?

_____

_____

_____

_____

Information to record from your visit:

Your child's diagnosis: _____

_____

Treatment instructions and prescribed medications: _____

_____

_____

_____

_____

_____

_____

When should she start getting better? _____

_____

_____

_____

_____

_____

What signs should you look for that may mean your child is getting worse?

_____

_____

_____

_____

When should you return for a recheck? _____

_____

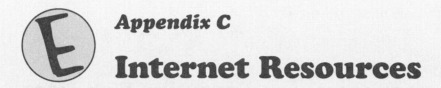

Appendix C

Internet Resources

The following Web sites can help you get more advice and tips on becoming a loving and supportive father.

Web Sites for Fathers

About Fatherhood

A complete guide to all aspects of fatherhood, including help for dads in all situations, from new dads and stay-at-home dads to divorced dads.

✍*fatherhood.about.com*

National Fatherhood Initiative Home

An organization that encourages dads to get more involved in the lives of their children. It also includes a section called "Fatherly Advice" that most new fathers will find helpful.

✍*www.fatherhood.org*

Fatherville

An online community for all types of fathers.

✍*www.fatherville.com*

fathers.com

Tips from the National Center for Fathering to help you become a better dad.

✍*www.fathers.com*

Fathering Magazine

An online magazine for fathers.

✍*www.fathermag.com*

mrdad.com

Ask questions and read articles by Armin Brott, author of many books about fatherhood.

✍*www.mrdad.com*

Slowlane.com

A great resource for stay-at-home dads.

✍*www.slowlane.com*

Father's World

Advice on becoming a better father and parent.

✍*www.fathersworld.com*

Parenting Web Sites

In addition to Web sites specifically for fathers, the average dad will need a lot of the more general parenting and medical advice from these parenting sites.

About Pediatrics

Pediatric parenting and medical information from Dr. Vincent Iannelli.

✍*pediatrics.about.com*

Keep Kids Healthy

Dr. Iannelli's guide to your children's health and safety.

✍*www.keepkidshealthy.com*

KidsHealth

A comprehensive guide for parents about their children's health.

✍*www.kidshealth.org/parent*

Parent Stages

Information and advice from some of the leading parenting Web sites, including iVillage, BabyCenter, and iParenting Media.

www.parentstages.com

About Parenting

Find advice about parenting newborns to teens.

about.com/parenting

Family Source

A search engine to find family-friendly parenting Web sites.

family-source.com

Dr. Spock

Get advice and information based on the philosophical approach of Dr. Benjamin Spock.

www.drspock.com

Ask Dr. Sears

General parenting and health-care advice from the Sears Pediatricians.

www.askdrsears.com

Index

THE EVERYTHING SERIES!

BUSINESS & PERSONAL FINANCE

Everything® Budgeting Book
Everything® Business Planning Book
Everything® Coaching and Mentoring Book
Everything® Fundraising Book
Everything® Get Out of Debt Book
Everything® Grant Writing Book
Everything® Homebuying Book, 2nd Ed.
Everything® Homeselling Book
Everything® Home-Based Business Book
Everything® Investing Book
Everything® Landlording Book
Everything® Leadership Book
Everything® Managing People Book
Everything® Negotiating Book
Everything® Online Business Book
Everything® Personal Finance Book
Everything® Personal Finance in Your
        20s & 30s Book
Everything® Project Management Book
Everything® Real Estate Investing Book
Everything® Robert's Rules Book, $7.95
Everything® Selling Book
Everything® Start Your Own Business Book
Everything® Time Management Book
Everything® Wills & Estate Planning Book

COOKING

Everything® Barbecue Cookbook
Everything® Bartender's Book, $9.95
Everything® Chinese Cookbook
Everything® Chocolate Cookbook
Everything® College Cookbook
Everything® Cookbook
Everything® Dessert Cookbook
Everything® Diabetes Cookbook
Everything® Easy Gourmet Cookbook
Everything® Fondue Cookbook
Everything® Grilling Cookbook

Everything® Healthy Meals in Minutes
        Cookbook
Everything® Holiday Cookbook
Everything® Indian Cookbook
Everything® Low-Carb Cookbook
Everything® Low-Fat High-Flavor Cookbook
Everything® Low-Salt Cookbook
Everything® Meals for a Month Cookbook
Everything® Mediterranean Cookbook
Everything® Mexican Cookbook
Everything® One-Pot Cookbook
Everything® Pasta Cookbook
Everything® Quick Meals Cookbook
Everything® Slow Cooker Cookbook
Everything® Soup Cookbook
Everything® Thai Cookbook
Everything® Vegetarian Cookbook
Everything® Wine Book

HEALTH

Everything® Alzheimer's Book
Everything® Anti-Aging Book
Everything® Diabetes Book
Everything® Hypnosis Book
Everything® Low Cholesterol Book
Everything® Massage Book
Everything® Menopause Book
Everything® Nutrition Book
Everything® Reflexology Book
Everything® Stress Management Book

HISTORY

Everything® American Government Book
Everything® American History Book
Everything® Civil War Book
Everything® Irish History & Heritage Book
Everything® Middle East Book

HOBBIES & GAMES

Everything® Blackjack Strategy Book
Everything® Brain Strain Book, $9.95
Everything® Bridge Book
Everything® Candlemaking Book
Everything® Card Games Book
Everything® Cartooning Book
Everything® Casino Gambling Book, 2nd Ed.
Everything® Chess Basics Book
Everything® Crossword and Puzzle Book
Everything® Crossword Challenge Book
Everything® Cryptograms Book, $9.95
Everything® Digital Photography Book
Everything® Drawing Book
Everything® Easy Crosswords Book
Everything® Family Tree Book
Everything® Games Book, 2nd Ed.
Everything® Knitting Book
Everything® Knots Book
Everything® Motorcycle Book
Everything® Online Genealogy Book
Everything® Photography Book
Everything® Poker Strategy Book
Everything® Pool & Billiards Book
Everything® Quilting Book
Everything® Scrapbooking Book
Everything® Sewing Book
Everything® Woodworking Book
Everything® Word Games Challenge Book

HOME IMPROVEMENT

Everything® Feng Shui Book
Everything® Feng Shui Decluttering Book, $9.95
Everything® Fix-It Book
Everything® Homebuilding Book
Everything® Landscaping Book
Everything® Lawn Care Book
Everything® Organize Your Home Book

All Everything® books are priced at $12.95 or $14.95, unless otherwise stated. Prices subject to change without notice.

EVERYTHING® KIDS' BOOKS

All titles are $6.95

Everything® Kids' Animal Puzzle & Activity Book
Everything® Kids' Baseball Book, 3rd Ed.
Everything® Kids' Bible Trivia Book
Everything® Kids' Bugs Book
Everything® Kids' Christmas Puzzle & Activity Book
Everything® Kids' Cookbook
Everything® Kids' Halloween Puzzle & Activity Book
Everything® Kids' Hidden Pictures Book
Everything® Kids' Joke Book
Everything® Kids' Knock Knock Book
Everything® Kids' Math Puzzles Book
Everything® Kids' Mazes Book
Everything® Kids' Money Book
Everything® Kids' Monsters Book
Everything® Kids' Nature Book
Everything® Kids' Puzzle Book
Everything® Kids' Riddles & Brain Teasers Book
Everything® Kids' Science Experiments Book
Everything® Kids' Sharks Book
Everything® Kids' Soccer Book
Everything® Kids' Travel Activity Book

KIDS' STORY BOOKS

Everything® Bedtime Story Book
Everything® Bible Stories Book
Everything® Fairy Tales Book

LANGUAGE

Everything® Conversational Japanese Book (with CD), $19.95
Everything® French Phrase Book, $9.95
Everything® French Verb Book, $9.95
Everything® Inglés Book
Everything® Learning French Book
Everything® Learning German Book
Everything® Learning Italian Book
Everything® Learning Latin Book
Everything® Learning Spanish Book
Everything® Sign Language Book
Everything® Spanish Grammar Book
Everything® Spanish Phrase Book, $9.95
Everything® Spanish Verb Book, $9.95

MUSIC

Everything® Drums Book (with CD), $19.95
Everything® Guitar Book
Everything® Home Recording Book
Everything® Playing Piano and Keyboards Book
Everything® Reading Music Book (with CD), $19.95
Everything® Rock & Blues Guitar Book (with CD), $19.95
Everything® Songwriting Book

NEW AGE

Everything® Astrology Book
Everything® Dreams Book, 2nd Ed.
Everything® Ghost Book
Everything® Love Signs Book, $9.95
Everything® Meditation Book
Everything® Numerology Book
Everything® Paganism Book
Everything® Palmistry Book
Everything® Psychic Book
Everything® Reiki Book
Everything® Spells & Charms Book
Everything® Tarot Book
Everything® Wicca and Witchcraft Book

PARENTING

Everything® Baby Names Book
Everything® Baby Shower Book
Everything® Baby's First Food Book
Everything® Baby's First Year Book
Everything® Birthing Book
Everything® Breastfeeding Book
Everything® Father-to-Be Book
Everything® Father's First Year Book
Everything® Get Ready for Baby Book
Everything® Getting Pregnant Book
Everything® Homeschooling Book
Everything® Parent's Guide to Children with ADD/ADHD
Everything® Parent's Guide to Children with Asperger's Syndrome
Everything® Parent's Guide to Children with Autism
Everything® Parent's Guide to Children with Dyslexia
Everything® Parent's Guide to Positive Discipline

Everything® Parent's Guide to Raising a Successful Child
Everything® Parent's Guide to Tantrums
Everything® Parent's Guide to the Overweight Child
Everything® Parenting a Teenager Book
Everything® Potty Training Book, $9.95
Everything® Pregnancy Book, 2nd Ed.
Everything® Pregnancy Fitness Book
Everything® Pregnancy Nutrition Book
Everything® Pregnancy Organizer, $15.00
Everything® Toddler Book
Everything® Tween Book
Everything® Twins, Triplets, and More Book

PETS

Everything® Cat Book
Everything® Dachshund Book, $12.95
Everything® Dog Book
Everything® Dog Health Book
Everything® Dog Training and Tricks Book
Everything® Golden Retriever Book, $12.95
Everything® Horse Book
Everything® Labrador Retriever Book, $12.95
Everything® Poodle Book, $12.95
Everything® Pug Book, $12.95
Everything® Puppy Book
Everything® Rottweiler Book, $12.95
Everything® Tropical Fish Book

REFERENCE

Everything® Car Care Book
Everything® Classical Mythology Book
Everything® Computer Book
Everything® Divorce Book
Everything® Einstein Book
Everything® Etiquette Book
Everything® Great Thinkers Book
Everything® Mafia Book
Everything® Philosophy Book
Everything® Psychology Book
Everything® Shakespeare Book

RELIGION

Everything® Angels Book
Everything® Bible Book
Everything® Buddhism Book
Everything® Catholicism Book

All Everything® books are priced at $12.95 or $14.95, unless otherwise stated. Prices subject to change without notice.

Everything® Christianity Book
Everything® Jewish History & Heritage Book
Everything® Judaism Book
Everything® Koran Book
Everything® Prayer Book
Everything® Saints Book
Everything® Torah Book
Everything® Understanding Islam Book
Everything® World's Religions Book
Everything® Zen Book

SCHOOL & CAREERS

Everything® After College Book
Everything® Alternative Careers Book
Everything® College Survival Book, 2nd Ed.
Everything® Cover Letter Book, 2nd Ed.
Everything® Get-a-Job Book
Everything® Job Interview Book
Everything® New Teacher Book
Everything® Online Job Search Book
Everything® Paying for College Book
Everything® Practice Interview Book
Everything® Resume Book, 2nd Ed.
Everything® Study Book

SELF-HELP

Everything® Dating Book
Everything® Great Sex Book
Everything® Kama Sutra Book
Everything® Self-Esteem Book

SPORTS & FITNESS

Everything® Fishing Book
Everything® Fly-Fishing Book
Everything® Golf Instruction Book
Everything® Pilates Book
Everything® Running Book
Everything® Total Fitness Book
Everything® Weight Training Book
Everything® Yoga Book

TRAVEL

Everything® Family Guide to Hawaii
Everything® Family Guide to New York City, 2nd Ed.
Everything® Family Guide to RV Travel & Campgrounds
Everything® Family Guide to the Walt Disney World Resort®, Universal Studios®, and Greater Orlando, 4th Ed.
Everything® Family Guide to Washington D.C., 2nd Ed.
Everything® Guide to Las Vegas
Everything® Guide to New England
Everything® Travel Guide to the Disneyland Resort®, California Adventure®, Universal Studios®, and the Anaheim Area

WEDDINGS

Everything® Bachelorette Party Book, $9.95
Everything® Bridesmaid Book, $9.95
Everything® Creative Wedding Ideas Book
Everything® Elopement Book, $9.95
Everything® Father of the Bride Book, $9.95
Everything® Groom Book, $9.95
Everything® Mother of the Bride Book, $9.95
Everything® Wedding Book, 3rd Ed.
Everything® Wedding Checklist, $9.95
Everything® Wedding Etiquette Book, $7.95
Everything® Wedding Organizer, $15.00
Everything® Wedding Shower Book, $7.95
Everything® Wedding Vows Book, $9.95
Everything® Weddings on a Budget Book, $9.95

WRITING

Everything® Creative Writing Book
Everything® Get Published Book
Everything® Grammar and Style Book
Everything® Guide to Writing a Book Proposal
Everything® Guide to Writing a Novel
Everything® Guide to Writing Children's Books
Everything® Screenwriting Book
Everything® Writing Poetry Book
Everything® Writing Well Book

We have Everything® for the beginning crafter!
All titles are $14.95.

Everything® Crafts—Baby Scrapbooking
1-59337-225-6

Everything® Crafts—Bead Your Own Jewelry
1-59337-142-X

Everything® Crafts—Create Your Own Greeting Cards
1-59337-226-4

Everything® Crafts—Easy Projects
1-59337-298-1

Everything® Crafts—Making Cards with Rubber Stamps
1-59337-299-X

Everything® Crafts—Polymer Clay for Beginners
1-59337-230-2

Everything® Crafts—Rubber Stamping Made Easy
1-59337-229-9

Everything® Crafts—Wedding Decorations and Keepsakes
1-59337-227-2

Available wherever books are sold!
To order, call 800-872-5627, or visit us at *www.everything.com*.
Everything® and everything.com® are registered trademarks of F+W Publications, Inc.